PARLIAMENTS AND LEGISLATURES

Janet M. Box-Steffensmeier and David T. Canon, Series Editors

CHALLENGING PARTIES, CHANGING PARLIAMENTS

*Women and Elected Office in
Contemporary Western Europe*

MIKI CAUL KITTILSON

THE OHIO STATE UNIVERSITY PRESS
Columbus

Library of Congress Cataloging-in-Publication Data

Kittilson, Miki Caul.
Challenging parties, changing parliaments : women and elected office in contemporary Western Europe / Miki Caul Kittilson.
   p. cm.—(Parliaments and legislatures)
Includes bibliographical references and index.
ISBN 0–8142–1015–5 (cloth : alk. paper)—ISBN 0–8142–5148–X (pbk. : alk.
paper)—ISBN 0–8142–9091–4 (cd-rom) 1. Women in politics—European Union
countries. 2. Women legislators—European Union countries. 3. Political parties—
European Union countries. I. Title. II. Parliaments and legislatures series.
HQ1236.5.E85K57 2006
324.2082'094—dc22
                    2005025702

Cover photo and design by Jason Moore.
Text design and typesetting by Jennifer Forsythe.
Type set in Times New Roman.

The paper used in this publication meets the minimum requirements of the American
National Standard for Information Sciences—Permanence of Paper for Printed Library
Materials. ANSI Z39.48–1992.

9 8 7 6 5 4 3 2 1

For Michael and Nikolas

contents

list of illustrations

LIST OF ILLUSTRATIONS

Tables

acknowledgments

I would like to express my deepest appreciation to Russell Dalton, who provided incredibly helpful advice from the planning to data analyses stages and beyond. His insights have been invaluable. Katherine Tate provided both substantive and professional advice, which is greatly appreciated. I would also like to thank Martin Wattenberg and Bernard Grofman for their thoughtful feedback on this project. Financial support was provided by the German Marshall Fund and The Center for German and European Studies. Insights into party processes were provided through interviews with party officials and politicians, and by materials given by the parties. I am grateful for the time granted to this project by several individuals. Although I agreed not to quote or mention some of them by name in the text, many did grant me permission to offer them the thanks they deserve. MP Maria Kaisa Aula, Vice President Parliamentary Party KESK; Peter Coleman, former Labour Director of Organization and European Parliamentary Labour Party leader; Leena Eerola, Finnish Green Party activist; MP Tarja Filatov, SDP; Sandra Hartman, German FDP, Bundesfraktion; Lisa Husu, former Finnish National Coordinator of Women's Studies; Aki Hyodynma, Finnish Green Party; Ronnie Jaeckel, German Alliance 90/The Greens; Peter Jepson, Labour Party member; Christa Karras, Die Grünen; Stefan Kapferer, Head of Strategy and Campaigns, FDP; MP Tarja Kautto, SDP; Deborah Lincoln, former Labour Party National Women's Officer and Director of Public Relations; Rachel McLean, Labour National Women's Officer; Heli Paasio, SDP; Val Price, President, Labour Women's Network; Eeva Raevaara, Kristina Institute for Women's Studies at the University of Helsinki; MP Susanna Rahkonen, SDP; Helena Riutta, KOK; Meg Russell, former Labour Party National Women's Officer; MP Tertuu Savolainen, SDP; MP Anni Sinnemaki, Finnish Green Party; Caroline Abel Smith, Conservative Party Women's Organization leader; MaryAnn Stevenson, Director of Campaigns, Fawcett Society; Madame Speaker, MP Katja Svarinen, Vice President of Finnish Left Alliance Party; Stefan Thomas, Director of Public Relations, German Bundestag; Mrs. Riita Uosukainen, Speaker of Eduskunta and KOK nominee for Finnish President; Lord Larry Whitty, former Labour Party General Secretary; and Annette Widman-Mauz, Chair of Frauenunion Baden-Württemberg CDU. Several individuals and organizations made available materials that were essential to this research. Professor Richard Matland, University of Houston, gathered data on women in parties from several party and country experts in Scandinavia. Professor Paul Webb, University of Sussex, provided information on the British Conservative Party. The Labour Party Archives provided assistance in locating minutes from women's organization meetings. For statistics on Denmark, Karina Pedersen, University of Copenhagen, was tremendously helpful.

I would also like to thank my parents, who gave me the opportunity to pursue this research, and a career in academia more broadly. I am grateful to Greg for his moral support, which makes it possible for me to balance both a professional and a personal life. Finally, thank you to my sons, Michael and Nikolas, for the sacrifices they do not even know they've made.

1

Women, Parties, and Political Power

Political parties—the gateways to political office—are the key to advancing women's full participation in the political process. It is not enough for parties to establish women's wings or place women at the bottom of party lists; they must develop real avenues for women's leadership roles.

—MADELINE K. ALBRIGHT, Chair, National Democratic Institute and former Secretary of State and Ambassador to the UN, as quoted in the National Democratic Institute's "Win With Women: Strengthen Political Parties"

In May 2000 British Prime Minister Tony Blair and his wife Cherie welcomed a newborn son to their family. Just before the baby's birth, Cherie Blair praised then Finnish Prime Minister, Paavo Lipponen, for a taking a week of paternity leave to care for his baby, and she called for the "widespread adoption of his fine example" (Hoge, 2000). Yet in his public response, Prime Minister Blair said, "I've got a country to run. . . . I know what people want me to say, but the truth is, if I went away and stopped taking calls, or having conversations, it just wouldn't be real . . . I cannot stop being Prime Minister" (Hoge, 2000).

The implications of this story go beyond the issue of paternity leave. Blair's refusal followed an intensive, decade-long effort by the Labour Party to portray itself as the "woman-friendly" party in Britain. In addition to emphasizing gender-related policies, Labour has taken great strides in promoting women candidates for Parliament, and Blair has appointed an unprecedented number of women, sarcastically dubbed "Blair's Babes" by the British press,

1

to high-profile government positions. By taking a parental leave upon the birth of his son, Blair might have signaled his commitment to gender equality and a socially progressive "New" Labour Party. Even *The Mirror* ran front-page headlines urging parental leave for the Prime Minister—"Show New Dads the Way, Tony."

The Blair parental leave story illustrates the ongoing struggle between women and party politics. Not only was this a botched opportunity for Labour to demonstrate its support for women's changing roles in society, and perhaps to attract the much sought-after women's vote, but it also represents the larger picture of party gender politics. On the one hand, the Blairs' case illustrates how far political parties have come for the prime minister to even consider paternity leave. On the other hand, it also illustrates just how far party politics has to go in order to move beyond rhetoric to create a truly "woman-friendly" environment. An environment conducive to women's participation will encourage a greater number of women to enter party politics and run for elected office.

Past explanations for women's lower participation levels in both parties and parliament, relative to men's levels, often focus on a shortage of women stepping forward to run for office. Several studies attribute the problem of women's underrepresentation in part to women's lower levels of participation in the types of professions (e.g., law) that serve as springboards to office (Rule, 1994; Darcy et al., 1994; Taagepera, 1994; Norris and Lovenduski, 1995). Yet Pamela Paxton's (1997) large cross-national analysis finds that women's general numbers among the labor force and in higher education have little impact on their parliamentary presence. But more specifically, women's rising presence among the traditional pool of applicants in high-profile professions will gradually bring greater gains in parliament. Importantly, the inadequacy of the "supply side" reasoning is that it places the onus for change solely on women themselves. This book flips this question on its head to ask how political parties can be transformed to encourage women's participation—especially as members of parliaments. Certainly women must play an active role in creating opportunities for themselves, but in addition, as the gatekeepers to elected office, parties can facilitate or impede women's participation in parliament. I will argue that women's efforts to gain a foothold in party politics and parliament are most effective where women recognize favorable conditions within the party and the party system, and where they devise context-contingent strategies for inclusion. Certainly there is no one-size-fits-all strategy across parties, and this book examines how women's strategies most effectively interact with party and political environments.

Identifying the ways political parties can facilitate women's access to national legislatures has recently become a pressing issue among academics, democratic activists, and political leaders alike. A December 2003 National

Table 1.1 Increases in Representation of Women in National Legislatures

	% Women MPs, 1975	% Women MPs, 1997	% Points Increase
Australia	0.0	22.4	+22.4
Austria	7.7	26.2	+18.5
Belgium	6.6	12.0	+ 5.4
Canada	3.4	20.6	+17.4
Denmark	5.6	33.7	+18.1
Finland	23.0	33.5	+10.5
France	2.7	10.9	+8.2
Germany	5.8	30.9	+25.1
Greece	2.0	6.3	+4.3
Iceland	5.0	25.4	+20.4
Ireland	2.8	12.0	+9.2
Israel	6.7	7.5	+0.8
Italy	3.8	11.1	+7.3
Japan	1.4	4.6	+3.2
Luxembourg	5.1	20.0	+14.9
Netherlands	9.3	36.0	+26.7
New Zealand	4.6	29.2	+24.6
Norway	15.5	36.4	+20.9
Portugal	8.0	13.0	+5.0
Spain	6.0	21.6	+15.6
Sweden	21.4	42.7	+21.3
Switzerland	7.0	21.0	+14.0
United Kingdom	4.3	18.4	+14.1
United States	3.7	13.3	+9.6
Average	7.1	21.3	+14.2

Note: Data collected from Inter-Parliamentary Union statistics on women in parliaments. The first time point is the election before and closest to 1975. The second time point represents the election closest to 1997.

Democratic Institute (NDI) forum, entitled "Win With Women: Strengthen Political Parties," brought together female political leaders from around the world to address the role of political parties in women's political advancement. Madeline Albright, NDI Chair and a former U.S. secretary of state and ambassador to the United Nations, led the forum, asserting that "there have been many initiatives to promote women's political leadership, but little attention has been paid to reforming and modernizing the way political parties operate . . . After all, political parties are the gateway to political office, and are key to advancing women's participation" (NDI, 2004).

3

Women in Parliament

In this book I assess the degree of women's integration into political parties and parliamentary office in ten Western European nations from 1975 to 1997, and the conditions under which their entrance occurred.[1] This is both a study of how women pressed for greater representation and how democratic party systems responded to their demands. The activism of women and the actions of political parties work together as catalysts for change.

Although the women's movement has made dramatic progress in improving opportunities, women are still numerically underrepresented in the national legislatures of all established democracies (IPU, 1997). Thus, women participate little as elected representatives in the national decision-making process.

For a set of twenty-four post-industrial nations, table 1.1 presents the percentages of women in the lower house national legislature at two time points—1975 and 1997—and the percentage point difference between those two time points. On áverage, the percentage of women in office in 1975 was only 7, and this number grew by fourteen points, to 21, by 1997.

It is most striking that in each nation, the proportion of women in parliament has grown since the 1970s. In comparison with the larger set of postindustrial nations, Western European nations demonstrate some of the highest levels of parliamentary participation by women, and some of the greatest increases. The Netherlands and Germany made the greatest strides. In 1975 the German Bundestag had only 6% women, but by 1997 women made up 31% of the lower house. Similarly, in 1975, 9% of the members of the Dutch parliament were women, yet this figure climbed to 36% by 1997. By contrast, by the late 1990s, the United States had only 13% women in the House of Representatives. However, there is a great deal of variation across Western Europe. For example, under similar electoral systems, Austria and Belgium differ substantially, registering increases of eighteen and five percentage points, respectively. Britain, with its plurality electoral system, realized a larger increase than Belgium, Finland, or Ireland, all nonplurality systems.

Comparative research on the number of women in national parliaments has primarily focused on the structure of electoral systems to explain cross-national patterns. Several studies have established that party list proportional representation (PR) systems produce higher percentages of women in parliament than single-member district plurality systems (Reynolds, 1999; Lakeman, 1994; Duverger, 1955; Beckwith, 1992; Caul, 1997). One example of a national-level finding that supports this relationship is the German case. Half of the Bundestag is elected by a plurality system and the other half by PR. In 1994, women won 19.1% of the seats by plurality election and 26.2% by PR. The standard explanation for this finding is that parties in plurality systems are reluctant to nominate a woman for fear they will lose the seat to a male competitor from another party. In contrast, parties in PR systems are more willing to add women to the party list in hopes of broadening the party's appeal to different groups. The perceived electoral risk with a female candidate decreases when she is part of a group, rather than the sole candidate (Lakeman, 1994; Lovenduski and Norris, 1993).

Supporting this explanation, studies have demonstrated that as the number of candidates elected in a district (district magnitude) increases, so does the number of women nominated to the list and elected (Beckwith, 1992; Matland, 1993; Rule, 1981). Three or more seats per district means that more than one person on the party list might win a seat. Czudnowski (1975) broadly theorized that party lists allow parties to balance the ticket to represent a number of groups within the party (p. 226). This logic applies to striking a gender balance on the ticket; women can be added to the party list to broaden appeal without unseating men with established positions. Even if women are not ranked first on the list, a woman may still be elected to office if the party wins more than one seat. Hence, research suggests that large, multimember districts and party lists are most conducive to women's representation in legislatures.

The bulk of previous comparative empirical research on women's representation focuses on these national-level patterns of women's representation. By comparing the static percentages of women in national parliaments, prior research misses an important point in explaining women's representation; while the electoral systems of most nations have remained stable over the past twenty years, the proportion of women in office has climbed. Thus, explanations based on fixed institutional characteristics deliver little leverage in explaining change over time.

An important new book by Ron Inglehart and Pippa Norris (2003) attributes women's rise toward equality to changing attitudes towards women's roles across postindustrial societies. Systematically examining the mass publics of seventy nations worldwide (agrarian, industrial, and postindustrial), the authors argue that in nations where there are more egalitarian attitudes, there are more women in political leadership positions. Similarly, Paxton and Kunovich (2003) create an index of gender attitudes and find this index highly correlated with women's political representation. Inglehart and Norris's data show that Western European nations display some of the highest levels of support for women's equality. In fact, "all of the postindustrial nations . . . are clustered at the top right-hand corner" of the graphs showing support for gender equality. Thus, there is little variation among Western European nations when it comes to gender attitudes. Certainly attitudes and values matter for rising levels of women's representation, and they must be taken into account in any study of women's representation. Yet among the set of nations within the scope of this book, cultural attitudes and values provide a fairly even and common force for change over time.

5

Table 1.2 Increase in Women MPs by Party, 1975–97

Party Name	% Women MPs 1975	% Women MPs 1997	% Point Change	Time Period	Number of Elections
Austria					
People's Party (OVP)	6.3	19.2	+13.0	1975-95	6
Freedom Party (FPO)	0	19.0	+19.0	1975-95	6
Socialist Party (SPO)	9.7	31.0	+21.3	1975-95	6
Greens (GA)	62.5	55.6	-6.9	1987-95	3
Belgium					
Christian People's (CVP)	12.0	21.0	+9.0	1974-87[a]	6
Liberty (Flemish) (PVV)	0	4.0	+4.0	1974-87	6
People's Union (VU)	9.0	11.0	+2.1	1974-95	7
Denmark					
Socialist People's (SF)	22.2	23.1	+1.1	1975-94	8
Social Democrats (SD)	11.3	38.7	+27.4	1975-94	8
Social Liberals (RV)	30.7	50.0	+19.3	1975-94	8
Christian People's (KRF)	33.3	N/A	—	1975-89	7
Center Democrats (CD)	0	40.0	+40.0	1975-94	8
Liberal (V)	16.7	31.3	+14.6	1975-94	8
Conservative (KF)	20.0	29.1	+9.1	1975-94	8
Progress Party (KRP)	12.5	27.3	+14.8	1975-94	8
Finland					
People's Democrat (SKDL)	22.5	14.3	-8.2	1975-95	6
Social Democratic (SPD)	24.0	36.5	+12.5	1975-95	6
Center Party (KESK)	18.0	27.3	+9.3	1975-95	6
Swedish People's (SFP)	22.2	25.0	+2.8	1975-95	6
National Coalition (KOK)	25.0	43.6	+18.6	1975-95	6
Germany					
Social Democratic (SPD)	5.4	33.7	+28.3	1972-94	7
Christian Democratic (CDU)	7.5	14.8	+7.3	1972-94	7
Christian Social (CSU)	2.1	12.0	+9.9	1972-94	7
Free Democratic (FDP)	4.8	17.0	+12.2	1972-94	7
Greens (G)	35.7	59.2	+23.5	1983-94	4

Table 1.2 Increase in Women MPs by Party, 1975–97 (*continued*)

Party Name	% Women MPs 1975	% Women MPs 1997	% Point Change	Time Period	Number of Elections
Ireland					
Worker's Party (WP)	0	0	0	1973-89	7
Labour (LAB)	5.3	6.0	+0.7	1973-97	8
Fianna Fail (FF)	1.4	4.4	+3.0	1973-97	8
Fine Gael (FG)	1.9	6.7	+4.8	1973-97	8
Netherlands					
Communist Party (CPN)	0	33.3	+33.3	1972-94	7
Labour Party (PvdA)	3.3	19.6	+16.3	1972-94	7
Pacifist Socialist (PSP)	0	2.1	+2.1	1972-89	6
Christian Democrats (CDA)	3.3	17.0	+13.7	1977-94	6
Democrats 1966 (D 1966)	1.0	35.5	+34.5	1972-94	7
People's Party (VVD)	2.0	18.5	+16.5	1972-94	7
Norway					
Socialist People's (SV)	18.8	33.3	+14.5	1973-97	7
Labour Party (DNA)	19.4	49.2	+29.8	1973-97	7
Center Party (SP)	14.3	36.3	+22.0	1973-97	7
Christian People's (KRF)	5.0	45.8	+40.8	1973-97	7
Liberals (V)	0	16.7	+16.7	1973-97	7
Conservative (H)	17.2	30.4	+13.2	1973-97	7
Progress (FRP)	0	8.0	+8.0	1973-97	7
Sweden					
Communist Party (VPK)	17.6	45.5	+27.9	1973-94	8
Social Dem Worker (S)	17.2	47.8	+30.6	1973-94	8
Center Party (C)	12.7	37.0	+24.3	1973-94	8
People's Party (FP)	10.3	34.6	+24.3	1973-94	8
Right Party (M)	9.8	27.5	+17.7	1973-94	8
UK					
Labour (LAB)	5.0	24.2	+19.2	1974-97	6
Liberal Dem (LIB/SDL)	0	6.5	+6.5	1974-97	6
Conservatives (CON)	2.8	8.6	+5.8	1974-97	6

Source: Katz and Mair (1992) and Inter-Parliamentary Union (1997).

ªFor Belgium the percentage of women in the 1991 and 1995 elections is not available for most parties. Data for the following Belgian parties are not published: BSP, PSB, AGA, and ECO.

Cross-national studies miss the substantial variations in women's parliamentary presence between parties. Across parties and within the same parties over time, parties differ substantially in the number of women they nominate, where they rank women on party lists, and in the number of women they send to parliament (Lovenduski and Norris, 1993; Norris and Lovenduski, 1995). The variation in the proportion of women to men is even greater across parties than across nations. Table 1.2 displays the number of women *by party* in the national legislatures of the nations in this study in the elections closest to 1975 and 1998; the third column displays the percentage point difference between these two time points. The variation in parties, even within the same nation, is often quite striking. For example, in Norway in 1997 the Progress Party had only 8% women in its delegation to parliament, while the Labour Party had 49% women. In stark contrast, the Irish Labour Party had only 6% women in its delegation.

Of the parties under investigation, forty-seven out of fifty registered an increase from 1975 to 1998. The percentage of women decreased only in the Austrian Green and Finnish People's parties, and it remained stagnant at zero in the Irish Worker's Party. However, in the case of the Austrian Greens, the period of time under study is shorter than for the other parties in the project—1987 to 1995. Further, in 1987, of their delegation to parliament, 63% of the MPs were women. In short, the Austrian Greens experienced a "regression toward the mean"—a 1995 move toward 50% women registered a decline. Thus, this case does not constitute a significant loss over time for women in Green Party politics. Likewise, the percentage of women in the Finnish People's Party began at a high level in 1975—23%—and the level fell to 14% in 1997.

Overall, the change in women's parliamentary participation over the last two decades can be characterized as a widespread and sustained increase. An exemplar of this increase in women's participation in parliament at the party level is represented by the Dutch Communist Party which, in 1975, sent no women to parliament, yet this number increased to 33% by 1997.

To present the variation across parties more concisely, figure 1.1 displays the average percentage of women MPs for several general "families," or types, of political parties. The three bars for each family represent the average percentage of women during the periods 1975–81, 1982–89, and 1990–97. As one can observe, all categories except religious parties register an increase. Surprisingly, Socialist parties did not start out with the highest percentage of women, but this percentage rose to the highest level during the 1990s. Rural and conservative parties averaged especially high proportions of women in the 1970s, relative to the other party types, yet they did not display the substantial gains evident among the Socialist parties. Even the ultra-right parties increased their proportion of women over the 20-year time period—although

Figure 1.1 Party Types and the Increase in Women in Parliament

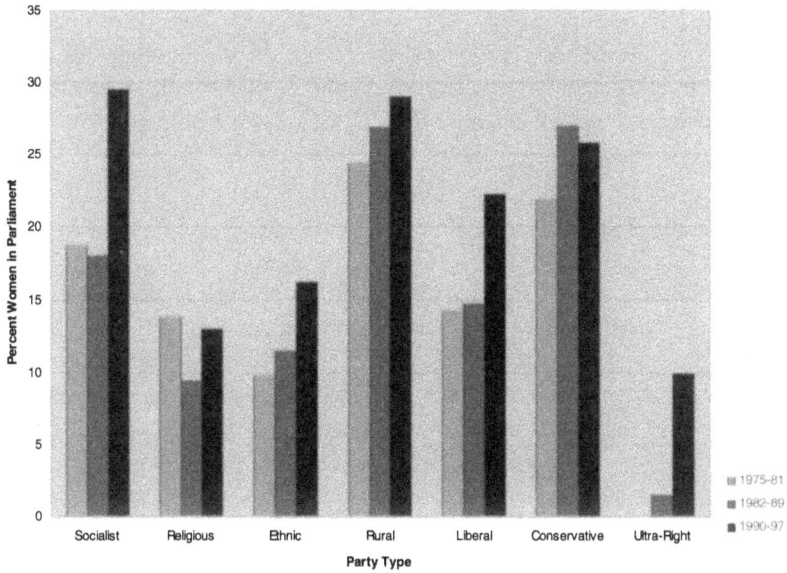

Source: Katz and Mair (1992) and IPU (1997); party type follows Lane and Ersson (1991).

they began at a very low percentage and only ended up averaging 10% women in the 1990s.

These increases in the proportion of women to men in certain parties often result from new party measures designed to make it easier for women to enter politics. Many parties adopt formal policies to promote women candidates, and these measures denote a process of changing attitudes toward women in politics. The implementation of policies to encourage women candidates not only reflects the acceptance that women are underrepresented; it also demonstrates a willingness to fix the problem. Parties have not only adopted gender quotas for candidates, but also for internal party positions. In addition, parties have founded women's branches within the party organization, changed their method of recruiting candidates, and offered special training programs and fundraising assistance for potential women candidates. Policies to promote female candidates have diffused across nations and within party systems. The Inter-Parliamentary Union (IPU) reports that by 1995, eighty-four parties in thirty-six nations had enacted quotas to increase the proportion of women in their delegations to the national legislature.

One example of party efforts to assist women candidates is illustrated in the British party system. Beginning in the mid-1980s, the Labour Party ran weekend training programs for potential women candidates to improve their confidence and speaking skills. The British Conservative Party followed

Labour's lead in the early 1990s by beginning to take steps to promote women. Rather than waiting for qualified women to come forward, the Tories began to "talent spot," choosing women who would make good MPs, recruiting them, and offering them special training. In addition, the central party leadership provides training seminars to selection committee members in order to reduce their bias toward women and minorities in the selection process.

Goals of the Book

Rising numbers of women in parliaments are commonly attributed to the efforts of women's movements, and to growing numbers of women in the workforce, universities, and law schools. Certainly these social processes are necessary, but they are not always *sufficient* explanations for why women's parliamentary representation increased when it did. In most cases, women's parliamentary presence has not grown in a strictly incremental fashion, but rather in punctuated and sometimes dramatic increases (Studlar and McAllister, 2002). Klausen and Maier (2001) theorize that the basic tenets of liberal democratic theory lead to the expectation that gender-blind rules produce equal opportunities that would bring women equality over time. Yet inequalities persist. A growing force within both democratic theory and in the democratic process calls for direct mechanisms to alleviate inequalities for women (Klausen and Maier, 2001). I will argue that the key mechanism for increases in women's parliamentary representation is the political party. As the "gate-keepers" to elected office, parties in Western Europe control which candidates are recruited and nominated, and they can take action to promote women. In short, parties can make or break women's efforts to run for office.

This book presents a more complete theoretical argument and empirical picture of how parties influence women's parliamentary presence. I bring new theory and data to uncover the party-level mechanisms that explain the growth in women in parliaments since the 1970s. Most prior research addressing the role of parties is limited to case studies of individual parties or countries. My systematic comparison of women's representation across parties and over time illuminates some common characteristics of parties that lead to increases in women's parliamentary presence. Party efforts are often attributed to mounting pressures from activists and public opinion at large. This book contradicts the conventional wisdom by showing that women's gains within parties flow not only from pressure from party supporters, but also from calculated efforts made by the central party leadership in a top-down fashion under specific circumstances. Certainly women's efforts are essential, and they can be most effective when they are framed, timed, and pitched toward the most opportune targets within the party hierarchy.

This book has broad implications at two levels. First, it examines how and why political parties respond to challenges from new contenders by focusing on change in one arena—the inclusion of women in party and parliamentary office. At another level, the findings shed light on how women, and new contenders more generally, find access within party politics, and how institutions shape their choices. To examine these questions, I bring together two growing bodies of literature—women and politics, and party change.

Research on women's parliamentary participation has largely focused on the national level. In a seminal volume on parties and women in politics in Western Europe, Joni Lovenduski and Pippa Norris (1993) offer illuminating insights into the characteristics of parties that facilitate women's participation in party politics, and the evidence is based on discrete case studies of individual countries. This book builds upon Lovenduski and Norris's important findings by systematically comparing the role of the party in women's parliamentary representation across ten European nations.

Another body of research addresses how parties change in the face of new challenges. Herbert Kitschelt (1994) examines the electoral fortunes of Socialist parties in Western Europe and argues for the centrality of the party as an active agent in shaping its own destiny. I build upon Kitschelt's contention that the most effective strategy results from a match between political environment and the structure of the party organization. I apply these theoretical insights from a new perspective—from the view of new contenders trying to make inroads within party politics.

Methodological Approach

This research calls for a multimethod approach. I use two types of evidence. At one level, cross-national, cross-party statistics allow for systematic analysis of several sets of explanations for increases in women's representation. I assemble national surveys and aggregate statistics from various published sources. Data are drawn from such diverse sources as The Eurobarometer surveys, the Inter-Parliamentary Union, and data handbooks assembled by party scholars (Katz and Mair, 1992; Laver and Hunt, 1991; Lane and Ersson, 1992). Details on the sources of data can be found in the Appendices.

At another level, qualitative case studies complement the broad statistical analyses. I examine select parties in Britain, Germany, and Finland. While aggregate data reveal patterns among the conditions and characteristics that lead to women's integration into parties, it is also important to understand the way in which power was yielded to promote women. By focusing on a few well-selected cases in detail, I uncover the processes and debates behind party decisions to promote (or not promote) women candidates for office.

Furthermore, for purposes of broad, cross-national comparison, the statistical analysis explains women's numerical representation. In contrast, the case studies can focus both on women in parliament and on an important intervening step—party campaigns to increase women's representation.

In late 1999, I spent nearly a month in each nation interviewing party officials, party workers, members of parliament (MPs), and women's movement coordinators. Only by interviewing those involved in the efforts to promote women candidates could I establish why certain parties decided to take action when they did. Specifically, I interviewed twelve MPs, five heads of party women's organizations, two party vice presidents, four party directors, a party general secretary, a campaign coordinator, the speaker of the Finnish Eduskunta and presidential nominee, seven party activists, and five representatives from independent women's groups. In addition, I analyzed a great deal of written material from party archives and government agencies. For example, I combed through minutes from meetings of women's organizations in the British Conservative and Labour parties. I visited the offices of the ombudsman for equality in Finland, and I read several reports. I scoured countless political pamphlets from parties in Britain, Germany, and Finland.

Case Selection

The book focuses on a set of Western European nations (Austria, Belgium, Denmark, Finland, Germany, Ireland, Netherlands, Norway, Sweden, and Britain) that are common to four comprehensive, party-level datasets (Katz and Mair, 1992; Inter-Parliamentary Union, 1997; Laver and Hunt, 1992; Lane and Ersson, 1991). The cross-national analysis is based on fifty parties in those ten nations (see table 1.2 for a list of parties). Because this group of nations is not a random sample of postindustrial democracies, my conclusions can only be cautiously generalized beyond these ten cases. Further, I examine the period from 1975 to 1997 because beginning in the 1970s, women dramatically stepped up pressures on parties for greater political representation (Jenson, 1995; Lovenduski and Norris, 1993: 5). During the 1970s, gender equality became part of the social agenda of advanced industrial societies, and a growing number of women took their demands for increased representation to political parties.

From this set of countries, I selected three for in-depth investigation: Britain, Germany, and Finland. In order not to introduce bias into the research design, I selected these nations, and several parties within each nation, based upon key explanatory variables (see King, Keohane, and Verba, 1994). Previous research on the role of parties in women's representation suggests that the most important influences are the party's ideology, the presence or absence of candidate gender quotas or targets, and the number of women among the party's highest decision-making body (Caul, 1999; Lovenduski and Norris, 1993).

Because ideology is a key variable, I included parties from across the ideological continuum in Britain, Germany, and Finland. In Britain, I included the Labour and Conservative parties. In Germany, I selected the Social Democratic (SPD), Free Democratic (FDP), and Christian Democratic/Christian Social Union (CDU/CSU) parties. In Finland, I selected the Social Democratic (SDP), Center (KESK), and National Coalition (KOK) parties.

Another important mechanism in explaining change in the inclusion of women candidates is the adoption of candidate gender quotas. As such, party systems have been chosen to maximize variation in the use of quotas or less stringent targets for the proportion of women candidates. At the high end, in Germany all of the parties (except the CSU) have adopted some form of gender quotas or targets. The use of quotas began with the Green Party and diffused across the party system. In contrast, in Finland none of the parties implemented formal candidate gender quotas or targets. Between these two extremes, in Britain the Labour Party adopted a version of quotas for shortlisting candidates, but quotas failed to diffuse across the ideological spectrum to the Conservatives.

Next, the proportion of women on the party's highest body was considered. In Finland the proportion of women on the National Executive Committees (NECs) of most parties began at a high level, relative to the levels of other parties. Germany witnessed substantial increases; the number of women on the NEC in the Social Democratic Party rose dramatically after 1975, while the number in the remaining German parties increased more moderately. By contrast, the number of women on the NEC in the Labour and Conservative parties has remained virtually stagnant.

The Importance of the Representation of Women in Parliament

This book hinges on the contention that the numerical, or descriptive, representation of women in national legislatures is essential to the quality of the democratic process. Yet how are women most effectively represented by their elected officials? In her seminal book, *The Concept of Representation,* Hannah Pitkin (1967) argues that a correspondence between representative and constituent on issues ("substantive" representation) is more critical than a match based upon personal characteristics, such as race or gender ("descriptive" representation). Anne Phillips (1995) argues for the addition of the "politics of presence," or descriptive representation. Several arguments underpin the call for "presence." The most persuasive contends that traditionally excluded groups raise new issues, and therefore their participation at the

13

agenda-setting and debate stages of policymaking is essential to the quality of the democratic process (Mansbridge, 1999). The groups that are represented in the legislature shape the issue agenda, alter the salience of certain issues, and influence the nature of the debate surrounding issues.

Specific to this research, many women elected officials may raise and support issues that are shaped by their life experiences. In a cross-national study of women's presence in the national legislatures of industrialized nations, Valerie O'Regan (2000) finds that the higher the proportion of women, the more likely are stronger policies such as employment and wage protection policy, and equal wage legislation. In addition, case study evidence shows that women elected officials highlight issues that are distinct from those emphasized by their male counterparts. For example, in Britain, female MPs, regardless of partisan affiliation, prioritize health and education and oppose nuclear energy more than male MPs (Norris and Lovenduski, 1989). In more recent research, on the basis of more fundamental values, British female MPs, regardless of party, differ from their male counterparts on support for affirmative action and gender equality issues (Norris and Lovenduski, 2001). Research on state legislatures in the United States finds that female legislators are more favorable toward expanding welfare programs than male legislators, and this gender difference is especially pronounced among Republicans (Poggione, 2004). Similarly, research on the United States Congress shows that although women members tend to vote along party lines at the same rate as men, women appear to raise new issues that are important to women as a group (Thomas, 1993; Dodson, 1995). And women in Congress show greater intensity of commitment to these "women's issues" in the legislative process, even when controlling for their party affiliation (Swers, 2002). Importantly, interviews with former and current congresswomen reveal that these women most often share a group identity as women and feel a special responsibility to represent women's interests in Congress (Carroll, 2002).

Research on the Scandinavian nations, who lead the world in the percentage of women in parliament, confirms that women's presence makes a difference. At the municipal level in Norway, Bratton and Ray (2002) find that the proportion of women elected is positively related to the percentage of children in state-funded childcare facilities, especially during the process of formulating a childcare policy. Hege Skjeie (1991) documents how a significant number of women in the Norwegian parliament first raised the issue of quality daycare in the legislature. Although Conservative women favored one policy outcome, and Labour women another, the significant breakthrough was that the national legislature took up the issue of daycare coverage and kept it on the agenda until a policy was passed. Further, through the eyes of elected officials themselves, women's presence impacts politics. In a survey of MPs from all parties in all five Scandinavian nations, Lena Wangnerud (2000) finds the majority of those surveyed confirmed that their party had indeed changed issue positions because of an increase in the number of women MPs among them.

The argument for a politics of presence is linked to another body of comparative politics literature that concentrates on group representation based on shared ethnic background, cultural heritage, or even language. Arend Lijphart's (1977) "consociational democracy" calls for elite power sharing among politically relevant segments of society to encourage full inclusion, thus decreasing the need for protest outside political channels. A representative body that includes women may signal the importance of their input, thereby lending legitimacy to the regime and thus encouraging democratic stability.

Lijphart's (1999) more recent research shows that across thirty-six nations, consensus-based governments lead to higher quality democracy. Specifically, consensus governments are more likely to have more women in parliament, be welfare states, have fewer citizens in prison, and protect the environment. Here, I argue that in addition to being a measure of the outcome (democratic quality), having more women in office is also part of the inclusive dimension of the consensus-based model. Where power is shared with new contenders such as women, rather than held exclusively by entrenched interests, the policymaking process itself is transformed.

Importantly, women's numerical representation in parliament may also empower women as democratic citizens and encourage their participation. Schwartz (1988) argues that descriptive representation brings constituents into the process and unites them into a political group. Some research on women's political participation in the United States supports this contention. Women are more highly engaged in politics in states where women candidates have run visible and competitive races (Atkeson, 2003). High-Pippert and Comer (1998) find that in districts where a woman is elected, women voters are more likely to be interested in and participate in politics, and to have a greater sense of political efficacy and competence. However, Lawless (2004) controls for party congruence among representative and constituent and finds little support for the idea that descriptive representation encourages efficacy or activity among women.

Further evidence for the importance of descriptive representation is found among other underrepresented groups. At the presidential level, Katherine Tate's (1991; 1994) research reveals that Jesse Jackson's presidential campaign stimulated turnout among blacks. At the congressional level, in separate studies Lawrence Bobo and Frank Gilliam (1990) and Claudine Gay (1997) show that African-American participation rates are higher in districts that are represented by an African-American. The mechanism behind higher participation appears to be the engagement of the marginalized group through a symbolic cue of likely responsiveness to racial concerns. Katherine Tate (2001) provides powerful evidence for this explanation by showing that

African-Americans in descriptively represented districts are significantly more knowledgeable about their representatives.

A final argument for encouraging women's candidacies is based on equality of opportunity, or equal access to the national legislature, for *all* citizens. In other words, if the democratic process is to be truly democratic, then all groups, including women, should have an equal chance of running for office. Thus, if norms and rules are consistent for all, then women's low levels of representation might be attributed to women's lack of motivation or interest. However, if there are barriers to women's parliamentary representation, then those barriers must be broken down to encourage women's representation. Although the legal barriers to women's participation have long been dismantled, this project examines some of the more subtle party norms and rules that historically inhibited women's participation, and the institutional and political context that encourages women's entrance into party politics.

Overview of the Book

This book uncovers the process of women's increasing participation in party politics and parliamentary office. In chapter 2, I draw on party, institutional, and social movement theory to develop a new framework for explaining how and why parties incorporate new contenders. I will argue that parties are more likely to incorporate women when women's organized strategy takes into account the institutional and political "opportunity structures" of both the party and the party system. To examine the timing of party change, I then tie the structure of opportunity into two analytical models of the sequence of party change, derived from the broad literature on comparative parties.

The second part of the book applies this theory to the systematic study of ten Western European nations. Previous research shows women's power in top decision-making bodies within the party improves women's opportunities in parliament (Caul, 1999). As women gain power within the party, they gain resources to pressure for further representation. Therefore, lobbying efforts from the top party ranks appear to be a powerful mechanism for increasing women's parliamentary participation. But how do women rise to these positions of power within the party in the first place? Chapter 3 turns to the conditions under which women made the most progress inside the party hierarchy. The multivariate statistical analysis uncovers the party institutions that encourage women's ascendance to the top ranks.

Candidate gender quotas spread across many parties in Western Europe in recent years; they signal a party's commitment to women's numerical representation. In chapter 4 I not only build upon and update previous studies to determine which parties are most likely to adopt quotas (Caul, 2001), but I also discuss how quotas fit into the process of change among parties, women in top-level party positions, and increases in women's representation in parliament.

The third part of the book applies my theory in depth to three nations. Chapters 5, 6, and 7 investigate how women challenged parties and accessed parliament in Britain, Germany, and Finland, respectively. The data in these chapters are derived from extensive interviews and party records and materials in each nation, and from national election studies and Eurobarometer Surveys. In each case, I identify the conditions under which parties have intensified efforts to run women candidates for office, and where these candidacies translated into office holding. I assess the impact of electoral pressures, party competition, the party's women's organization, key women in party leadership positions, and party rule changes.

Broad similarities and differences make these nations ripe for comparison. All three offer capitalist economic systems that have undergone similar socioeconomic transformations in the postwar period, hold similar Western values, share long-standing democratic processes, and are members of the European Union. Importantly, all three witnessed a dramatic transformation in women's roles over the past fifty years. With rising economic affluence, restructuring of the labor force, and secularization, women have come to play a larger role in the public sphere, entering the workforce and institutions of higher education in unprecedented numbers. Yet at the same time, the three systems vary greatly. Their rich and unique histories and intricate governmental structures allow adequate variation to uncover the differences that underpin women's distinct strategies and parties' varying responses to women's demands.

The final section of the book represents the culmination of the project's efforts to explain the role of parties in increasing women's presence across ten Western European parliaments. Chapter 8 presents a multivariate analysis based on party-level time series cross-sectional data, with observations for all national elections between 1975 and 1998. The most important factors identified in the previous chapters are combined with opportunity structure variables to model both the variation and change in women's parliamentary presence across parties.

Finally, in chapter 9 I connect the case study and statistical findings, tying this evidence into the opportunity structure theory. This concluding chapter addresses how the case of women's representation has broader implications for a unified theory of party adaptation to new demands, and for how new contenders can best press their claims for presence within the party and parliamentary office.

2

Opportunity Structures:
The Key to Women's Access

After World War II, Western European societies were divided largely along class, religious, and urban and rural lines (Lipset and Rokkan, 1967; Rose and Urwin, 1970). Beginning in the 1970s, these reliable groupings gradually diversified (Dalton et al., 1985; Crewe and Denver, 1985). Citizens became increasingly concerned with new issues such as environmental quality, alternative lifestyles, and gender equality (Inglehart, 1977; 1997). Much previous research has concentrated on the role of new parties, namely New Left parties, in representing these new concerns (Mueller-Rommel, 1989; Kitschelt, 1989). However, we know less about the effects of new issues on established parties. Although new issues may have the potential to disintegrate the existing partisan alignment, Mair and Smith (1990) argue that most new issues are absorbed within the framework of traditional left and right ideology. "For all the changes experienced in recent years, it is clear that left and right not only remain the major organizing principles in modern West European politics, but also help to create a uniform foundation for contemporary patterns of political competition" (175).

Empirical research supports this claim that established parties in Western Europe have adopted many of these new issues. Klingemann et al. (1994) find that the percentage of references to issues such as environmental quality and minority rights has steadily increased in party manifestos over the past several decades. Likewise, Rohrschneider (1993a) finds that, across four nations,

18

established leftist parties are "considerably more able than previously assumed to absorb the environmental challenge." Given that established parties are addressing issues beyond the traditional socioeconomic concerns that have historically defined their agendas, it is essential to examine the process by which parties incorporate these new concerns.

The campaign for gender equality represents one prominent new issue. In the 1960s and 1970s, feminism resurged as a strong social movement in most postindustrial societies (Gelb, 1989). Although the movement has been composed of diverse ideologies, forms of action, and organization, one common theme has been the demand for the democratization of social and political life (Jenson, 1995). Some wings of the women's movement eschewed working within established political channels, but many groups pressed political parties for political representation of women (Lovenduski and Norris, 1993). Women's demands for representation are both programmatic and organizational, and this book centers on the latter. With varying degrees of success, women made concerted efforts to be included in parties, even at the highest rank—parliamentary office.

This chapter proceeds as follows. First, I draw from existing scholarship to set out the components of party opportunity structure. Second, I point out some of the limitations of previous theories of party change and conceptualize the sequence of change within parties. Finally, I combine structure and sequence to offer a model for women's gains in elected office.

Conditions of Party Change: The "Opportunity Structure"

So why do some established parties respond to the challenges of new demands? More specifically, *why did some political parties react to the pressure to promote women candidates for parliament while others did not?* And why did those parties take action at the time they did? The role of the party in increasing women's access is a case of a broader process of party organizational change, or incorporation of new contenders.

The established party literature does not offer a clear, systematic theory to account for how and why political parties incorporate new contenders. This book offers an integrated and dynamic theory that considers both the direction of dominant forces for party changes and the way those forces interact with the party's opportunity structure. I argue that the likelihood and sequence in which a party will either absorb or create new constituencies is shaped by the set of rules, norms, and political conditions in which the party is embedded. Taken together, these factors structure opportunities for both parties and women. Simply put, opportunity structure shapes the degree to which efforts, both from the top and bottom of the party organization, will succeed or fail.

Considering the receptivity of parties to women's demands explains, in large part, why political parties promote women candidates when they do.

The importance of an opportunity structure to timing the translation of citizen demands is rooted in Sidney Tarrow's (1989; 1994) research on social movements. Tarrow develops the concept of "political opportunity structure" to explain why collective action emerges in some instances and not others. This opportunity structure framework has been applied to the women's movement (Katzenstein and Mueller, 1987; Gelb, 1989; 2002), the environmental movement (Kitschelt, 1986), new social movements in general (Kriesi et al., 1992), and the civil rights movement in the United States (McAdam, 1982).[1] Similarly, Herbert Kitschelt (1994) argues for the efficacy of opportunity structure within political parties in his analysis of the divergent electoral fortunes of nine socialist parties in Western Europe. In this book, I build upon this framework for opportunity structure by examining the entrance of a new group of contenders vying for a voice within the party, and ultimately in parliament.

Specific to this research, opportunity structure sheds light on the constraints and incentives that condition women's strategies within political parties. Certainly these contextual characteristics do not act as agents of change, but they do intervene in the process of political change to make it more or less likely for a group of party leaders to take strategic action. I break down the concept of opportunity structure into two categories, political and institutional. Political opportunity structure describes the broader ideological environment within which political parties operate and focuses on shifts in the balance of political power between contending groups, which open up windows of opportunity for change. Institutional opportunity structure consists of both the "rules of the game" that shape party behavior and the efforts of new contenders.

Furthermore, each set of structures operates both within the party, and in the party system at large. The set of exogenous factors includes a dense set of external rules that guide party behavior. In a similar fashion, the set of endogenous factors offers some reasons for how and why party elites may exercise control over party change. Table 2.1 summarizes the specific set of conditions I expect to constitute the "political opportunity structure" and the "institutional opportunity structure," both within and outside of the party, and I draw out these expectations in the sections below.

This book focuses less attention on how parties differ in these characteristics, and more on how the characteristics intervene in the process of change. In the following sections, these theoretical "opportunity structures" will be linked to hypotheses about the ability and willingness of a party to incorporate women.

Table 2.1 Opportunity Structure for Increasing Women's Representation in Parliament

	Political Opportunity Structure	Institutional Opportunity Structure
Exogenous to Party	· Electoral Instability · New Issues · Party System Competition	· Electoral System Rules
Endogenous to Party	· Reorganization of Power within Party · Changing Perceptions of Party Leadership	· Internal Party Structure

Political Opportunity Structure

Political opportunity structure describes the broad power balance within which actors operate—either at the elite or at the mass level. Sidney Tarrow (1989) aptly describes this power balance as the "ebb and flow of political tides" (25). These are the broad political conditions that surround women's efforts to gain greater representation and to influence the priority given to this issue by political parties.

Electoral Instability

New challengers can make greater inroads within political parties during periods of electoral instability. For example, Piven and Cloward's (1977) research in the United States on Civil Rights points toward the importance of electoral volatility in the South in altering the Democratic Party's strategy to attract a new group of supporters. Likewise, party realignment is key to changing the power balance in Sidney Tarrow's (1994) theory of the rise and decline of social movements.

Social divisions based on class and religion once structured party competition in Western Europe (Lipset and Rokkan, 1967). The shift from industrial to service-dominated economies, rising levels of affluence and education, and secularization undercut these traditional divisions. In the post–World War II period, citizens were less likely to align with parties based on strong class loyalties (Franklin et al., 1991), and a declining proportion of unionized workers in most postindustrial democracies (Griffin, McCammon, and Botsko, 1990; Gray and Caul, 2000) left parties seeking new groups to supplement their electoral bases. The declining strength of the traditional class-based groups has opened the door for new contenders to become important to the party.

21

Further, women's voting patterns have shifted over this same period. The early research on women's voting behavior in Western Europe established that in the 1960s and 1970s, women were more conservative than men, both in their attitudes and in their partisan loyalties (Duverger, 1955; Lipset, 1962; Butler and Stokes, 1974: 160; Inglehart, 1977: 229). Scholars often attributed this conservative, or "traditional," gender gap to structural factors, such as women's higher rates of church attendance and their low participation in the paid workforce (DeVaus and McAllister, 1989; Inglehart, 1981; Baxter and Lansing, 1983).

During the 1980s, however, differences between women's and men's electoral behavior gradually faded. Women were no longer consistently more conservative, and in some cases moved toward the Left (Jelen, Thomas, and Wilcox, 1994). Increasing similarity between men and women in both partisanship and the vote was identified in Britain (Heath et al., 1985; Hayes and McAllister, 1997; Norris, 1999) and in Western Europe overall (deVaus and McAllister, 1989; Studlar, McAllister, and Hayes 1998). Scholars often link the transformation in women's conservatism to the transformation of women's lives in the postwar period. Religiosity and church attendance among women decreased, and their collective educational and workforce participation levels increased.

By the late 1990s, empirical research suggested that women were moving to the left of men in their vote and partisanship. This new gender gap was first identified in the United States in the early 1980s (Klein, 1985). Inglehart and Norris's (1998) comprehensive study from 1980 to 1995 shows that in the early 1980s, women were more right-wing than men in most advanced industrial democracies, yet by 1995 women were more left-wing in most nations. Further, unlike the findings of deVaus and McAllister (1989), Inglehart and Norris found that the gender gap is less reliant on structural forces, but rather on the shift in attitudes and values associated with feminism and postmaterialism. And among younger generations, young women tend to be more left-wing than young men, and one might expect that the gender gap will continue to grow over time.

Thus, the "unanchoring" of women's votes has created an atmosphere of new opportunity, and the possibility for parties to court women's votes as a group. Past case study research on women and politics in Britain and Germany begins to link shifts in women's voting behavior to women's parliamentary representation (Kolinsky, 1992; Norris, 1999). Yet previous research has neither fully drawn out the links between the two nor tested this relationship systematically.

Certainly where women coordinate their efforts to visibly show their electoral support for women-friendly parties, parties are most likely to take notice. Mona Lena Krook's (2002) research in Sweden shows that competition between the Swedish parties over women's votes intensified after women threatened to form their own women's party if they did not make substantial gains on the party lists. In response, five Swedish parties began alternating the names of men and women on the party lists.

The Rise of New Issues

These broad social transformations and their concomitant shifts in values and attitudes have altered the political issue agenda (Inglehart, 1977; 1997). Specific to women's representation, as women entered higher education and the paid workforce en masse, women's changing roles in the public sphere became a more salient issue. Based on identity rather than economic status, concern for women's representation attracts supporters based upon concerns for equality or for empowerment. Women's empowerment is part of a larger package of "New Left" issues in Western Europe that also includes environmentalism, nuclear proliferation, and alternative lifestyles.

These "New Left" issues are often carried to mainstream politics by social movements. The women's movement "resurged" in the late 1960s across Western Europe and intensified efforts to gain a foothold in partisan politics. Underneath the broad pattern of resurgence of the women's movement in the 1970s, research on the women's movement in Western Europe reveals variation in the amount and type of pressure on parties across both parties and nations (Gelb, 1989; Kaplan, 1992). Once women began to concentrate efforts in party politics, they gained greater power, resources, and opportunities to directly pressure for representation at the highest level of the party. Further, a shift in focus from "separatism" in the 1970s toward greater "integration" and partisan politics in the 1980s and 1990s heightened the salience of the issue of women's representation (Krook, 2001).

In addition, inequalities in the presence of men and women in national legislatures gained international recognition as an enduring problem. The key organizational force in bringing the issue of women's parliamentary representation to the world agenda has been the United Nations, which sponsored several international conferences addressing women's global status in 1975 in Mexico City, in 1980 in Copenhagen, in 1985 in Nairobi, and in 1995 in Beijing. The United Nations declared 1975 the "International Women's Year," which soon expanded to the "Decade for Women," 1976 to 1985. In 1979 the United Nations General Assembly adopted the Convention on the Elimination of All Forms of Discrimination Against Women (CEDAW), and, 187 nations have signed it. Women's activism initially sparked United Nations attention to women's equality, and in reciprocal fashion, the United Nations conferences and parallel nongovernmental organization forums have fostered the growth of a global feminist movement that addresses women's representation among other women's issues (Keck and Sikkink, 1998). The United Nations' activities and women's international networking have heightened the importance of women's equality at the national level. In an event history analysis of 157 nations from 1975 to 1998, True and Mintrom (2001) find that greater transnational networking increases the likelihood that a country will adopt formal agencies and rules to consider the impact of new legislation on women's equality.

Structure of Party System Competition

In a similar fashion, competition between parties often opens up new windows of opportunity for women in political parties. Several scholars suggest that competitive pressures generated by rival parties motivate party change (Harmel and Svansand, 1997; Appleton and Ward, 1997). In a strategic process, one party motivates another to change its behavior. The expectation is that an established party will adopt a new issue after a successful entrepreneurial party "steals" part of its traditional voting bloc on the basis of that issue(s). Further, the new party has the greatest impact on the established party when they are neighbors on the ideological continuum. For example, Rohrschneider's (1993) cross-national study of leftist parties in four European nations reveals that electoral successes by New Left parties stimulated the established Old Left parties to respond to environmental issues. Likewise, Harmel and Svansand's (1997) research suggests that even the introduction of a new rightist party can pressure neighboring established parties. In both Norway and Denmark, the entrance of a new Progress Party motivated the larger Conservative Party to respond to new issue demands. The new ideologically-driven party was able to get its issues onto the mainstream agenda without gaining a large vote share, but rather by pushing the major party to perceive the new party as a future problem.

Specific to parties' incorporation of women, case study evidence points toward a process of change across the party system—where one party initiates change to seek competitive advantage, rival parties may follow suit. Krook (2002) aptly titles the parties that initiate the competition through innovative policies as the "pro-active" parties, and those that follow the "reactive parties." The emergence of a New Left party that competes for women's votes may elevate women's representation to heightened salience and spur an established party to respond. Matland and Studlar (1996) detail this "contagion" effect within the party systems of Norway and Canada. After a small entrepreneurial party in each system began promoting women, larger rival parties anticipated a loss of votes and responded by running higher numbers of women themselves. In France in 1992, the Greens began running lists of candidates with equal numbers of women and men, heightening the visibility of claims for parity (Jenson and Valiente, 2003). Although party-level quotas were initially deemed unconstitutional in 1982, efforts culminated in state-level policies to bring more women to the National Assembly. In June 2000, France amended its Constitution to change Article 3, allowing for positive action to bring a balance among men and women elected officials (Jenson and Valiente, 2003). Likewise, Lisa Baldez (2003) examines the adoption of a national gender quota law in Mexico and theorizes that a party-level contagion in quotas may even give parties incentive to push for a national candidate quota policy. Parties across the spectrum may favor such a law in an effort to neutralize the electoral advantage that one individual party might gain. In other words, parties may seek state intervention to even the playing field for all.

Reorganization of Power within the Party

Party elites are those within the decision-making groups of the party; they shape the positions parties will take on issues, and the image the party will project to voters. Party elites are concerned with the party's electoral fortunes, and as such, they act in a strategic manner to align the party with issues that they expect will expand the party's base and secure votes. The party leadership, whether by conversion or turnover, may change their calculus concerning how support for an issue may contribute to their ability to attract support.

First, new leadership often leads to new policies and behaviors. New leaders may make deliberate and conscious choices to consolidate their power and to advance the party's goals (Harmel and Janda, 1994). Christina Wolbrecht (2000) argues that this replacement of the old guard with newcomers—elite turnover—was instrumental in changing party positions in the United States. In comparative perspective, evidence from six parties in the United Kingdom and Germany from 1991 to 1993 reveals that decisions made by new internal leaders or new dominant factions are an important force in bringing change in the status quo (Harmel et al., 1995). Further, even when electoral losses are taken into account, changes in the party leadership exert an independent and powerful influence on party change. For example, in a case study of the Austrian Socialist Party, Wolfgang Mueller (1997) shows that the party's transition from mass communications to professionalized campaign techniques flowed directly from the decisions of new leaders. After a poor electoral performance, Socialist leaders assessed the party's problems and designed strategies to increase the party's vote share in the next election.

With regard to women's claims within party politics, elites have often pursued a strategy of neglect, and this is the pattern of elite behavior that Harvey (2003) finds in the early half of the twentieth century in the United States. Similarly, even since the 1970s, Sanbonmatsu (2001) finds Democratic and Republican party leaders have still largely ignored most women's equality issues, choosing not to build electoral support based on gender alignments. However, the addition of women to the subset of party elites may introduce a new perspective on the utility of women's votes. Past research in the United States shows that women in office are more likely than their male counterparts to introduce women's rights legislation (Burrell, 1994), to include representing women's interests in their understanding of their role as representative (Thomas, 1994), and to sponsor women's rights legislation (Wolbrecht, 2000).

Rather than turnover, a subset of existing party elites may gain a new understanding of the importance of certain issues, and their potential for party support. To explain divergent party responses to issues, it is essential to consider the *perceptions* by political actors that responding to new issues will benefit the party. In other words, party leaders must come to see their interests in a new light. This process is analogous to the "perceived presence of support" that is an aspect of Tarrow's (1989) opportunity framework for social movements. For example, in an investigation of the different responses of European Socialist parties to new economic conditions, Frank Wilson (1994) argues for the importance of shifts in the attitudes of party leaders, who prioritized the needs of their parties, chose among a variety of tactics and strategies to address the problem, and then persuaded party members to follow them.

Importantly, new contenders' efforts can alter party leaders' perceptions of the value of the group's support. Doug McAdam (1982) argues for the importance of "new frames of meaning" in gaining support for the demands of an insurgent group. McAdam et al. (2001) contend that framing "mediates between opportunity and action" (41). In other words, new contenders make gains when they pitch their demands in a manner that connects the group and its leaders under a common ground. For political parties, that common ground is most likely electoral support. Therefore, women's efforts within political parties may be most likely to gain favor among party leaders when they are couched as part of a larger strategy to benefit the party at the polls.

Institutional Opportunity Structure

Institutions also condition access to party hierarchies, and the party itself may be said to have an "institutional opportunity structure." Furthermore, parties are embedded in a larger set of electoral rules that shape party strategy. The importance of institutions in shaping divergent responses to common challenges is emphasized by the "new institutionalist" literature (March and Olson, 1989; Powell and DiMaggio, 1991). Steinmo et al. (1992) state that "institutions constrain and refract politics, but they are never the sole 'cause' of outcomes." As such, institutions mediate, or filter, the relationship between political actors' efforts and outcomes. Following North's (1990) seminal definition, institutions include both norms and formal rules—whether consciously designed or unintended consequences. Clearly such features of parties as standard practices, organizational structures, and formal rules fall under this definition. The importance of intraparty institutions such as these has been highlighted in past research—but the focus has been limited to how power structures shape a party's electoral fortunes or policymaking (Panebianco, 1988; Kitschelt, 1994).

Electoral System Rules

The electoral system represents a key set of rules outside the party. Several studies have established that party list PR electoral systems with large, multi-member districts yield higher numbers of women in parliament than plurality (single-member district) systems (Rule, 1987; Matland, 1993). Women and politics scholars have long theorized that parties are less likely to run a woman in a single-member district system because they can only run a single candidate and fear losing the seat to a male competitor. In contrast, in party-list system parties, where parties nominate several candidates, parties are more likely to add women to the list of candidates in order to broaden the party's appeal and to balance the ticket. A woman candidate can be seen as a benefit to the ticket by attracting votes, without requiring that established politicians step aside. The logic behind the strong relationship between electoral system and women's representation attributes a great deal of explanatory power to party leaders, who presumably act in the best electoral interest of their parties.

Importantly, electoral rules also structure competition across the party system, which in turn affects institutions within parties. A proportional representation (PR) system encourages new parties, while single-member district, winner-take-all systems discourage third parties, because voters fear third-party votes will be wasted (Duverger, 1955). The ability of a marginalized group to take its demands to a small, entrepreneurial party, or even to form its own party, may motivate established parties to respond to the challenges of the marginalized group.

In addition, electoral rules pace the rate of turnover among elected officials. In this way, single-member districts can act as a drag on women's progress. In single-member districts, elected officials act as representatives of geographically based constituencies. Through the candidate-centered process, bolstered by individual case work and name recognition, incumbents gain great advantage and normally retain their seats for several terms in office. Thus, a district with an incumbent often earns the title "safe seat." An abundance of safe seats means few open seats for new challengers such as women (Darcy and Beckwith, 1987, as cited in Darcy et al., 1994).

Internal Party Structure

Specific institutional forms both influence the permeability of the party to new challenges and shape the processes through which decisions are made (Weaver and Rockman, 1993). Certain organizational characteristics within the party constrain the ability and the willingness of a party to respond to new pressures, and they control the form of that response. Together, the degree of centralization, factionalization, institutionalization, and party ideology are the most important rules and norms within parties vis-à-vis the institutional opportunity structure for new contenders.

The first internal structure, the party's degree of centralization, describes the distribution of control over decision making among the levels of the party hierarchy. Epstein (1980) theorized that more decentralized parties will be more likely to change. The stimulus for change is usually detected at the local level, and centralized parties could miss this stimulus. Bolstering this theory, in an empirical study of the changing nature of four European social democratic parties, Kitschelt (1994) finds that the ability of parties to change is a function of the openness of the party organization at the grassroots level. A more decentralized, loose structure encourages the influx of new ideas and "innovation from below."

Although party activists at the local level may perceive a need for the party to adapt, local activists in a centralized party have little power to enact that change. Thus it may be a more centralized party organization that facilitates the flow of information between party units and directs information toward the top of the organization, thus enabling party leaders to encounter new challenges (Appleton and Ward, 1997). Further, Kitschelt (1994) finds that autonomy of the party leadership from collateral organizations allows party leaders to act strategically upon the impulses received from the grass roots. Thus, ties and previous commitments to outside groups may conceivably constrain a party in its response to newcomers.

In addition, parties with structures capable of recognizing new challenges quickly are often more likely to respond to new groups (Kitschelt, 1994). Parties with a greater number of strong ties to outside groups (more highly factionalized) and a tradition of allowing organized interest groups to have a say in party decision-making processes should be more likely to extend this access to newcomers. Panebianco (1988) argues that parties with a great deal of internal conflict learn to more easily absorb new demands. Similarly, through a case study of the intraparty decision making of Austrian parties, Mueller and Meth-Cohn (1995) theorize that highly factionalized parties tend to develop integrating strategies to reduce the potential for and the effects of conflict.

Likewise, parties with deeply engrained ideological orientations and fixed

rules absorb fewer challenges. This aptitude for ideological and rule flexibility is a party's "degree of institutionalization." Panebianco (1988) hypothesizes
that reliance on standardized rules impedes change, because parties that integrate new issues must be flexible and open to new demands. Where leaders
are subject to many bureaucratic rules, their strategic flexibility is inhibited.
And strict adherence to the party program may be linked to factionalism—if
a party is entrenched in the functional specialization of roles, this situation
may also discourage factionalism, and the party may have trouble responding
to new challenges (Kitschelt, 1994).

Further, rigid procedures shape the nature of the process by which MPs are
recruited. Highly regulated parties provide all potential MPs, especially those
without ties to the power center, with a set of understandable rules. Czudnowski (1975) reasons that the more institutionalized the selection process,
the easier it is for any outsider to understand how the selection process works.
The aspiring officeholders anticipate the criteria by which each applicant will
be judged. In addition, party leaders have less leeway to bend the rules in favor
of certain candidates. Weakly institutionalized parties tend to bias candidate
nomination in favor of those who have accumulated "personal political capi-
tal," resources based upon personal status or external group support
(Guadagnini, 1993).

Finally, a party's ideology shapes its ability to change. The seminal
research of Duverger (1945) first highlighted the importance of ideology in
shaping party behavior. Similarly, Kitschelt (1994) argues that a party's
response is constrained by its existing framework of ideas and traditions. The
party's past ideological debates frame the new debates and condition the willingness of party to listen to new demands. In short, a party's solution to a new
problem or challenge is conditioned by its history.

The ideological congruence between movement and party is key to the
process of change. In the case of women's representation, leftist parties, which
harbor more egalitarian ideologies overall, are more sympathetic to the interests of a marginalized group. The party leadership in leftist parties finds it easier to absorb and channel an issue that is consistent with the party's present
values.

Opportunity Structure and the Sequence of Party Change

Certainly the conditions for opportunity are important, but one must also consider the efficacy of different sources of pressure for change. How do
women's efforts and party leaders' efforts interact with the opportunity structure? Two simplified theories of the flow of change within political parties can
be extracted from the broader literature on the sequence of political change

and adaptation. The two analytical models loosely follow those outlined by Wolfgang Mueller (1997), who traces their development to organizational theory literature. The first, the "Societal Change" approach, theorizes that parties and other political institutions react to new challenges in a largely bottom-up process. In contrast, the "Elite-led" approach views parties as actors who alter their environment in a predominantly top-down process. Specific to women's access, the Societal Change approach would suggest that pressure generated by the party's grass roots forced parties to respond by promoting women candidates for office. In contrast, the Elite-led approach suggests that party leaders selected the issue of promoting women candidates in anticipation that these women would benefit the party at the polls.

It is important to note that the two approaches are simplified versions of a compilation of rich theories. Rather than being mutually exclusive alternatives, these two categorizations are designed to act as analytical tools in understanding how existing scholarship has conceptualized party change, and how considering forces from one direction, to the exclusion of the other, severely limits our understanding of political parties. Certainly forces from both the top and the grass roots are necessary for party change, but past accounts often focus on one or the other. Herbert Kitschelt (1994) cogently notes that "both sociological determinism and political voluntarism shun a more complex reconstruction of the relationship between social structure and politics." Specifically, elite-led forces have often been given short-shrift. Thus, by depicting parties as empty vessels that react to social forces, past research has missed the productive role party elites can play in steering party efforts to promote women candidates.

The Societal Change Approach

Theories that give credence to social forces highlight the fundamental and ultimate role of the electorate. From this perspective, social movements, citizen groups, and party supporters pressure the party to incorporate their issues. The party responds, or does not respond, to those challenges at its own peril. From this perspective, a political party is a set of institutions that reflect changes in the environment, rather than controlling that environment (Katz and Mair, 1992).

The seminal studies of party transformation in the European setting envision change in response to shifts in society. A common theme underpins both Otto Kirchheimer's (1966) catch-all prophecy and Leon Epstein's (1967) theory of a "contagion from the right": the attenuation of links between social groups and parties yields changes in party behavior, most notably a shift toward centrist politics in a race for electoral success. Similarly, in their early research on the ability of parties to emulate the "responsible parties model," Robert Harmel and Kenneth Janda (1982) envisioned party adaptation to new demands as a process in which changes in broad environmental factors, such as mass values, influence a party system. Using data on the ideology and organization of ninety-five parties from 1957 to 1962, Harmel and Janda contend that regarding change and political parties, "causal primacy resides in the environment."

Specific to the literature on women's issues and parties, Christina Wolbrecht's (2000) research on the United States finds a similar bottom-up pattern. She concludes that with the rise of the women's movement, Democrats and Republicans absorbed and channeled demands from their existing constituencies, causing them to shift their positions on women's rights. Yet it should be noted that Wolbrecht does not ignore top-down forces, and her addition of the role of party elites is described in the following section.

Theories based on social forces provide only a partial understanding by focusing on how political parties "respond" to changes in mass values and demands of women activists for greater numerical representation of women. From the social forces perspective, broad changes in society in terms of women's increasing participation in the workforce and higher education fostered changes in public attitudes towards women's roles. Shifts in aggregate attitudes toward the role of women in society brought more positive attitudes toward the role of women in politics more specifically. In addition, the women's movement has pressured for women's representation.

Importantly, by limiting its focus to the role of social forces, past research has often assumed that women's gains in parliament are inevitable (albeit slow) as their roles in society and general attitudes shift over time. Yet the empirical evidence presented in chapter 1 shows that women's gains have neither been incremental, nor automatic, nor widespread. Instead, women make gains in certain parties at certain points in time. Clearly social forces do not paint the full picture.

The Elite-led Approach

Theories that emphasize the role of political leaders add the importance of conscious party efforts, decisions, and strategies in the process of change. In this top-down process, new issues often first emerge as struggles between rival party leaders or factions, and then filter down to the party rank and file. Rather than simply responding to environmental changes, parties consciously create or alter the environment in which they compete. In other words, social forces are neither a necessary nor a sufficient condition for party change (Mueller, 1997). As Sheri Berman cogently writes, "while exogenous socioeconomic and cultural changes may . . . force parties to confront a distinct set of challenges, they do not determine how parties will actually respond to those challenges" (105).

This perspective on party change stems from the seminal works of Downs (1957) and Riker (1965), who both view political actors as rational decision makers who calculate the consequences of their acts and pursue their own self-interests. Riker (1965) theorizes that the party (or parties) out of power always has the incentive to improve its situation by breaking the status quo, and the most effective method is to bring new cross-cutting issues onto the political agenda. Thus, the party leadership itself initiates change, marketing its new ideas to the electorate.

The elite perspective on the process of adaptation is most evident in the work of Edward Carmines and James Stimson (1989), who reason that many issues compete for recognition, and those that become salient are promoted by strategic politicians. Then, the electorate responds to some issues and not to others, analogous to natural selection in the biological world. Relying on measures of party positions derived from party platforms, presidential stances, and congressional votes, Carmines and Stimson find that the change in popular perceptions of party position on the racial issue registered only after the party elites had polarized on the racial issue. In short, division among elites (although likely based upon projected electoral concerns) led to a change in the mass perceptions of party positions, which in turn led to a new alignment among voters. Carmines and Stimson assume citizens are neither sufficiently informed nor sufficiently involved to change parties. Instead, political elites mobilize the mass public on a new issue in order to increase their power.

Thus, the Elite-led approach begins with the premise that if all parties in a system are presented with the same challenges and demands, then internal party dynamics may explain why parties respond differently. The incentive for the established party to change may not be based upon a party's composition of voters, as suggested by the Social Change approach, but rather the established party's anticipation that to win new votes, it must target a new group of voters. I argue that neither changes among the electorate nor losses in votes alone spur parties to make changes; the critical element in change is the shifting priority of those votes to party leaders. I will show that in certain contexts, increases in women's parliamentary presence occurred after party leaders anticipated that women's votes could be won by selecting more women candidates. Where party leaders recognized the potential for gender issues to provide new bases of voter support, and/or to provide new bases of political appeal, they pressed for policies to offer more female candidates. And where the political and institutional opportunities allowed, these party elites then decisively altered their environment, resulting in elevated numbers of women candidates and women MPs.

A Theory of Party Inclusion of New Groups

Party theory gains a new perspective when it goes beyond identifying the dominant sources for change to look at the way those pressures interact with the opportunity structure. In the following chapters, I will demonstrate that party change occurs in both a bottom-up and a top-down process within parties. Importantly, the process is conditioned by the rules and balance of power within which the party is embedded. Bottom-up efforts alone are effective only in a particular context, and top-down party efforts are an essential addition in others. Key political opportunity structures and forces for change suggest a sequence of influences as shown in figure 2.1. Forces operating outside the party, such as growing electoral support for women's equality at the mass level, underpin the rise of new issues to the political agenda. Shifts in voting patterns leave parties searching for new bases of support. Grassroots pressure within the party for the inclusion of a group representing this new issue often comes through an existing ancillary organization, which effectively becomes an intraparty interest group. Rising from within this interest group, members climb to higher positions within the general party structure. Ascension to the top leadership is facilitated by the political opportunity structure. Changes are most likely during internal party upheavals where the party faces increasing electoral uncertainty, heated competition from an entrepreneurial party, and/or declining support based on traditionally reliable voting blocs. Elite turnover is more likely under certain internal institutional opportunity structures, as well. Parties with many disparate factions and interest groups in the first place provide more points of access and norms of inclusion. In addition, parties that are less rule-bound and ideologically rigid find it easier to accommodate new interests. Further, where the new groups' claims fit in with existing party ideology, change is facilitated.

A partial replacement of party elites translates into a shift of power within the party. At this point, top-down party forces exert pressure as well. Elite replacement infuses the party with innovative ideas. Entrenched party elites

Figure 2.1 Sequence of Influences in Party Change

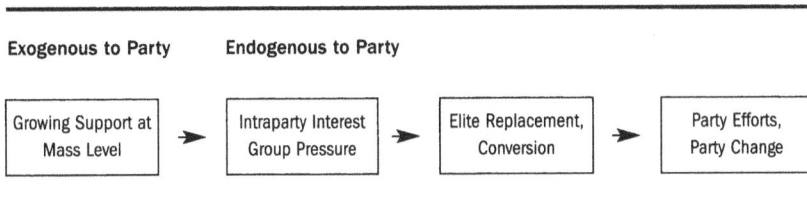

Exogenous to Party   Endogenous to Party

| Growing Support at Mass Level | → | Intraparty Interest Group Pressure | → | Elite Replacement, Conversion | → | Party Efforts, Party Change |

may also come to see their interests in a new light when effectively lobbied by internal interest groups.

Finally, a reorganized party leadership most likely makes new policies to reinforce its power. Party rule changes and efforts to promote the descriptive representation of new challengers are most likely in a flexible, pragmatic, open party structure. Likewise, in a centralized party, the leadership has the ability to make and enforce the new rules, even if local party organizations are reluctant to upset entrenched power holders.

Finding Access in Political Parties

The flow chart in figure 2.1 depicted inclusion from the perspective of the party, and this model also offers some practical strategies for how new contenders, such as women, or even environmental interests or ethnic minorities, might best find access in a party system, and how institutions shape these choices. As activists challenge the political system for presence in decision making, they often meet barriers presented by entrenched interests and institutions. Where new contenders do not make automatic gains as a result of changing social environments, they can take concrete claims to political parties. By entering party politics, these new contenders translate informal movement tactics and demands to more formal and institutionalized intraparty interest group lobbying. Overall, most effective strategy within parties resembles the chart shown in figure 2.2. First, the most facilitative opportunity structure is one in which the party's existing ideological orientation matches up with that of the new challenger. New groups do best to take their demands to the more sympathetic parties. In the case of women, minorities, or environmental interests, parties that already hold some New Left values are the best targets. Parties that lean more toward Old Left politics of class struggle may still share the closest relationships with labor groups, and new issues subordinated to the old dominant economic issues.

Still, new challengers may favor a variety of different parties across the ideological spectrum, and parties have many other structures that make them

Figure 2.2 Effective Strategy for Party Change

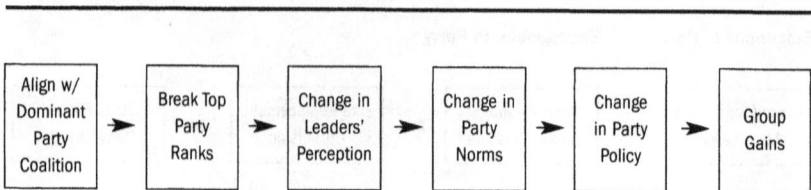

34

more or less permeable to new challengers. Parties guided by an overall ethos toward relying on various interest groups will be more amenable to new group demands. And a centralized leadership creates a central target at which the new group can aim its demands. This structure minimizes the number of levels at which the group will have to lobby, thus concentrating the full force of their demands in one place, and holding those central authorities accountable if their demands are not met.

To begin to make inroads, a new group's best strategy is to align with the dominant faction within the party, rather than the out-groups. This strategy may mean a trade-off toward more pragmatic claims for organizational advancement. Forging ties with the dominant faction is especially important in a centralized party structure, where the party leadership has the power and control to meet the new group's demands.

To move toward the end goal of parliamentary seats, it is key for the new group to break the top party ranks, thus reorganizing the traditional power structure. By gaining new positions of power, new challengers also gain the ear of party leaders. By strategically framing their claims, these new party elites can often change entrenched leaders' perceptions of the need to offer new contenders among the party's slate of candidates. This approach is most likely in an environment of electoral instability or heated competition in the party system. The new contenders within the party can pitch their claims for greater power in terms of winning the support of the larger group they represent, as a symbol of the party's commitment. By placing claims within a vote-getting strategy, the new contenders can take advantage of the opportunities provided by outside forces.

Once a few token newcomers have gained power within the party, it is imperative that they pressure for active measures and formal rule changes that favor them. That is, new challengers seek to reinforce their gains on party decision-making bodies with some internal quotas. Positive action strategies such as quotas are most likely to gain support in parties with an ideological tradition supportive of proactive remedies for structural injustices. Often, leftist parties are more amenable to quotas than their rightist counterparts, who eschew preferential policies of any form. Further, centralized parties find it easier to implement such rules. Once internal quotas further increase the challengers' power inside the party, challengers press for candidate-level quotas. Candidate quotas work best in PR systems, where party lists can be balanced to reflect both new and entrenched office seekers.

Mechanisms for Increasing Women's Parliamentary Gains

Specific to women's inclusion, several mechanisms work together to increase

Figure 2.3 Opportunities and Mechanisms for Increasing Women's Representation in Parliament

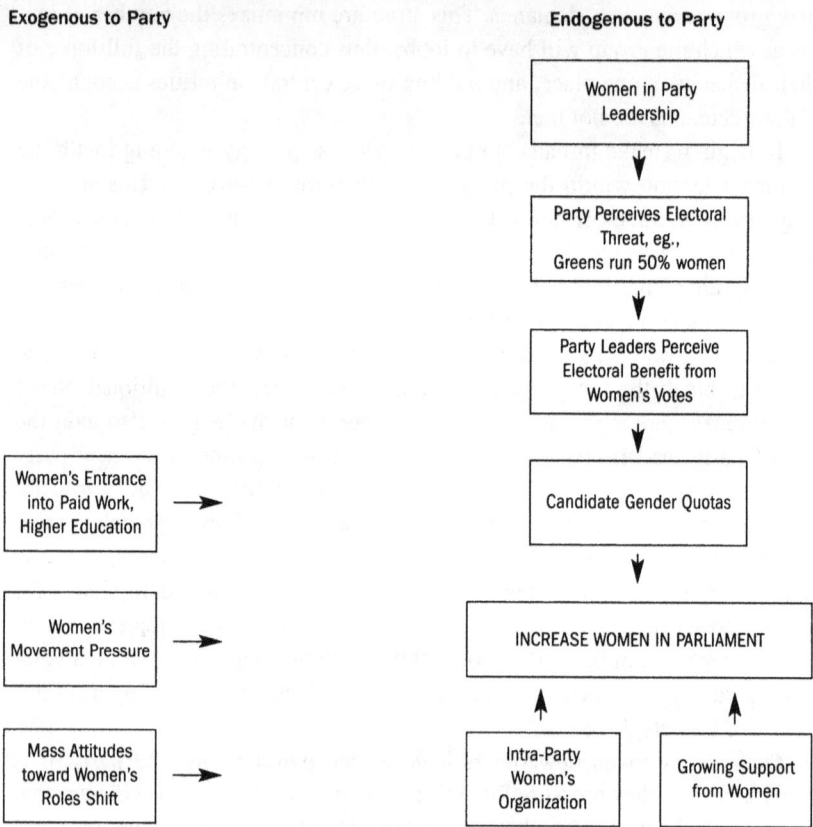

Exogenous to Party   Endogenous to Party

```
                                          ┌─────────────────────────┐
                                          │   Women in Party        │
                                          │   Leadership            │
                                          └─────────────────────────┘
                                                     ▼
                                          ┌─────────────────────────┐
                                          │ Party Perceives Electoral│
                                          │ Threat, eg.,            │
                                          │ Greens run 50% women    │
                                          └─────────────────────────┘
                                                     ▼
                                          ┌─────────────────────────┐
                                          │ Party Leaders Perceive  │
                                          │ Electoral Benefit from  │
                                          │ Women's Votes           │
                                          └─────────────────────────┘
                                                     ▼
┌───────────────┐                         ┌─────────────────────────┐
│ Women's Entrance│ ──────▶               │ Candidate Gender Quotas │
│ into Paid Work, │                       └─────────────────────────┘
│ Higher Education│                                  ▼
└───────────────┘
┌───────────────┐                         ┌─────────────────────────┐
│ Women's        │ ──────▶                │ INCREASE WOMEN IN PARLIAMENT│
│ Movement Pressure│                      └─────────────────────────┘
└───────────────┘                              ▲              ▲
┌───────────────┐              ┌─────────────┐      ┌─────────────┐
│ Mass Attitudes │ ──────▶     │ Intra-Party │      │ Growing Support│
│ toward Women's │             │ Women's     │      │ from Women   │
│ Roles Shift    │             │ Organization│      └─────────────┘
└───────────────┘              └─────────────┘
```

the proportion of women in a party's delegation to parliament. The main mechanisms are depicted in figure 2.3. These mechanisms are conditioned by opportunity structure variables. For the clarity of presentation, some of these structures are not shown in the figure and will be added to the discussion. Together, these pressures and structures suggest a sequence of events. The broader and more indirect influences, which are exogenous to political parties, are depicted down the left side of the figure. While not the focal point of this book, the processes of societal transformations, pressure for reform from the women's movement, and changes in mass attitudes toward women's roles in society and political life are certainly essential to sparking pressure for greater representation in party politics. As discussed in chapter 1, broad social transformations such as women's increasing levels of higher education, paid employment, and entrance into elite occupations combined to create a pool of politically aware women. These changes and growing concern for women's oppression are represented by the women's movement, which increasingly concentrated on mainstream political channels throughout this period. Pressures generated from this movement sustain demands on the party to increase women's voice in the democratic process. Certainly the demands and strategies of the national women's movement condition women's entrance into party politics.

In a particular context, where there are few barriers to women seeking election, these social forces bring women substantial gains in parliamentary seats. Yet in most cases, social forces are necessary but not sufficient. In the past, many parties effectively blocked some women's election to office, especially in single-member districts where entrenched males proved a safer bet, or in closed-list PR systems by placing women at the bottom of party lists, where they had little chance of being elected, except in an unexpected landslide. However, where proportional systems allow for preferential voting through an open list, parties can provide balanced lists without threatening entrenched office holders, and voters can cast their ballots for women if they wish. Under these circumstances, direct appeals to the electorate to increase women's parliamentary representation can be effective. Few countries use open lists, so women's candidacies are most often in the hands of the party gatekeepers.

Women's concerted efforts to lobby from within political parties are most often an essential addition. At the bottom right-hand side of the flow chart in figure 2.3, I highlight the importance of party grassroots forces. First, the party women's organization is a key access point for women as a group. Though traditionally designed to recruit new female members, the women's organization provides a ready-made infrastructure for new demands for women's presence among the party leadership and in parliament. In addition, the women's organization holds an available pool of party women for leadership spots when they open up, and growing electoral support among women voters pressures parties to run female candidates. As class-based voting declined, opportunities arose as parties looked to draw support from new voting blocs, and women can become a more important electoral asset.

Party efforts from the top down often bring significant gains, which are depicted at the top right-hand corner of figure 2.3. Women's presence among the party leadership is the single most important mechanism for initiating women's gains in parliament. Of course, these first women must be willing to "let the ladder down" to other women within the party. In a top-led fashion, increasing numbers of women among the party's highest ranks heighten women's power and resources to gain parliamentary representation. Within the party, this reorganization of power is crucial in terms of breaking up the historically male-dominated party leadership circles.

Particular institutional opportunity structures facilitate women's rise from supporters and activists to leadership positions. A more factionalized, interest-group-oriented party structure facilitates this bottom-up pressure from the party women's organization. Further, a more flexible party may adopt internal party gender quotas in an effort to appease female party activists who seek higher positions. And these quotas are much more likely in a party with some New Left values that are already sympathetic to women's inequality as a structural problem in need of direct remedy.

Adding fuel to the fire, competition across the party system for women's votes will spur parties to present a more "woman-friendly" image through symbolic representation. Specifically, if an entrepreneurial New Left party sets a gender quota and runs a large number of women for office, the deficiencies of the established parties are magnified, and the issue of gender equality is heightened to greater importance. This sort of competitive pressure represents a shift in the political opportunity structure and highlights the importance of competitive party leaders as agents of change.

With more women in party leadership positions, women gain access to party leaders, and thus they gain the ability to change leaders' perceptions of the utility of running more women for office. Party leaders are most likely to initiate top-down efforts to promote women candidates when they come to see the electoral benefit from women's votes.

Women at the top of the party organization have often pressed for party policies to mandate more women candidates in winnable spots. And where these efforts are successful, women gain parliamentary seats. Importantly, women have changed the rules of recruitment in many parties across Western Europe, thereby institutionalizing and ensuring their future gains in office. Again, more flexible parties with leftist values are most likely to adopt gender quotas, and centralized parties can implement new selection rules. Further, candidate gender quotas work best in party-list PR systems, where candidate lists can be balanced. In single-member districts, mandating a "female" seat to the exclusion of all males is often seen as discriminatory and a threat to local party autonomy.

Conclusions

This chapter provides a conceptual map to plot the path on which women are most likely to make the greatest gains through political parties. This is an ideal set of circumstances. In practice, women are unlikely to confront a chain of solely favorable circumstances. Yet by identifying which factors are favorable and which are not, we take a major step toward understanding how women and other new challengers can make gains. Importantly, by tying these forces together, it is possible to identify the way strategies interact with structures. The following chapters will test this framework for party change and women's access, both systematically with party-level statistics, and in-depth with some critical case study comparison.

3

Change from the Inside Out: Women in Party Leadership

Organizations invariably serve to guarantee, perpetuate, or increase the social power of those who control them, e.g., the elites that guide them.

—Angelo Panebianco (1988, xii)

While some segments of the women's movement have eschewed participation in male-dominated mainstream political institutions, others have viewed political parties as centers of power. Women have been active within the parties of Western Europe for many years, especially since the suffrage movement, and in many instances since the party's inception. Yet with the heightened emphasis on equality born from the New Left social movements, during the 1970s women moved toward party politics and began to intensify their organized demands for equality in the decision-making processes of the party (Randall, 1987; Kaplan, 1992; Lovenduski and Norris, 1993; Lovenduski and Randall, 1993). In many parties, women began to rise to powerful positions within the party hierarchy.

Women's power in top decision-making bodies appears to improve women's opportunities in the national legislature. Previous research found a consistent relationship between women in the top party bodies and women in the party's delegation to parliament across industrialized democracies (Caul, 1999).[1] As women gain power within the party, they also acquire greater opportunities and resources to pressure for further parliamentary representation. Therefore, lobbying efforts from within the top party ranks may be a *mechanism* for increasing women's representation in the national legislature.

This chapter aims to uncover the opportunity structures that facilitated women's progress in the party organizations of ten Western European nations. I describe the patterns of women's presence in top-level positions and identify the common characteristics of parties with higher numbers of women in the leadership. I then test several sets of influence in a multivariate model.

Women in Top Party Positions across Western Europe

For women, gaining power within the highest echelons of the party organization has been a difficult and sometimes tumultuous process. In some parties, moving into the party leadership, an arena long dominated by entrenched interests represented by men, has in some respects been more difficult than getting "women-friendly" legislation onto the party platform. As other research suggests, it may be easier for parties to incorporate new issues than to fundamentally reorganize the power distribution within the party organization (Rohrschneider, 1993). Demands for positions of power threaten the established interests, and as such may present more obstacles.

This section systematically analyzes women's patterns of representation on the national executive committees (NECs) of fifty Western European parties. As an important decision-making body within parties, the national executive committee represents a center of power, and thus a central aim for women with political aspirations, or a desire to affect party policy. In some parties, officially there are higher ranking bodies. For example, among the Finnish parties the highest ranking body is the party congress. Yet the party congress meets only annually, and it is a large and unwieldy body. The intention of selecting the NEC for analysis is to pinpoint the highest decision-making body with day-to-day decision-making powers and a manageable number of members.

The proportion of women on the NEC is important because if a "critical mass," or sizable number from an underrepresented group, enters into a political institution, that underrepresented group may gain enough power to further its gains (Dahlerup, 1988; for a review of the literature see Studlar and McAllister, 2002). Studlar and McAllister (2002) find that "critical mass," in terms of a numerical threshold in parliament, has little impact on future parliamentary gains. Yet where women with the power to affect candidate nominations can advocate for other women, gains are likely. Women with power inside the party can gain the ear of the other party leaders, and they can even press to institutionalize their gains through some type of gender rules, such as quotas.

Figure 3.1 Average Percentage of Women on Party NECs, 1975–1997

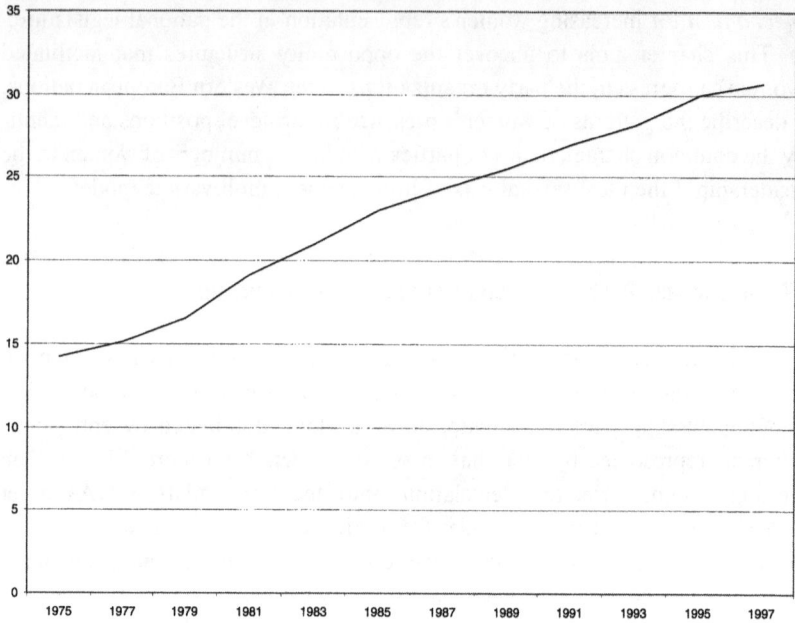

Women's presence on the national executive committees of parties has been growing across Western Europe. Figure 3.1 displays the aggregate percentage of women on the NECs of the parties in this study from 1975 to 1997. The graph reveals a steady climb in women's progress, in an almost linear fashion. In 1975 women composed about 15% of the NECs, on average, and over the next twenty years that average doubled, culminating in women making up about 30% of the NECs in these parties.

Yet below the surface of this aggregated figure, there is a great degree of variation in women in top decision-making bodies at the party level. Table 3.1 displays the percentage of women on the national executive committees in 1975 and 1997 for the fifty parties in this book, as well as the percentage point difference between these two time points.

With a few exceptions, the percentage of women grew in each party. Only in Denmark's Progress Party did the percentage of women fall by a few percentage points. The percentage of women on NECs climbed to nearly 50% in a number of countries. For example, for three parties in Norway the number climbed to 50%, and for three others it climbed into the 40% level, while the Norwegian Progress Party remained stable. Similar substantial gains were made in the Netherlands and Germany, where parties such as the Dutch Pacifist Socialist Party climbed by thirty-five percentage points.

Table 3.1 Women on Parties' NECs, 1975 and 1997

Party Name	% Women on NECs, 1975	% Women on NECs, 1997	% Point Change	Time Period	Number of Elections
Austria					
People's Party (OVP)	9	18	+9	1975-95	6
Freedom Party (FPO)	7	14	+7	1975-95	6
Socialist Party (SPO)	13	31	+18	1975-95	6
Belgium					
Christian People's (CVP)	13	15	+2	1974-87	6
Flemish Socialist Party (BSP)	6	12	+6	1977-95	7
Franco (Socialist) Party (PSB)	N/A	N/A	–	–	–
Liberty (Flemish) (PVV)	N/A	N/A	–	–	–
People's Union (VU)	7	19	+8	1974-95	8
Flemish Greens (AGA)	N/A	N/A	–	–	–
Franco Greens (ECO)	N/A	N/A	–	–	–
Denmark					
Socialist People's (SF)	20	39	+19	1975-94	8
Social Democrats	11	35	+24	1975-94	8
Social Liberals (RV)	21	40	+19	1977-94	7
Christian People's (KRF)	20	40	+20	1981-94	5
Center Democrats	10	17	+7	1975-94	8
Liberal (V)	7	15	+8	1975-94	8
Conservative (KF)	17	30	+13	1977-94	7
Progress Party (KRP)	17	14	-3	1975-94	8
Finland					
People's Democratic (SKDL)	13	27	+14	1975-95	6
Social Democratic (SPD)	8	33	+25	1975-95	6
Center Party (KESK)	13	20	+7	1975-95	6
Swedish People's (SFP)	14	52	+38	1973-95	6
National Coalition (KOK)	18	22	+4	1975-95	6
Germany					
Social Democratic (SPD)	14	47	+33	1972-94	7
Christian Democratic (CDU)	3	33	+30	1972-94	7
Christian Social Union (CSU)	4	26	+22	1972-94	7
Free Democratic (FDP)	9	19	+10	1972-94	5
Greens (G)	6	56	+50	1980-94	5
Ireland					
Worker's Party (WP)	3	16	+13	1977-89	5
Labour (LAB)	3	26	+23	1973-97	8
Fianna Fail (FF)	6	18	+12	1973-95	7
Fine Gael (FG)	24	24	0	1982-97	5
Progressive Dems (PD)	22	39	+17	1991-97	4

continued on next page

Table 3.1 Women on Parties' NECs, 1975 and 1997 *(continued)*

Party Name	% Women on NECs, 1975	% Women on NECs, 1997	% Point Change	Time Period	Number of Elections
Netherlands					
Communist Party	8	25	+17	1972-94	7
Labour Party (PvdA)	23	38	+15	1972-94	7
Pacifist Socialist (PSP)	5	40	+35	1972-94	7
Christian Democrats (CDA)	19	29	+10	1981-94	5
Democrats '66 (D'66)	14	22	+8	1972-94	7
People's Party (VVD)	19	28	+9	1972-94	7
Norway					
Socialist People's (SV)	47	50	+3	1973-97	7
Labour Party (DNA)	33	50	+17	1973-97	7
Center Party (SP)	36	50	+14	1973-97	7
Christian People's (KRF)	18	40	+22	1973-97	7
Liberals (V)	29	45	16	1973-97	7
Conservatives (H)	0	33	+33	1973-97	7
Progress (FRP) 13	13	13	0	1973-89	5
Sweden					
Communist Party (VPK)	18	52	+34	1973-94	8
Social Dem Worker (S)	11	50	+39	1973-94	8
Center Party (C)	29	43	+14	1973-94	8
People's Party (FP)	29	44	+15	1973-94	8
Right Party (M)	26	39	+13	1973-94	8
UK					
Labour (LAB)	24	48	+24	1974-97	6
Liberal/Liberal Dem (LIB/SDL) 13	13	N/A	–	1974	–
Conservatives (CON)	17	20	+3	1992-97	2

Source: Katz and Mair (1992) updated with data from Steinenger (2000) for Austria and data from Galligan (1998) for Ireland. Data on Denmark collected by Karina Pedersen, University of Copenhagen. Data from parties' self-reported records (Denmark's Radikale Venstre and Liberals, Norway's Liberal, DNA, Hoyre, and the UK's Conservative and Labour Paraties). In some instances data were unavailable for 1975 or 1997, and in such cases the nearest available data point was substituted as noted in the final two columns of the table.

Examining Party-Level Differences in Women's Leadership

Women's gains on the NEC are more than simply a function of their activism; the level of representation is also shaped by the opportunity structure. Herbert Kitschelt (1994) theorizes that those parties with the structures capable of recognizing new challenges quickly are more likely to respond to new groups. This section examines which party characteristics make a party more likely to recognize and accept women's pressures for greater presence among the party elite.

Party Women's Organization

As an intraparty interest group, the party's women's organization often calls for more of a voice among the higher party ranks. The women's organization channels and organizes women's claims. Further, it provides a visible pool of women for positions in higher party posts. Alternatively, some women might contend that women's organizations isolate and effectively marginalize women within the party structure, keeping them from the avenues of true power. It is important to test whether the presence of a party women's organization is conducive to women's gains in the upper party echelons. One must keep in mind the limitations of this overly simplified dichotomous measure. Ideally, one could also systematically test the strategies, strength, claims, and choice of allies of the women's organizations cross-nationally. Yet no such published comparative measures for party women's organization exist, and it would be disingenuous to create a flawed measure to demonstrate their importance. As such, the dynamic role of the women's organization is probably better captured by the case study chapters in this book.

Party Ideology

A party's ideology may also play an important role in conditioning party responses to the demands of women for positions within the organizational hierarchy. Kitschelt (1994) argues that the ability of a party organization to respond to new demands is constrained by the historical, established ideological orientations of the party. The party's past ideological debates frame the new debates and condition the willingness of the party to listen to new demands.

One might expect leftist parties, rather than rightist parties, to be more open to newcomers such as women for two reasons. First, leftist parties have a tradition of espousing egalitarian ideologies in general, and this trait has carried over into their rhetoric regarding women's representation (Duverger, 1955; Beckwith, 1986; 1992; Matland and Studlar, 1996; Caul, 1999). Rule (1987) argues that rightist parties hold a more traditional view of women's roles in society more generally, and in politics more specifically. Second, historically the women's movement has been linked to leftist parties, and they have proven to be more supportive of feminist issues than parties of the Center or the Right (Jenson, 1982; Katzenstein and Mueller, 1987:6). Yet there have been tensions between the Left and the women's movement, as the Left had long argued that women's lives would be most improved if the party would concentrate on women's material conditions as part of the overall Socialist framework, rather then focusing on women's rights as a group.

Further, both Lovenduski and Norris (1993) and Matland and Studlar (1996) posit that while a leftist ideology might once have been a strong predictor of a party's likelihood to adopt gender policies, it is no longer as strong. Leftist parties may not be the only parties to have a high number of women among their top officials as support for women spreads across the ideological spectrum of the party system.

Further, the traditional unidimensional Left/Right ideological continuum may be too simple to describe how ideology affects women's representation. The lines of political conflict were once based upon "Old Politics" cleavages of class conflict. Old Left parties are oriented toward the concerns of the working class, and Old Right parties are oriented toward business interests. The rise of a "New Politics" cleavage adds a new dimension to our conceptualization of ideology (Inglehart, 1977). The New Politics dimension involves conflict over a new set of issues, among which are minority rights and gender equality. This new cleavage has spurred new parties, especially New Left parties that have been active proponents of women's issues. The New Left and its parties—such as Green parties—are even more closely linked to the women's movement than are the traditional leftist parties such as Labor and the Social Democrats.

Hence, a *left* party in general may not necessarily favor policies to support women. New Left parties, as representatives of postmaterialist values, may be more amenable to implementing strategies to quickly promote women candidates. Therefore, I test summary measures for both Old Left values and New Left values, developed from scores assigned by party experts (see Appendix A).

Party Structure

Previous literature emphasizes four different components of a party's structure that may impact its ability to change: the degree of centralization, pragmatism, fractionalization, and the presence of formal party rules. Centralization describes the distribution of control over decision making within the party hierarchy. Does a centralized or decentralized party organization better facilitate women's ascendance to the top ranks? Harmel and Janda (1982) state that there are competing theories regarding the role of centralization. On the one hand, a decentralized party organization may provide for greater input from the grass roots, giving women more points of access to enter the party ranks. Local party organizations may serve as a springboard for women to work their way up to national party offices. On the other hand, a centralized party structure may be more conducive to women entering the top echelons of the party. The central elite have the power to impose change upon the subnational party units. A more highly centralized level may give party leaders the ability to select women as key decision makers—when the party leaders see fit to do so. Matland and Studlar (1996) point out that as a consequence, a central party organization can be held more directly accountable for the party's failure to take steps to promote women; the buck stops with the party leadership. In a more decentralized party, party leaders can point fingers at one another to escape responsibility for adding more women to the top ranks.

The second party characteristic, party pragmatism, describes the extent to which the party's program guides the party when acting on issues (Lane and Ersson, 1994). Parties with a high degree of pragmatism are considered flexible and may be more open to the demands of women.

The third component, the degree of fractionalization, refers to the ties a party has with organizations outside the party. A highly fractionalized party has organized relations with a number of groups and relies on these outside groups to attract party members and supporters. For example, parties with ties to powerful unions find it difficult to be flexible to women's claims because of their long-standing commitment to labor issues. Specifically, Rohrschneider (1993) points out that unions often oppose social movement goals because unions put a priority on economic issues at the expense of social issues, and especially those associated with the postmaterialist New Politics. Therefore, we expect that strong ties to outside groups will impede a party's ability to incorporate women into its higher ranks.

Finally, formal rules may shape who enters the top ranks of the party. Some parties have established internal party rules regarding the gender composition of party committees. For example, in 1989 at its annual party conference, the British Labour Party passed a resolution that mandated that women make up from one-third to one-half of selected party bodies at the local, regional, and national levels. Parties can adopt quotas or more informal recommendations regarding the number of women required on different committees. It is logical that parties with internal gender quotas for the party hierarchy are more likely to have a large number of women on their decision-making committees.

Data Analysis

This section systematically analyzes the mechanisms that influence change in the proportion of women on the national executive committees of fifty parties from 1975 to 1995 in ten Western European democracies. I pool a cross-section of data that includes observations for the gender composition of the NECs in each national election between 1975 and 1997 in these ten nations.[2] The application of this data to a meaningful statistical procedure required some careful methodological reasoning. The use of 375 cases allows for the legitimate use of ordinary least squares regression (OLS). Measures were collected for each

Table 3.2 Multivariate Model Explaining the Number of Women in Party Leadership

Explanatory Variable	% Women on NEC by Party
Women's Mobilization	
Presence of a Party Women's Organization	.01
Party Structure	
Degree Party Centralized	.09*
Degree Party Fractionalized	.11**
Degree Party Pragmatic	.02
Party Ideology	
Old Left Politics Scale	.08
New Left Politics Scale	.24***
Party Rules	
Internal Party Gender Rules	.54***
Adjusted R-Squared	.40
Number of Cases	375

Note: Table entries are standardized regression coefficients.
Significance level: *** = $p < .01$, ** = $p < .05$,* = $p < .10$

of the independent and dependent variables from published national statistics and other data sources. A full explanation of variables and sources is contained in Appendix A.

Multivariate Analyses

Using the hypotheses outlined in the previous section, I created a multivariate model to test the combined influence of these explanatory factors. Table 3.2 presents the results of the model. Combined, these indicators explain 40% of the adjusted variance in the proportion of women on the parties' NECs. The second column displays the standardized OLS regression coefficients. The results reveal that the presence of a women's organization is not a significant predictor of women's representation on the NEC. As discussed in the previous section, the mere presence of a women's organization cannot measure its strength, demands on the party leadership, or choice of allies within the party.

The table shows that party structure, ideology, and rules all influence women's presence on the NEC. The results support the hypothesis that more centralized and factionalized parties create more opportunities for women in top party positions. Both indicators achieve statistical significance, while the degree of pragmatism does not. The data suggest that, controlling for the other influences, in a centralized party the leadership has the authority to promote women to the top echelons when pressured. Further, a party with strong ties to more outside groups is more likely to have more women on its NEC. This finding runs counter to our hypothesis that ties to groups limit a party's autonomy. It appears that parties with ties to outside groups provide more points of access, so that women can climb to positions of power.

The second set of influences reveals that a leftist ideology is more conducive to women on the NEC, but specifically, a leftist ideology based on the New Politics issues is significantly related to the proportion of women on the NEC. Parties that incorporate new noneconomic issues from social movements are, by extension, more likely to incorporate women into their centers of power. Finally, the strongest impact comes from the presence of party rules, specifically internal gender quotas. Formal rules that ensure women's presence throughout the party help to bolster women's progress to the top party hierarchy.

Conclusions

Women's efforts to gain power are embedded in a set of institutions—formal rules, party structures, norms, and ideological traditions—that shape the effectiveness of their demands for equality. Past research on women's numerical representation in national legislatures found that electoral rules are important; women are more likely to be nominated and elected in party-list, proportional representation systems with large district magnitudes (Duverger, 1955; Lakeman, 1994; Rule, 1987; Beckwith, 1987; 1994; Matland, 1993; Matland and Studlar, 1996). Although there is substantial variation across parties, there has been little systematic research conducted on party institutions. From this research, it is clear that the institutional structures of some parties are more conducive to women's advancement; party organizational structures and ideology both condition women's efforts. Women are more likely to reach the top ranks of a centralized, fractionalized party with New Left values and formal rules for women's participation in the lower party bodies. A party with a strong leadership is better able to respond to women's demands. And a party with New Left values is more likely to view women's demands as legitimate and to share a closer historical relationship with the women's movement. Finally, it is logical that where women have enough power and the party is willing to adopt formal measures to ensure women's representation in internal party bodies, there will be more women on the party's highest decision-making body, the national executive committee.

4

Rule Changes to Increase Women's Parliamentary Presence: The Diffusion of Candidate Gender Quotas

The most effective way to increase the percentage of women in parliament seems to be formal or informal gender quotas on candidate lists set by political parties.

—Council of the European Union, 1999

Gender quotas for parliamentary candidates first emerged in 1975 in Norway, where the proportion of women in parliament has traditionally been highest. As parties across Europe looked to the leader, the number of parties adopting quotas rose sharply in the 1980s—diffusing across nations and within party systems. Gender quotas are the most visible way for parties to symbolically demonstrate their commitment to women. The use of gender quotas and targets denotes a process of changing attitudes within parties toward women in politics that has led to a change in the formal rules.

Importantly, gender quotas appear to have their desired effect. For example, in Germany the Green Party adopted quotas in 1986. By 1994 the delegation the Greens sent to the Bundestag consisted of nearly 60% women. In 1988 the German Social Democrats adopted quotas, and the percentage of Social Democratic women MPs rose from 18% in the prequota 1987 election to 27% in the postquota 1990 election. Likewise, the establishment of a light form of

Table 4.1 Political Parties and Candidate Gender Quotas

	Year Quota Adopted	Other Affirmative Action Policy
Austria PR-List **(20)**		
1. People's Party (OVP)	1995	
2. Freedom Party (FPO)	—	
3. Greens (GA)	1987	
4. Socialist Party (SPO)	1985	
Belgium PR-List **(12)**		
5. Christian People's (CVP)	1993	
6. Socialist (Flemish) (BSP)	—	
7. Socialist (Francophone) (PS)	—	
8. Liberty (Flemish) (PVV)	—	
9. People's Union (VU)	—	
10. Christian Social (PSC)	—	
11. Ecology Party (Flemish) (AGA)	1991	
12. Ecology Party (Francophone)	1991	
Denmark PR-List **(25)**		
13. Socialist People's (SF)	1989	
14. Social Democrats (SD)	—	1984
15. Social Liberals (RV)	—	
16. Christian People's (KRF)	—	
17. Center Democrats (CD)	—	
18. Liberal (V)	—	
19. Conservative (KF)	—	
20. Progress Party (KRP)	—	
Finland PR-List **(13)**		
21. People's Democratic (SKDL)	—	
22. Social Democratic (SDP)	—	
23. Center Party (KESK)	—	
24. Swedish People's (SFP)	—	
25. National Coalition (KOK)	—	
Germany MMP **(10)**		
26. Social Democratic (SPD)	1988	
27. Christian Democratic (CDU)	—	1987
28. Christian Social Union (CSU)	—	
29. Free Democratic (FDP)	—	1987
30. Greens (G)	1986	

Continued on next page

Table 4.1 Political Parties and Candidate Gender Quotas *(continued)*

	Year Quota Adopted	Other Affirmative Action Policy
Ireland STV **(4)**		
31. Workers' Party (WP)	1991	
32. Labour (LAB)	1991	
33. Fianna Fail (FF)	—	
34. Fine Gael (FG)	—	1987
35. Progressive Democrats (PD)	—	1992
36. Greens (G)	—	
Netherlands PR-List **(110)**		
37. Communist Party (CPN)	—	1982
38. Labor (PvdA)	1987	
39. Pacifist Socialist Party (PSP)	—	1983
40. Radical Political (PPR)	—	1988
41. Christian Democrats (CDA)	—	1986
42. Democrats '66 (D'66)	—	
43. People's (VVD)	—	
44. Green Left (GL)	1985	
Norway PR-List **(8)**		
45. Socialist People's (SV)	1975	
46. Labor (DNA)	1983	
47. Center (SP)	1989	
48. Christian People's (KRF)	1993	
49. Liberals (V)	1975	
50. Conservatives (H)	—	
51. Progress (FRP)	—	
Sweden PR-List **(12)**		
52. Communist (VPK)	—	1980
53. Social Democrat Worker (S)	—	1960
54. Center (C)	—	
55. People's (FP)	—	1972
56. Right (M)	—	1975
57. Environmental Party (MP)	—	1991
UK Plurality–FPTP **(1)**		
58. Labour (LAB)	1992	1989
59. Liberal/Lib Dem (LIB/SLD)	—	1988
60. Conservative (CON)	—	

Source: Katz and Mair (1992) and Inter-Parliamentary Union (1993) supplemented with data from country experts collected by Professor Richard Matland.

quotas by the British Labour Party in 1993 is credited with a ten percentage point increase in female Labour MPs from the 1992 to the 1997 elections.

If parties can use candidate gender quotas and targets to substantially improve women's representation, then it is important to ask *why certain parties have adopted these policies while others have not.*[1] Further, *why did those parties take action at the time they did?* I employ event history analysis (EHA) to statistically model the adoption of these new quotas. Candidate gender quotas are an intervening variable in increasing women's representation. If we are to understand this increase as a process, then it is important to isolate and examine this intermediary step.

A Systematic Examination of Quotas across Western Europe

Several parties in Western Europe changed their selection rules to improve the gender balance in their delegations to parliament. Table 4.1 lists the sixty parties included in this analysis, indicating if and when quotas were adopted. Gender quotas are often associated with the Nordic countries and with Green parties. The data in table 4.1 show that quotas are certainly not limited to these cases. Strikingly, although candidate gender quotas have diffused across the Norwegian party system, Denmark has only one party with quotas, and no Swedish nor Finnish parties have adopted formal quotas. Further, quotas are not limited to New Left Parties. For example, the Christian People's Party in Belgium and the Austrian People's Party adopted quotas, as did the mass leftist parties in Austria, Germany, Ireland, the Netherlands, Norway, and Britain.

The second column of table 4.1 notes whether and when parties have adopted another form of policies intended to increase the number of women in office. Some parties adopted affirmative action measures that fall short of qualifying as candidate gender quotas. Yet the presence of these "recommended" percentages of women, such as the "targets" set by the German FDP or the "quorum" of the CDU, have helped to increase the number of women in office.[2] Of the parties in this dataset that had not adopted the more formal quotas, sixteen adopted some form of a "target" number of women candidates. Because the strict nature of quotas makes them controversial, many parties have turned to these softer targets. The party leadership can recommend a certain percentage of women candidates in the party policies, thus giving the localities incentive to recruit women, without diminishing the power of the localities to select their own candidates. Because these targets are unevenly enforced, this statistical analysis is limited to formal quotas.

The electoral rules shape the conditions under which these parties have (or have not) adopted quotas. Because most countries in this study are party list proportional representation (PR) systems, the average district magnitude is also reported in table 4.1. These nations vary substantially in terms of district magnitude, ranging from 1 to 75.

Influences on the Adoption of Candidate Gender Quotas

This section examines the conditions under which parties adopt quotas. A party's decision to adopt candidate gender quotas may be influenced by several factors, both at the level of the political system and at the level of the party. These factors are grouped into two categories, political and institutional opportunity structures.

Political Opportunity Structure

Women's political power in the party increases women's resources to mobilize for policies such as quotas to ensure greater representation in the future. The concept of a critical mass may link parties with initially higher levels of women in top positions to a tendency to adopt quotas. If a "critical mass," or a sizable number from a minority group, enters into a traditionally majority-controlled institution, that minority group may gain enough power to institutionalize itself (Dahlerup, 1988). Specifically, the new contender may further its gains by pressing for formal policies that are difficult to remove, even when those individual members are gone.

The influence of women's political activity exerts itself both at the national and at the party level. First, the historical proportion of women in a legislative body might signify the power of women in the nation to pressure parties for more support. Second, the individual party's proportion of women MPs may have more direct impact. Once women begin to enter the top party ranks, they can directly pressure the party leaders to take formal steps to promote women.

When this idea is tested empirically across nations, Studlar and McAllister (1999) find little support for the effects of a critical mass on furthering women's seat gains. Yet it remains to be seen whether the critical mass might affect party *policies*. Previous literature on the impact of a critical mass points more solidly toward the minority's effect on policy, rather than on numerical representation (see Dahlerup, 1988, for a review). This finding is because sizable numbers of the minority now participating in decision making can more effectively lobby for the intermediate step of concrete rules, rather than for the ultimate outcome.

In a different manner, quotas may follow a process of diffusion. Taken from Duverger's (1954) conception of a "contagion" among parties, Matland and Studlar's (1996) research suggests that parties are more likely to adopt gender quotas and/or targets when pressured with the adoption of these rules by a rival party. Competing parties fear losing women's votes if they do not match the gender policies of their rivals. In response, other parties adopt the quotas, and this policy diffuses across the party system. In an analysis of four Western European nations, Davis (1996) determines that parties react to the positive efforts of their electoral competitors.

The diffusion of an innovative policy such as quotas may occur simply because there is a prototype. For example, the German Greens' introduction of quotas set the stage for rival parties in the system. If the process of adoption of quotas is simply one of diffusion, then a simple indicator of the year the first party in the system adopted quotas should help to explain the adoption by other parties. The earlier one party in the party system adopts targets or quotas, the more likely it is that other parties in the system will subsequently adopt similar party policies.

Institutional Opportunity Structure

An important institutional structure, exogenous to the party, that conditions its ability to adopt candidate gender quotas and targets is the electoral system. In contrast to a single-member district system, a party-list PR system may improve the ability of a party to adopt candidate rules, because achieving gender balance on a list should be more feasible than mandating that one particular seat be filled by either gender (Lovenduski and Norris, 1993). Previous scholarship finds that party-list PR systems are positively associated with parties' adoption of candidate gender quotas (Caul, 1999).

The mechanism that links the type of electoral system to the presence of quotas may be the number of seats per district within a nation (district magnitude). As Matland and Studlar (1996) point out, parties in a system with a low district magnitude, such as the single-transferable vote system (STV) in Ireland, may have a more difficult time installing quotas, because in order for women to be mandatory in the party's parliamentary delegation, the incumbents, usually men, must lose seats. In contrast, where there are many MPs per district, established politicians within the party may not have to be deposed in order to make room for newcomers such as women. Thus, one expects that the higher the district magnitude, the more likely a party will be to adopt quotas. More specifically, Matland (1993; 1994) points out that it may not be the general district magnitude that impacts the election of women, but rather the "party magnitude"—the number of seats a party actually expects to win. That is to say, a party may only have a chance at winning one seat in a particular district, and if a woman is ranked second on the list, her opportunities for election are nil.

Another set of institutions is located within the party. Together, a party's ideology, organizational structure, size, and age may affect a party's propensity and capacity to adopt candidate gender quotas. As shown in chapter 3, leftist parties tend to be more supportive of women within their ranks. By extension, parties with leftist ideologies might be more likely to employ active strategies to increase women's representation, because an egalitarian ideology justifies intervention into recruitment in the name of balancing power. Both women activists and party leaders alike in these leftist parties reasoned that equal opportunity was not enough to help severely underrepresented groups. Instead, the rules change is deemed necessary to bring structural change. In contrast, more conservative parties may extend their "laissez-faire" approach to the economy to the gender composition of candidate lists, as well (Lovenduski and Norris, 1993, p. 320). Conservatives may continually eschew any form of quotas, contending that women's promotion must be based upon merit alone, and that quotas serve as a form of special protection not necessary for qualified women. However, both Lovenduski and Norris (1993) and Matland and Studlar (1996) posit that while leftist ideology might once have been a strong predictor of a party's likelihood to adopt gender policies, it is no longer as strong.

Further, as reasoned in chapter 3, the traditional, unidimensional Left/Right ideological continuum may be too simple to describe how ideology affects women's representation. The lines of political conflict, based upon "Old Politics" cleavages of class conflict, may be less conducive to the adoption of quotas than the new dimension, based upon a "New Politics" cleavage (Inglehart, 1977). Therefore, I include summary measures for both Old Left values and New Left values, which are the same measures of ideology used in the previous chapter (see Appendix A).

Another party-level influence is the organizational structure of a party. One component, level of nomination, characterizes the level at which candidates are selected by the party. A more centralized level gives party leaders more control to initiate gender quota policies—when they see fit to do so. Matland and Studlar (1996) point out that centralized party procedures in general allow party leadership to respond to pressures for measures to increase women's representation. In a more localized process, each region or locality must be pressured separately to adopt measures to promote women.

The second component, the degree of institutionalization, denotes the nature of the party organization. Using the same measure as in chapter 3, I consider highly institutionalized parties as rule-oriented and bureaucratic. More highly institutionalized parties should be more likely to resort to rules such as quotas to achieve goals and should be more likely to actually implement these rules.

Finally, one might expect that smaller and newer parties would be the first to adopt quotas and initiate the process of a contagion. Evidence from Norway supports this hypothesis (Matland and Studlar, 1996). Although not concerned specifically with women as an underrepresented group, Czudnowski (1975) more generally addresses the relative strength of parties in a national system and argues that majority parties would be less concerned with "problems of sociodemographic representation" than would a minority party (p. 181). His prediction can be extended to the problem of women's representation in the present—smaller parties that draw on women's support may have more to lose. They may be more concerned with maintaining their strength among women.

New parties may act as the "policy entrepreneurs" identified in the state policy diffusion literature (Mintrom, 1997). New parties must carve out a niche for themselves within the party system and attract voters if they are to survive. Therefore, new parties may try to lure female voters by making a commitment to ensure that the parties will have female candidates, and more broadly, to demonstrate their commitment to women's issues. Further, the smaller, newer parties also may have less to lose if the strategy fails. New parties may not have loyal groups whose support may be lost. Likewise, innovative policies, such as quotas, may meet with less resistance in newer parties because there are fewer established norms and few entrenched power holders who would be deposed by a policy such as quotas.

Data Analysis

The primary focus of this chapter is to describe the diffusion of quotas as an innovative policy across parties and to explain a party's adoption of candidate gender quotas for the national legislature. The statistical analysis is based on sixty parties[3] in ten Western European democracies.[4] Measures for each of the independent and dependent variables were collected from published national statistics and other data sources. A full list of variables and their sources is presented in Appendix A. The dependent variable in each case is the presence or absence of candidate gender quotas. The adoption of candidate gender quotas is examined from 1970 to 1995. The first candidate gender quota was adopted in 1975. Finally, systematic data on gender quotas is available only up to 1995.

Parties and the Adoption of Gender Quotas

Parties have adopted candidate gender quotas steadily over time. Figure 4.1 displays the cumulative number of parties adopting quotas from 1972 to 1995

Figure 4.1 Cumulative Quotas Adopted 1972–95

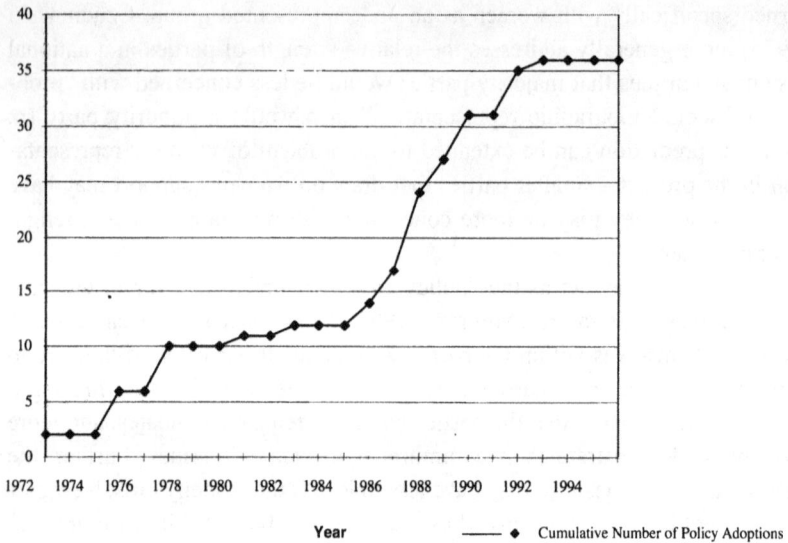

Source: Calculated by the author based on data obtained from Katz and Mair (1992) and Inter-Parliamentary Union (1993), supplemented with data from country experts collected by Professor Richard Matland.

for the sixty parties in this study. From 1975 to 1984, the number of parties with quotas remains below four and then begins to take off. The most rapid increase in the adoption of quotas occurred from 1985 to 1993, from five parties to eighteen. After 1993, the rate slows again.

This graph follows the characteristic "diffusion of an innovation," which is the process by which a new idea is communicated over time among members of a social system (Yamaguchi, 1991). The standard s-shaped curve displays a pattern in which adoption is slow and then reaches a takeoff point, rising toward a maximum rate of diffusion, and leveling off. A slowdown in the adoption rate is because there are fewer potential adopters left; thus the policy has reached a saturation point. This is the case with quotas. Those parties that are most likely to adopt quotas had likely done so by 1993, and the pool of favorable parties decreases, leading one to predict that fewer parties will adopt quotas in the future.

Event History Analysis

A special statistical procedure is needed to analyze the diffusion of gender quotas. Scholars of policy diffusion frequently use event history analysis

(Berry and Berry, 1990; 1992; Mooney and Lee, 1995). Event history analysis (EHA) is the best method to analyze this dynamic process. Where the standard ordinary least squares (OLS) regression uses interval/ratio variables as dependent variables, EHA allows one to use a dichotomized variable measuring the event we are interested in—quotas. Further, one can measure the presence or absence of quotas in each year within the study. Therefore, there is no need for a separate variable measuring time; it is built right into the dependent variable. In addition, EHA is an improvement over logistic regression because it handles "right censoring." That is to say, among the parties in the data set, there is a set of parties that never adopt quotas. In a standard regression, these cases are treated in the same manner as those parties that adopted quotas in the last year of our time period. Clearly the two sets of parties are quite different when it comes to quotas, and EHA distinguishes between the two in its analysis.

EHA allows us to look at both the cross-temporal pattern and the influences on the adoption of candidate gender quotas. For each party, EHA asks what determines the probability that quota adoption occurs. This probability is called the "hazard rate" in EHA, and it denotes the likelihood that a quota will be adopted at a given point in time, given that the event has not already occurred (Yamaguchi, 1991). EHA models produce maximum likelihood estimates, which provide a great deal of information about the likelihood that each party might adopt quotas through the defined time period (Box-Steffensmeier and Jones, 1997).[5]

An Event History Analysis Model of Candidate Gender Quota Adoption

I combine the four categories of hypotheses outlined in the literature review to predict the likelihood a party will adopt candidate gender quotas.[6] Although there are distinct reasons to believe that leftist values based on both Old and New Politics would make a party more likely to adopt quotas, I could not include both variables in the same model because they correlate too strongly with one another. Therefore, I include only the degree of leftist orientation based upon Old Politics. When I substitute the indicator of New Left Politics, it is highly statistically significant as well, and the impact of the other explanatory variables remains similar.[7]

Table 4.2 presents two models: Model I covers 1975 to 1995, and Model II covers only 1985 to 1995. Because the assumptions of EHA require that the set of cases not change throughout the observation period, only those parties that had gained seats in parliament by 1975 could be included in the first model. Those parties that gained their first seat in the national legislature after 1975 (e.g., several New Left parties[8]) are eliminated from this first model.[9]

Table 4.2 Logit Maximum Likelihood Estimates for Event History Analysis Model of Candidate Gender Quota Adoption

Independent Variables	Model I 1975-95		Model II 1985-95	
	B	Exp(B)	B	Exp(B)
% Women MPs–National	.02	1.028	.06	1.061
% Women MPs–Party	-.02	.978	-.01	.970
% Women Party Leadership	.07*	1.077	.04**	1.040
Electoral System Proportionality	-.02	.986	-.03	.965
Year First Quota in Party System	-.25**	.778	-.15**	.865
Leftist Ideology	-.42**	.656	-.38**	.682
Level of Candidate Nomination	1.97	1.055	.97	2.64
Degree of Institutionalization	-.49	.608	-.34	.706
Age of Party	.01	.997	-.01	.985
Number of Cases	61		66	
-2 (Log-likelihood ratio)	75.617**		76.42**	

Significance Levels:* = $p < .1$, ** = $p < .05$

Certainly one must take this exclusion into account when interpreting the results from the first model. The second statistical model limits the time period to 1985 to 1995 in order to include those parties established between 1975 and 1995. Hence, the first model sacrifices the inclusion of new parties for a greater span of time, and the second model the reverse.

The coefficients (B) are maximum likelihood estimates obtained through logit, and the signs of the estimates indicate whether a variable increases or decreases the "hazard rate" across time.[10] The most important explanations for the adoption of gender quotas are consistent across both models in table 4.2. A high number of women among the party's leadership, the year the first quota was adopted by a party in the system, and a leftist ideology strongly influence the likelihood that a party will adopt quotas. Because these three explanatory variables are the only statistically significant indicators, the discussion will focus on them. The results reveal that for each percentage point gain in the proportion of women among the party's leadership, or national executive committee, the likelihood that the party will adopt quotas increases by almost 8% in the first model and by 13% in the second model. Further, for each year closer to 1975 that the first quota in the party system was adopted, the likelihood that other parties will follow suit increases by 22% in the first model, and by 13% in the second. The degree of leftist values that a party holds, based upon Old Politics issues, shows that for every one point toward the left on the index, a party is 34% more likely to adopt quotas in Model I, and 32% more likely in Model II.

The strong and significant estimate yielded by the percentage of women on the national executive committee emphasizes the integral role of women within the party in pressing for measures to increase women's representation at the parliamentary level. Where women acquired power within the party by the mid-1970s, their presence at the decision-making table heightened the likelihood their party would adopt formal rule changes to advance women's gains in parliament. Further, other parties within the party system strongly impact the decision to adopt gender quotas. The earlier the first party (the prototype) adopts quotas, the more likely other parties in the system are to follow the innovator's lead. Finally, although quotas have spread across the ideological spectrum in some cases, when compared systematically, a leftist party is more likely to adopt quotas, and to adopt them sooner. These cross-national findings, controlling for other factors, support the "contagion theory" of Matland and Studlar (1996), who predict a contagion after a party from the Left sets the precedent for rival left parties to follow.

In short, leftist values, based on both Old Politics and New Politics issues, are important. By looking at two time periods, it is evident that it is not New Left parties alone that drive this process. In the first model (1975–95), a majority of New Left parties is omitted, because of their late entrance into parliament.[11] However, parties were adopting quotas, and women's activism and New Left values within established parties were quite important.

Establishing Sequence: Women on the National Executive, Parliament, and Rules

It is important to systematically assess the sequence of events that led to the adoption of quotas and to their effects. The multivariate analysis in chapter 3 made clear that *internal* party rules are strongly related to the presence of more women on the national executive committees of the parties in this study. And past scholarship shows that the number of women on the NEC is strongly related to the number of female party MPs. Further, the present chapter has linked the adoption of quotas to the percentage of female MPs. Yet one might question the sequence of events. Which comes first, quotas or women in high party posts? Women in high party posts, or women in parliament? Quotas or women in parliament?

While internal quotas are often credited with raising the proportion of women within the party, it may also be that parties with initially high levels of women in the top party echelons are the ones that are most likely to adopt quotas. Thus, we must test whether internal quotas achieve their desired effect.

Figure 4.2 Women on the NEC and Internal Party Rules, 1975–97

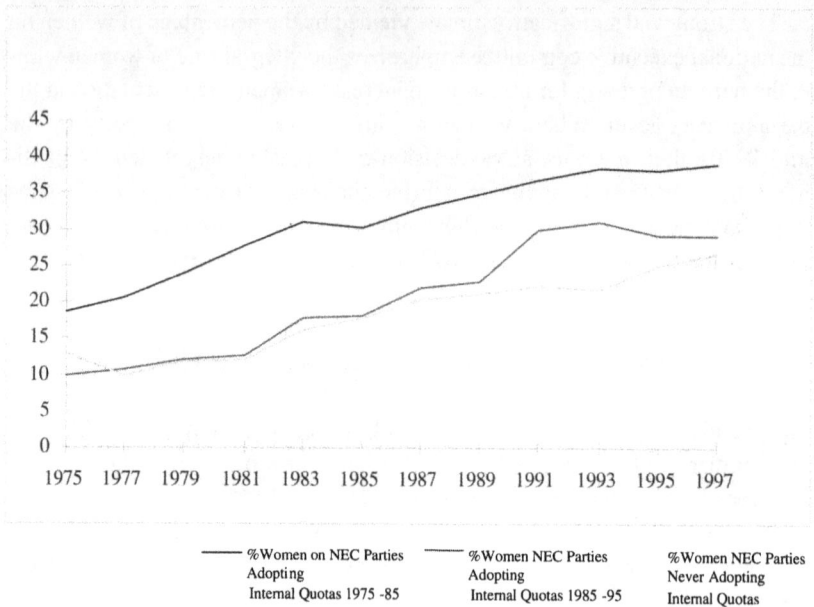

——— %Women on NEC Parties Adopting Internal Quotas 1975 -85	········· %Women NEC Parties Adopting Internal Quotas 1985 -95	%Women NEC Parties Never Adopting Internal Quotas

Source: See figure 4.1.

Figure 4.2 displays the trends in the proportion of women on the NEC in parties with and without internal quotas from 1975 to 1997. The three lines in figure 4.2 represent the average percentage of women on the NEC for: (1) parties
that adopted internal quotas from 1975 to 1985; (2) parties that adopted internal quotas from 1985 to 1995; and (3) parties that never adopted internal quotas. By breaking down parties with internal quotas into two periods of
adoption, we have two separate tests of the effect of quotas. In the period after
quotas are adopted, one can expect a jump in women's representation on the
NEC.

Each line in figure 4.2 shows an increase in the number of women in
office, yet the significant increases occur at different points for each group.
The first line shows that while all three subgroups began at similar levels, parties with internal quotas early on jumped far above the others shortly after
quotas were adopted. The takeoff point for the early quota parties is 1977, and
the average percentage of women on the NEC climbs steadily, but more slowly, into the 1990s. The second line reveals that parties that adopted internal
quotas from 1985 to 1995 averaged numbers of women on the NEC similar to
parties without quotas up to the late 1980s, when the average percentage of
women on the NEC jumps substantially for parties with internal quotas, rising

Figure 4.3 Percentage of Women in Parliament by Year in Which Women Reach "Critical Mass" on NEC

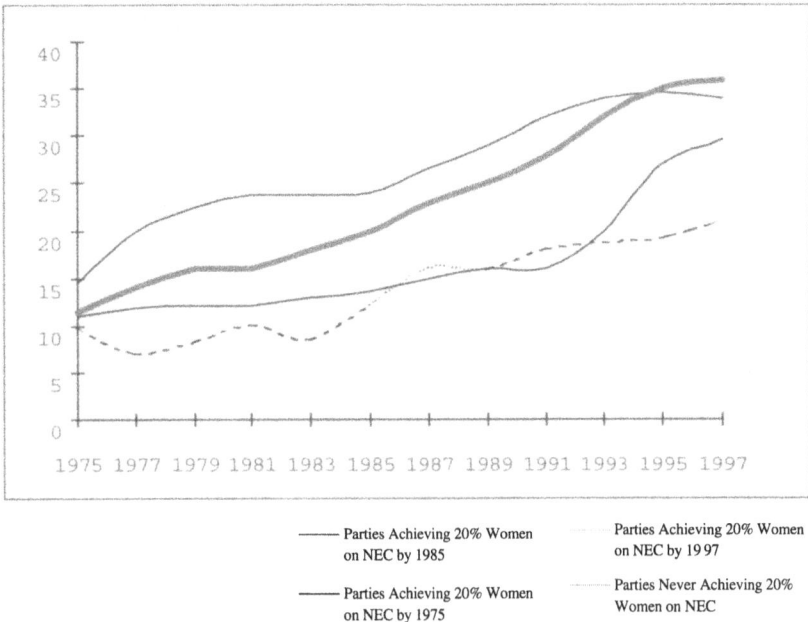

Parties Achieving 20% Women on NEC by 1985

Parties Achieving 20% Women on NEC by 1975

Parties Achieving 20% Women on NEC by 1997

Parties Never Achieving 20% Women on NEC

Source: See figure 4.1.

above those without quotas. Finally, the third line reveals that parties that never adopted internal quotas are nevertheless increasing their percentage of women on the NEC, yet these parties end up in 1995 with the lowest average. It is clear that internal quotas are a mechanism of increase in women's presence on the NEC across parties.

In a similar fashion, it is important to examine whether women's gains on the national executive committees of parties preceded their gains in the party's delegation to parliament. If attaining a "critical mass" of women on the NEC, or crossing a certain threshold, leads to gains in parliament, then it would appear that women's power within the party allows them to lobby for further gains in parliament. Past theorizing on what constitutes a critical mass sets the threshold at anywhere from 10% to 35% women in a given institution (for a thorough review of the literature, see Studlar and McAllister, 2002).[12] Given this variation, it seems most prudent to select a point between the two extremes, and thus the threshold for a critical mass of women has been set at 20%. It is hypothesized that when the composition of the NEC reaches 20% women, women's acquired power will translate into

Figure 4.4 Average Percentage of Women MPs by Adoption of Quotas, 1975–95

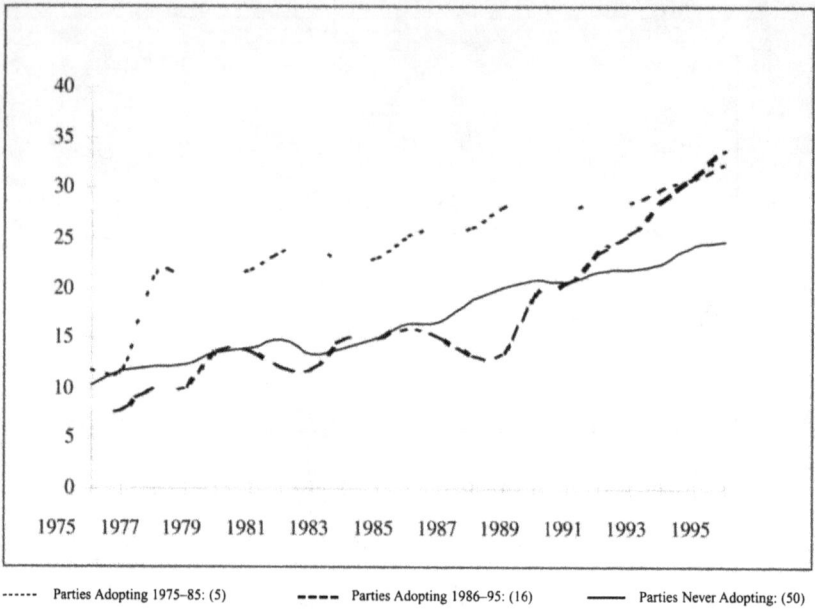

------ Parties Adopting 1975–85: (5)   ---- Parties Adopting 1986–95: (16)   —— Parties Never Adopting: (50)

Source: See figure 4.1.

further power, manifesting itself in significant increases in the proportion of women in the party's parliamentary delegation.

Figure 4.3 displays the trends in the average percentage of women MPs for parties: (1) that achieved 20% women on the NEC before 1975; (2) that achieved 20% women on the NEC between 1975 and 1985; (3) that achieved 20% women on the NEC between 1985 and 1997; and (4) that never achieved 20% women on the NEC. By breaking down parties into three eras in which women reached a critical mass on the NEC, we have three separate tests of the effect of women's internal power. In the period after women reach 20%, we expect a jump in women's representation on the NEC.

Each line in figure 4.3 shows an increase in the proportion of women in office, yet the significant increases occur at different points for each group. The first line shows that while all three subgroups began at similar levels, parties reaching a critical mass by 1975 jumped above the others straightaway, and then the rate of growth slows and then levels off. The second line reveals that parties reaching a critical mass by 1985 averaged intermediate numbers of women MPs up to the mid 1980s, when the average proportion of women MPs jumps substantially, rising far above the others and eventually matching the parties reaching a critical mass by 1975. The third line reveals that parties that do not reach a critical mass of women until 1997 do not realize gains in parliament until the mid-1990s, when there appears a steep upward slope. Finally, the fourth line reveals that parties never reaching a critical mass are only slightly increasing their percentage of women MPs. It is clear that having a substantial number of women on the NEC is a mechanism of increase in women's parliamentary representation across parties.

Finally, while quotas are often credited with raising the proportion of women in office, it may also be that parties with initially high numbers of women members of parliament (MPs) are the ones that are most likely to adopt quotas. Thus, we must test whether quotas achieve their desired effect. Figure 4.4 displays the trends in the proportion of women MPs in parties with and without quotas from 1975 to 1995. The three lines in figure 4.4 represent the average percentage of women MPs for: (1) parties that adopted quotas from 1975 to 1985; (2) parties that adopted quotas from 1986 to 1995; and (3) parties that never adopted quotas. By breaking down parties with quotas into two periods of adoption, we have two separate tests of the effect of quotas. In the period after quotas are adopted, we expect a jump in women's representation.

Each line in figure 4.4 shows an increase in the percentage of women in office, yet the significant increases occur at different points for each group. The first line shows that while all three subgroups began at similar levels, parties with quotas early on jumped far above the others shortly after quotas were adopted. The takeoff point for the early quota parties is 1977, and the average percentage of women MPs climbs steadily, but more slowly, into the 1990s. The second line reveals that parties that adopted quotas from 1985 to 1995 averaged lower numbers of women officeholders than parties without quotas up to the late 1980s, when the average proportion of women MPs jumps substantially, rising above all others. Finally, the third line reveals that parties that never adopted quotas are nevertheless increasing their percentage of women. However, although parties that never adopted quotas start off in the 1970s with similar percentages to all other parties, these parties end up in 1995 with the lowest average. It is clear that quotas are a mechanism of increase in women's representation.

Conclusions

The strongest explanatory variables may be linked logically in a sequential chain of influences to explain both why and when parties adopt policies to promote women candidates. First, the more women who establish themselves within the highest ranks of the party, the greater the chances the party will adopt quotas. These women may actively point out that there are too few women in parliament and directly pressure the party leadership to adopt formal measures to increase women's legislative representation. Further, parties with leftist values may be the same parties that have greater numbers of women among the party hierarchy to begin with, and they are the parties where the leadership is more likely to listen to the demands of women on their national executive committees. The strong influence of an entrepreneurial party in the system adopting quotas, and other parties following suit, suggests a process of contagion. And leftist parties may be more likely to initiate the process of contagion. These leftist parties appear to start the process of contagion, and they appear more likely to respond to the precedent set by their rivals.

It may be that parties adopt quotas merely as a symbolic act, in an effort to attract votes. Quotas for women candidates are a visible method of demonstrating support for women's issues. And quotas are often adopted in a process of competition. As such, quotas may be more of an election strategy and less a reflection of real support for women's parliamentary presence. Yet an institution initially designed for one end can often have unintended consequences. Once women are in positions of power, no matter how they got there, it will become more difficult in the future to exclude them. The increasing numbers of women MPs have set a standard for all parties to follow, and greater proportions of women in the party delegation will be expected in the future.

Although a contentious issue, the adoption of candidate quotas and targets reflects some changes that parties have undertaken regarding women's issues. As formal rule changes, gender quotas represent an institutionalization of changing attitudes toward women in politics. Once quotas are in place, there is less need for constant pressure for women's representation. In turn, it is possible that formal rules can turn into norms, reinforcing the changing attitudes toward women in politics.

5

Britain: Women, Parties, and the House of Commons

British women won the right to vote in two stages, in 1918 and in 1928, and the right to run for office in 1918. By 1974 women's voter turnout rates caught up with those of men (Lovenduski and Norris, 1993). Further, evidence from the 1987 British general elections reveals voters do not appear to be biased against women candidates (Studlar et al., 1988). Yet historically, few women have been elected to the House of Commons. The trends in women's presence in the House of Commons are displayed in figure 5.1. Until 1987 women constituted fewer than 4% of the members of the House of Commons. Although women made great gains in the number of candidates in the late 1980s, it was not until the 1997 election that these candidacies register as a substantial increase in seats in the House.

Neither legal barriers nor a lack of political interest can explain the lack of women's parliamentary presence. So why did women make great gains in Parliament in the 1997 election? Drawing on survey data on gender and voting patterns, I will show that shifts in women's voting behavior did not translate into automatic gains in office. Instead, grassroots forces were bolstered by top-down party efforts, especially in the British Labour Party, after women gained some power within the party and devised strategies that complemented the existing opportunity structure.

Figure 5.1 British Women in the House of Commons, 1970–97

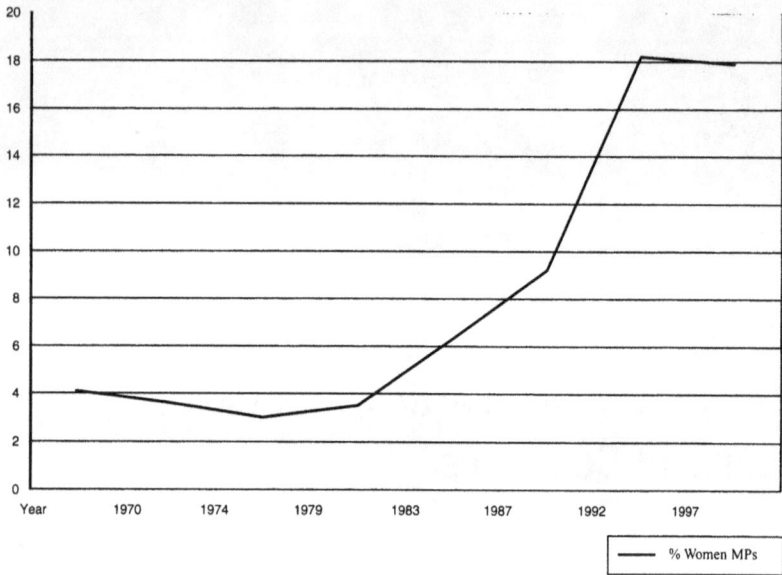

Source: Inter-Parliamentary Union (1997), updated with data from www.ipu.org.

Political Background

In the British parliamentary system, voters elect, with a plurality of votes, a single representative from their district to the House of Commons; this system is most commonly known as the "first past the post" (FPTP) system. The British party system approximates the "responsible party model" with its centralized and cohesive parties, where members of Parliament (MPs) most often vote along party lines.

As a result of the winner-take-all system, two major parties compete for control of the British government, the Labour Party and the Conservative Party. Although the plurality system works against third parties, the Liberal Democratic Party (or some allied form of this current party) routinely sent MPs to Parliament throughout the period of study in this book.[1] Still, under the FPTP system many voters perceive a vote for a third party candidate as essentially "wasted." To capture the greatest number of voters, both Labour and the Conservatives attempt to appeal to a broad stratum of the electorate by aggregating a diverse set of groups under the party structure.

Historically, social class structured the British political system. Traditionally, the Conservatives represent the middle class and business, and Labour, the working class and unions. While class has declined from its postwar high in structuring the vote, it still remains a dominant theme in British party politics (Norton, 1994). Yet changes in the composition of the electorate, based on a decline in the industrial sector and a weakening relationship between Labour and trade unions, are linked with the broad process of party "modernization"—a move toward a more centrist, centralized, professional party.

British Women's Voting Patterns and Parliamentary Presence

Existing party scholarship leads us to believe that parties react to shifts in voting patterns, as explained in chapter 2. One might logically expect that after parties gain a greater proportion of women's votes, they will offer more female candidates for office in winnable districts. In this section, I search for links over time between changes in the gender gap in voting and in women's gains in parliamentary seats. Figure 5.2 displays the trends in the gender gap in both and the trends in the number of Labour women in Parliament from 1970 to 1998. I measure the gender gap as the percentage of women who intend to vote for Labour minus the percentage of men who intend to do the same.[2] The higher the vote gap line reaches, the better Labour is faring among women voters. The graph shows that in the late 1950s and 1960s, British

Figure 5.2 British Trends in the Gender Vote Gap and Women MPs
from Leftist Parties, 1970–98

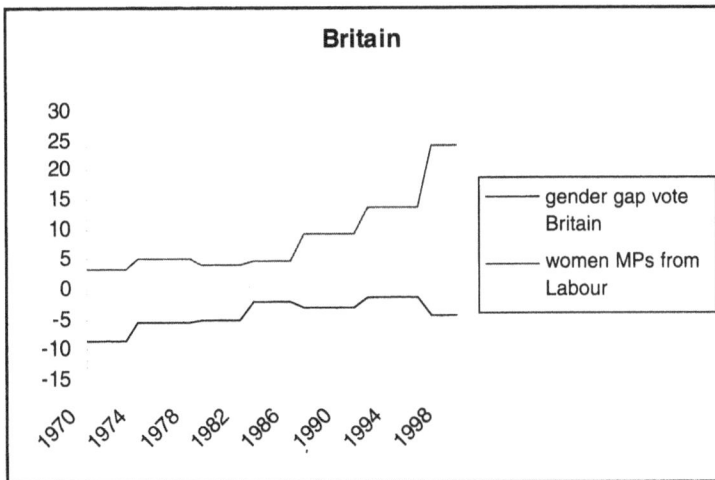

Source: British National Election Studies. Inter-Parliamentary Union. See Appendices for details.

69

women slightly favored the Conservatives. Inglehart and Norris (2003) call this the "traditional" gender gap. Although this gap weakened a bit, it persisted through the 1980s and somewhat into the 1990s. In 1970 the gender gap for Labour is at almost a ten point deficit, and in 1998 the deficit is only about five points. This weakening of the traditional gender gap, toward a "dealignment" of women's votes, is consistent with previous research (see Norris, 1999; Inglehart and Norris, 2003). The top line in the figure shows that Labour women made slight gains in Parliament in the mid-1980s and made a major leap in 1997. There is little evidence that a fading "traditional" gender gap in the 1980s is connected with more women in office in the 1990s. Indeed, gender provides little structure for the British vote in recent years as women's parliamentary presence has climbed.

Values and Party Preferences

It may be misleading to treat women as an undifferentiated group. Specifically, it may be a subset of feminists, rather than women in general, who developed a distinct set of values. Conover (1988) finds that American feminists are a distinct group of women with specific values, and that feminism is strongly correlated with party identification. Based on survey data in thirteen established democracies, Hayes et al. (2000) find that women are indeed more likely to hold feminist values. Thus, feminist attitudes may actually account for the apparent gender-based gap in voting behavior. Specific to Britain in 1992, Hayes (1997) finds that although gender had little impact on the vote in Britain in 1992, feminist attitudes do have an impact; those that are pro-feminist are significantly less likely to vote Conservative than for Labour or the Liberals. Women are also significantly more likely than men to adopt a feminist orientation.

So, past research suggests that perhaps attitudinal differences regarding women's role in society, or in politics more specifically, exerts greater influence than gender on party support. Those who favor women's equality presumably support women's parliamentary representation. To be sure, the women's movement is composed of several different strands, and some subgroups prefer different courses of action. Yet one common thread is the demand for the democratization of social and political life (Jenson, 1995). Hence, support for the women's movement may be more directly related to the proportion of women Labour MPs.

The one indicator of feminist values that is considered consistently from the 1970s to 1990s in the Eurobarometer studies is a measure of support for the women's movement.[3] Figure 5.3 displays the trends in the Labour vote among those who support the women's movement, similar to the analysis of

70

Figure 5.3 British Trends in the Left Vote among Supporters of the Women's
Movement and Women MPs from Labour Party, 1970–97

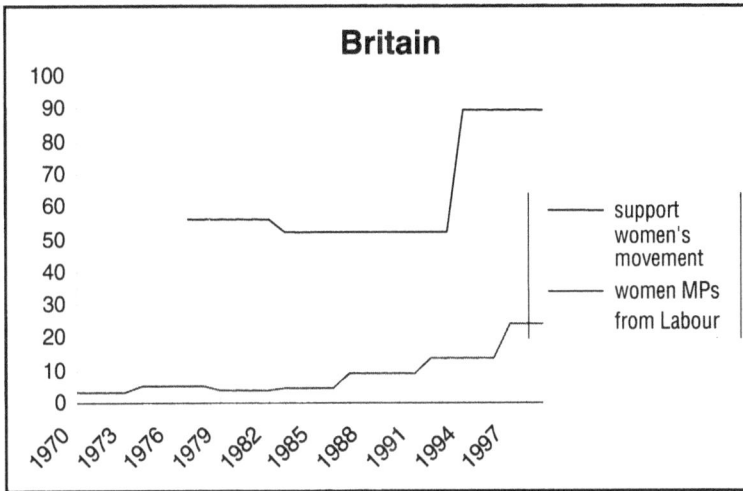

Source: Eurobarometer studies. Inter-Parliamentary Union. See Appendices for details.

voter support in the previous section. In addition, the trends in Labour women
MPs are graphed as well, for comparison. The graph shows that support for
the women's movement among Labour supporters did not increase in the
1980s, hovering around 55%, and then jumped considerably in the 1994 survey to 90% approval of the movement. Consistent with this change, the substantial increases in women MPs from the Labour Party began in the 1990s,
culminating in 1997—later than in Labour's sister Socialist parties across
Western Europe. A late show of support from leftist supporters for the
women's movement precedes the jump in women's representation. Certainly
these common trends do not constitute causality. Instead, there may be a spu-
rious correlation—a factor that explains both increases in support for the
women's movement and for women's parliamentary gains.

The British Women's Movement

Attitudinal forces and women's gains may be driven by the shift in tactics
within the movement itself. The British women's movement gained momentum in its "second wave"[4] in the late 1960s, and the first conference was held
in February 1970 (Randall, 1982). Past scholarship characterizes the British
movement as radical and autonomous, relative to movements in other Western
European nations (Gelb, 1989). In the 1970s, most women's movement

71

activists preferred to work at the grassroots level, independent of parties and mainstream politics (Randall, 1992; Lovenduski and Randall, 1993). Yet by the 1980s, responding to the attacks on the welfare state by the Thatcher government, an increasing number of movement activists sought alliances with the established parties (Jenson, 1982; Lovenduski and Norris, 1993; Beckwith, 2003). Indeed, a more mainstream movement is likely to garner more widespread public support and is more likely to make some inroads in established political arenas. Thus, changes in attitude may underpin women's gains in Parliament, but certainly other factors are at work as well.

Party-Level Forces for Increasing the Number of Women in Westminster

Women's voting behavior, mass attitudes, and the women's movement alone cannot explain why women's parliamentary representation increased when it did. Further, why were women's gains concentrated among Labour MPs? Certainly it is essential to look at party-level forces. As far back as 1965, the central party organizations of the Labour and Conservative parties advocated for women candidates, but stopped at encouraging rhetoric (as cited in Welch and Studlar, 1986). Charlot (1981) even argues that the central party elite may be ahead of the local party on women's representation, given the fact that women accounted for 13% of those appointed to life peerages in the House of Lords, compared with fewer than 4% in the House of Commons back in the late 1970s and early 1980s. An in-depth focus on the Labour and Conservative parties, and the role of the Liberal Democrats in stimulating party competition, will reveal the motivations for these parties to promote (or not promote) women candidates in winnable seats.

Party Competition

The previous section showed how the women's votes became "unanchored" in the 1980s, and electoral uncertainty may have generated some pressure to gain women's votes. However, it was not until a small third party promised to support more women candidates that Labour took notice. The Liberal Party was the first to run more women in the 1974 campaign, but largely in hopeless races, so women made few gains in Parliament (Hills, 1981). Likewise, in its search for new constituencies, the SDP (the Social Democratic Party) made a direct appeal to Labour's women voters, offering to nominate an unprecedented number of women candidates (Lovenduski and Randall, 1993). The SDP joined forces with the Liberal Party to form the Liberal Democrats, and this alliance campaigned to send more women to Parliament (Norris and Loven-duski, 1995). Although the party's initial intentions were not fully carried through, the important point is that the Liberal Democrats had made women's representation a salient political issue in attracting women's votes.

Studlar and Welch (1992) contend that the presence of a third party gener-ated greater electoral uncertainty than in the previous two-party system. Since 1974 the Liberal Democrats had increased their number of female candidates, yet most of them were defeated in hopeless contests (Studlar, 2004). As a con-sequence of this heated party competition, the Liberal Democrats' rival Labour Party took notice and followed suit by supporting more women can-didates as well. While the Liberal Democrats' pressure led to more women candidates, it did not improve women's chances of winning (Studlar and Welch, 1992).

Women in the Party Hierarchy: Gaining Power, Changing Perceptions

Yet even the addition of party competition does not tell the full story. It is essential to add the active role of women in advancing their claims for parlia-mentary presence. Women have long played a role in British party politics. Yet the women's movement's increasing focus on party politics in the 1980s and 1990s infused the Labour, Conservative, and Liberal Democratic parties with new demands for inclusion at all levels in the party hierarchy and for a place in Westminster.

The Labour Party

Although one might expect that Labour's egalitarian ideology would make it a conducive environment for women to gain voice, traditionally this has not been the case. Labour's close ties to trade unions often precluded the represen-tation of other interest groups within the party. British trade unions have not always been terribly supportive of women. In 1979 only one in thirty-two trade union officials was a woman, and women even had little decision-making power in unions where they made up most of the membership—for example, garment makers, health service employees, and teachers (Hills, 1981).

The Labour women's organization was founded in 1906, and it underwent a few name and organizational changes before it became more politically active in the 1970s (Hills, 1981). The women's section of the Labour Party began to play a vital role in pressing for women's opportunities in the early 1980s. The structure of the women's organization parallels the mainstream party organization. Even in the 1970s, Labour's women's organization was large (1400 local-level women's sections according to party pamphlets)—yet to this point they were powerless. Although the women's sections held meetings at the local and central levels, their meetings were traditionally uneventful social gatherings. Records from the women's section meetings reveal that the organization met infrequently, about half as frequently as the youth committee (Women's Section minutes, Labour Party Archives). In the late 1970s, limited discussions of women's need for greater access to party decision making surfaced. Women's claims were often considered less important than class-based issues (Perrigo, 1995). By the early 1980s the women's section was formulating plans to improve women's representation and began mobilizing around this issue (Women's Section minutes, Labour Party Archives). Yet it would take many years of work to finally get the issue of women's representation on Labour's agenda.

Gradually, more militant women began to demand greater access (Gelb, 1989). From 1979 to 1983, feminist organizations based outside Labour were well connected to women on the inside (Perrigo, 1995). In the 1980s feminists within the party, organized in the Labour Women's Action Committee (LWAC), joined forces with the more radical leftist party factions, who sought to take over the entire party apparatus. Yet this more militant women's organization still did not achieve the goal of substantially raising women's representation within the party or in Parliament. Several former high-ranking Labour Party officials stated that party leaders largely ignored the LWAC's claims because of its ties to the party's radical left faction. A former party general secretary revealed that at this time, women's claims were viewed as part of the "loony left," which was the faction that chained Labour to unpopular radical policy positions and thereby contributed to Labour's electoral losses. Moderate party factions were trying to rid Labour of the "loony left." During this period, women's gains within the party largely stagnated. One former Labour Party official commented that in the mid-1980s, there were not even enough women at the top levels to even qualify this as an era of tokenism.

Yet women within the party persisted, as they had for so many years, working to gain a foothold and to further the party's goal of recapturing government. Labour's first (and largely symbolic) response to women's demands was to appoint a women's officer and a shadow minister for women's affairs (Gelb, 1989). Yet the women who held this post—Jo Richardson and her successors, Joyce Gould, Clare Short, Vicky Phillips, Deborah Lincoln, Meg Russell, and Rachel McLean—used this newly gained power within the party to fight tenaciously to bring women's equality within the party to the forefront. Using the women's officer position as a springboard to higher office, Richardson, Gould, Short, and Phillips went on to assume new roles in the making of party policy.

With access to the party leadership, these women gradually gained more concessions. Responding to pressure from the activists, in 1982 the party made women's representation an official concern by drafting the National

Women's Charter, which called for more women to be promoted at all levels of the party. Still, party rhetoric was not enough to bring substantive changes. In an interview, a former national women's officer said that each year the women's conference would vote for some form of quotas, and each year the resolution would not make it through the national executive committee (NEC). Clearly, women needed some leaders on the NEC who were sympathetic to their demands.

By the late 1980s, women's presence on Labour's national executive committee rose to 30%. Although Labour had guaranteed women five of the twenty-nine seats (17%) on the NEC since 1918 (see Studlar, 2004), a larger presence in a new era created a new context for women in the party elite. With a new power base, women inside the NEC were instrumental in pushing for new rules to promote more women to positions within the party (Short, 1996). In 1989 Labour passed a resolution that, in summary, mandated that women make up from one-third to one-half of selected party bodies at the local, regional, and national levels. At first the local parties resisted, but with continued pressure, the intraparty quota policy was implemented. The effect of these new internal rules was two-fold. First, these quotas solidified women's presence within the higher echelons of the party, and second, they also ensured that women within the party had the power to press for increased representation at the parliamentary level.

With even more women well placed in the party hierarchy, the issue of parliamentary representation took the spotlight. The women who had attained those high positions among party officers and on the NEC, such as Clare Short, Tessa Jowell, and Barbara Follett, worked closely with the top party leaders and directly lobbied for more women candidates in winnable seats.

In interviews, a few former national women's officers emphasized Clare Short's role. Short had persuaded the party leadership to add research on women voters to their surveys and focus groups. The initial pollster refused to analyze women's opinions separately, and Short turned to her connections in academia to conduct a gender-specific analysis. In one report, two British political scientists, Joni Lovenduski and Pippa Norris, reported that Labour could have won the last election if women's votes had swung in their direction. Lovenduski later collaborated on a manuscript for the Labour Party, illustrating how the party could achieve gains in women's representation.

Focus group researchers presented Labour's leaders with new evidence that women often viewed Labour as male dominated and union controlled (interview with former aide to women's officer; Russell, 2003). Many women who agreed with Labour's policy positions failed to vote Labour because of their male-dominated images of the party. Women who perceived Labour as a group of confrontational men were more likely to vote for the Conservatives. Thus, it became quite clear to Labour officials that they must communicate more effectively with women in order to change their image among female voters (Short, 1996). Focus group research, to a certain extent, had created a new target issue group—women who had historically viewed Labour as male dominated, but would vote for New Labour if it became more female friendly. This potential swing-voter, dubbed the "Worcester Woman," was described as a working mother, in her 30s, and living in middle England, who had traditionally voted Conservative (Coote, 2001). Labour leaders became convinced they could attract her vote and swing the election in their favor.

To change their image among women voters in the 1997 campaign, Labour launched a party campaign called "Winning Words" (interviews with former women's officers). As part of the campaign, Labour trained its candidates to speak about issues in a manner that specifically appealed to women. Labour politicians were rehearsed on how to shift from more abstract language to discussing policies in more concrete terms, and in a form of language that women preferred. For example, rather than talking about a nebulous economic policy, Labor candidates discussed pocketbook finances and job opportunities. In addition, the campaign highlighted women politicians. Key sources within the party said that the strategy was to feature these women in policy discussions in the media. Thus, Labour needed more female candidates and MPs to successfully transform its image.

The analysis of the 1992 electoral loss, coupled with women's negative images of Labour in focus groups, finally persuaded Labour leaders to listen to women in the party hierarchy (Russell, 2003). After Clare Short and her colleagues framed women's votes as a key ingredient to winning the next election, the party's leadership took steps to close the gender gap in the next election. These women in high-ranking party bodies effectively moved the issue of women's representation from the "loony left" to the party's rising package of "modernization" issues. In the early 1990s, the Labour Party was in the midst of recasting itself as "New Labour"—a pragmatic, centrist, and progressive party. This key group of women presented its demands to a succession of Labour leaders, including Tony Blair, as congruent with the party's overall goals to gain wide appeal and win control of the government (Perrigo, 1995). Turning its back on promoting women candidates, a prominent women's officer reasoned, was couched as retreating to Labour's earlier, more old-fashioned and unsuccessful days. Meg Russell (2003) sums this idea up by saying that women pushing for greater presence shifted their "frame" from one centered on justice to one of electoral necessity.

In addition to women within the party, external women's groups both lobbied for and provided practical assistance in increasing women's parliamentary representation. The Labour Women's Network (LWN) was founded in 1987 by four women who had attempted to become candidates in the 1987 election but had encountered too many obstacles. According to the Network's leader, Val Price, the LWN uses the media to keep women's representation on the political agenda. Newspapers seek stories on women's roles in the party, and the LWN provides them with information and research. In addition, the LWN sponsored training sessions for potential candidates for office. The training seminars were so successful that Labour itself eventually took them over. Adding another dimension to support for Labour women candidates, Emily's List UK, modeled after its counterpart in the United States, was founded in 1993 by Barbara Follett to offer training and grants to women candidates to meet the costs incurred in running for office, such as travel, supplies, and childcare expenses (www.emilyslist.org.uk).

Women's sustained efforts to ascend to the top of the mainstream party hierarchy and gain a voice among the party leadership proved effective. Although Labour began with only about 20% women on the NEC in the 1970s, this percentage jumped to nearly 30% in the late 1980s and rose to 48% by the mid-1990s. In sum, these gains can be attributed, in part, to the decision of parts of the larger women's movement to align with Labour in the 1980s, the subsequent pressure generated by the more politicized women's organization, and the women's organization's eventual alliance with the party "modernizers."

Conservatives

Since women's enfranchisement, the Conservatives have mobilized women's electoral support by incorporating women at the grassroots level (Lovenduski et al., 1994). Women at the local level run meetings, campaign door-to-door, and serve on local committees. Conservative women are well represented in many positions in the lower rungs of party hierarchy, such as constituency chairs and councilors. Yet among the higher ranks, women have been severely underrepresented. As far back as 1965, the Conservative leadership paid lip service to women's underrepresentation. The Selwyn Lloyd Report recommended that each short list contain one woman, but the constituency organizations largely ignored the central leadership on this issue (Rush, 1969, as cited in Welch and Studlar, 1986; Hills, 1981).

Although more women are active among the Conservatives' local ranks than in those of the Labour Party, Conservative women are not as well represented at higher levels in the party and within Parliament. At the annual party conference, some spaces were set aside for women. The Conservatives have not released records on the number of women among the party's leadership in the 1970s, but according to scholars, women made up 20% of the Conservatives' NEC from the 1970s to the 1990s (Hills, 1981; Lovenduski and Norris, 1993).

Despite their fairly low and stagnant levels of representation in the national party hierarchy, women historically made few demands for greater representation within the Conservative Party (Lovenduski and Randall, 1993). The Conservatives' women's organization, the Conservative Women's National Committee (CWNC), avoided the LWAC model of mobilization for greater representation. The lack of internal divisions and feminist mobilization within the CNWC, and within the party more generally, not only stem from the party's more rightist ideology, but also the party's more authoritarian culture (Lovenduski and Norris, 1993). Comparisons of women's organization pamphlets from the 1980s from both the CWNC and LWAC reveal two contrasting styles of organization and goals. The CWNC stuck close to its original goals to recruit women party members and discuss mainstream party business. The CWNC sponsors an annual women's conference, and pamphlets from that event from the 1970s and 1980s emphasize how women across the country contribute to the party. In short, early party records indicate Conservative women were more likely to take the "good soldier" role within the party, rather than challenging the status quo.

While women in the party traditionally made few demands, external groups did lobby the Conservative Party. The most prominent, the 300 Group, was formed outside party institutions and initially was unaffiliated with either political party. Aptly titled, its goal was to increase the number of women in Parliament to 300. Founded in 1980, the 300 Group offers women training in campaign skills and policy education, and provides a forum for networking and developing mentor relationships (www.300group.org.uk). As more Conservative women entered the ranks of the group, key sources in British women's organizations revealed that it is now essentially a Conservative-dominated organization. To add to pressures from the 300 Group, over the course of the 1980s, a tide of discontent began to sweep across segments of Conservative women activists as younger generations of professional women joined the party. Some ten years after similar events in the Labour Party, segments of Conservative women activists began to press for greater representation on party bodies, and in the party's parliamentary delegation.

The Conservative Party's Women's National Committee (CWNC) pushed for several years in the late 1980s and 1990s to get the party to more actively recruit women candidates, to no avail. Because the Conservatives historically enjoyed a large bonus in women's votes, the party organization paid little attention to the paltry number of women they sent to Parliament. Yet with the Conservatives' defeat in 1997, party leaders took greater notice of women within the party. According to an interview with a key women's officer in the Conservative Party, after 1997 the Conservatives were eager to win back women's votes, and party leaders began to discuss strategies.

Increasingly focused on the gradual loss in their loyal base of women voters, the Conservatives began to hold special meetings to address regaining women voters by running more women candidates in the next election. The party adopted new recruitment structures designed to seek out potentially strong female candidates. Rather than waiting for women to step forward to run, the party organization has gone so far as to "talent spot" in certain constituencies for potential women candidates, urging them to run in the next election, and providing assistance and training. The Tories (the Conservatives) have also decided to emulate the "Winning Words" campaign of Labour and change the way that they talk about issues in order to appeal to women voters. However, focus group research (done by an independent political organization) suggests that the Tories' attempt to package their issues in a more "woman-friendly" way will be unsuccessful with women voters if the policies continue to be pitched only by men (interviews with Conservative women's officer and a leader of The Fawcett Society).

Party Rule Changes: Gender Quotas

Certainly attaining gender quotas is more difficult in a single-member district system like Britain, where quotas mean reserving a seat for a woman, rather than the list-balancing that characterized proportional representation systems. Yet Labour women persuaded the Labour Party to adopt a form of gender quotas for candidates, and the Conservatives have steered clear of any formal rule changes.

Labour

The road to changing party selection rules to promote women candidates in the Labour Party was long, and Labour women made many incremental steps. Beginning in the 1970s, each year the women's conference voted for quotas, and the measure passed to the NEC for a vote. Year after year the quota resolution failed. Since 1970, after each election the party general secretary sent a letter to all constituencies regretting the low numbers of women candidates and suggesting that more women be nominated (Brooks et al., 1990). However, these letters brought little change, and no rules for increasing women's representation were considered by the central party organization at this time. Those arguing for quotas were an isolated minority in the 1970s and in the early 1980s.

The first step toward quotas in the British Labour Party began within the party organization as part of an effort to increase the number of women in party offices and among party decision-making bodies, and these internal quotas were discussed in the last section. In 1989, the party conference passed Composite 54, which accepted, in principle, the idea of quotas within the party structure (Brooks et al., 1990). The 1990 party conference passed a resolution requiring that women make up 50% of the party officers at the branch level, three-sevenths of the party officers at the constituency level, and one-third of general selection committees. At first the local parties resisted these new rules, claiming that they could not find enough women to fill the spots. However, eventually the local party organizations found women and implemented the policy.

Gradually, the party flirted with watered-down versions of quotas for candidate lists. First, in 1988 the party ruled that each list of potential candidates, or short list, should contain one woman. The token woman policy had little effect on actual nominations. Then, in 1990 the party ruled that each short list should contain 50% women (Lovenduski and Norris, 1993). Yet the presence of women on a short list did not ensure that a woman would be nominated.

Support for a form of quotas for women candidates continued to build throughout the 1980s. A change in party leadership changed the climate within Labour. Interviews with former party officials highlighted the leadership of new party leader John Smith in legitimizing the idea of rule changes as part of a process of opening up Labour to traditionally underrepresented interests. Although Neil Kinnock ushered in the process of reform within Labour, Kinnock did not support any form of positive discrimination. In contrast, Smith strongly supported a temporary measure to directly get more women into office. Because most people characterized Smith as an old-fashioned lawyer who generally put limits on Kinnock's reforms, his support for a form of quotas surprised many within the Labour party, and contributed toward a new perception of quotas.

Yet the support of the larger body of party leadership was still necessary. Key Labour officials, including a national women's officer and former party secretary, revealed that Labour's NEC finally changed its attitude toward quotas in an attempt to change the party image among women voters. As part of a larger process in which Labour sought to construct a new image to appeal to a wider group of voters after the 1992 defeat, senior Labour figures began to prize women's votes. As a means to winning control of the government in the next election, putting forth more women candidates became part of Labour's strategy to attract those women's votes. Because the central party organization has only some control over the selection of candidates, they needed a mechanism to encourage local constituencies to run women candidates. The rules mandating 50% women on the short list had little effect on getting women nominated. Clearly more rigorous rules were necessary.

As part of Labour's "modernization" campaign, gender quotas shifted from a "loony left" policy to the mainstream agenda. Women on the NEC packaged gender quotas in a new way—as part of an image shift. Three members of the NEC Women's Committee were integral in achieving the quota policy—Rachel Brooks, Angela Eagle, and Clare Short. After Clare Short was named chair of the Labour Women National Executive Committee, a subgroup of the NEC that is elected by the Labour Women's Action Committee, she directly and effectively lobbied the National Executive to pass a form of gender quotas for parliamentary candidates. Together, Clare Short, with Labour MPs Brooks and Eagle, published a manuscript calling for quotas (Brooks et al., 1990). The manuscript not only lays out the legal and theoretical reasons that Labour should adopt quotas, but it also makes the pragmatic claim that Labour must find a mechanism to get more women into Parliament, or risk losing the next election without women's votes. This argument was integral to getting Labour leaders to listen to the women's committee demands. In several interviews with party insiders, it was emphasized that Clare Short, who would go on to be a Labour Minister, was the most publicly visible of the strong advocates, and her power within the party was a great strength to the eventual passage of a quota-type policy. In order to pass a quota policy, the NEC Women's Committee joined forces with the NEC Organization Committee—a move toward an alliance with the powerful forces within the party.

While the single-member district plurality electoral system did not preclude the introduction of a quota policy as generally assumed, the electoral rules necessitated a modification in the standard quota policy and made quotas more difficult for the party to implement. With single-member districts, the quota policy could not follow the typical gender balance on a party list, more common to quotas in Labour's sister Socialist parties across Western Europe. The plan that was devised, titled the "all-women shortlist" (AWS) policy, mandated that in one-half of the upcoming "inheritor seats" (vacancies resulting from retirement) and one-half of "strong challenger" seats (those deemed most winnable), the list of potential nominees must be composed of only women, ensuring that the nominee would be a woman (Studlar and McAllister, 1998; Norris, 2001; Russell, 2003). The goal was to get women nominated in forty constituencies, which were to be selected on an ad hoc basis.

With the backing of the NEC, the quota bill was finally passed on to the party conference for a vote. At the 1993–94 Conference, Labour leaders attached the AWS policy to the one-member one-vote (OMOV) policy, which was designed to take power away from trade unions and the hard left by removing the block vote. Knowing that OMOV would likely succeed at the conference, former national women's officers and their staff revealed in interviews that the two bills were strategically linked together. If a member voted against AWS, then he or she also had to vote against the popular OMOV resolution. In effect, the top Labour leaders gave the AWS policy a boost by slipping it by conference members as part of the OMOV bill, indicating that the Labour leadership supported the passage of gender quotas. Some party insiders even speculate that many members voting at the conference did not even know that they were also voting for AWS when they cast their ballot in support of OMOV. As a consequence, AWS passed and was popular in the following months.

The women-only short list became a difficult policy to implement, and AWS supporters increasingly found themselves targets of ridicule. Because only one candidate could be nominated in a given constituency, any form of quotas meant taking power away from men. Where the AWS policy was used, no men could apply for a seat in that constituency. Many men in those constituencies had worked for decades within the party, waiting for their chance to be nominated. With Labour's fortunes on the rise, many activists saw the upcoming election as their best opportunity to be elected. Labour's national women's officer traveled to several regions trying to "sell" the idea of AWS. Regional party officers were invited to a "consensus meeting" at which central party officials attempted to persuade the local party to agree to nominate only women to the party's short list of potential nominees (Russell, 2003). Because of the previous intraparty quotas, three of the local attendees at any meeting were guaranteed to be women. However, former party officials who had been commissioned to enforce the policy noted in interviews that Labour's national women's officer did not always gain the support of those women in attendance. In the end, some constituencies voluntarily adopted the AWS policy. Yet some resisted, and because there were not an adequate number of volunteers, the central party resolved to impose the new selection procedure. Thus began the bad publicity related to AWS.

The AWS policy was challenged by two male party members who claimed that the policy discriminated against them. They took their case to the Leeds Industrial Tribunal, which ruled that Labour acted unlawfully and contravened the Sex Discrimination Act (Lovenduski and Eagle, 1998). The tribunal struck down the AWS policy and ordered Labour to extend equal opportunities to men. Labour officials, including Tony Blair, decided against appealing the ruling, and the all-women short lists ended in January 1996. According to interviews with former members of Clare Short's staff, Blair was highly reluctant to push another quota policy, lest it be viewed as discriminatory. Yet thirty-four of the forty women had already been nominated under this policy, and their nominations stood. Given the proximity of the upcoming election, Labour could not afford to be uncertain about its candidates (Russell, 2003). After the defeat of AWS in the employment tribunal, gender quotas lost popularity among party members and leaders.

The quota policy achieved results—the number of female Labour MPs increased from 38 to 101 in the 1997 election as a result of the compulsory all-women short lists. In seats where AWS did not apply, men remained the favored candidates. Thus, we can assume that without AWS, women would not have fared nearly as well in the last election (Lovenduski and Eagle, 1998). Not only did AWS work to get more women elected, but also its controversial nature did not cause a backlash among British voters. Studlar and McAllister's (1998) analysis of 1997 voting data reveals that women selected through AWS averaged a higher percentage of votes than other Labour challengers—even other women on short lists.

The Liberal Democratic Party

Before the small British Social Democratic Party joined forces with the Liberals to form the Liberal Democrats, the Social Democrats demonstrated their support for women's parliamentary presence by stepping forward as the first party to mandate women on candidate short lists (Studlar and Welch, 1992). Once allied, the two parties employed this policy for the 1983 and 1987 elections. The impetus for this policy appears to be electoral competition. As a small party in need of publicity, such a policy served as a way to grab attention. Yet without key women protagonists pushing for stronger measures, no formal quotas were adopted. Importantly, as an entrepreneurial third party, the Liberal Democrats acted as policy entrepreneurs by introducing a mild (and largely ineffective) rule change onto the political stage. This rule change served as a precedent for subsequent moves to employ mechanisms within parties to directly raise the proportion of women candidates.

The Conservative Party

The Conservatives have not adopted quotas, and Britain did not witness a contagion of quotas across the party system. The Tories have not even adopted targets for women candidates. Instead, they rely on "talent spotting" and training programs for potential women candidates, and they encourage selection committees to consider women candidates through promotional videos.

The Conservative Party lacks many of the forces for quotas found in the Labour Party. First, Conservative ideology has long worked against quotas. The laissez-faire ideology that applies to government intervention logically works against any formal party policies mandating local party organizations to select candidates of a certain gender. Further, positive discrimination of any form is eschewed in favor of selection based upon merit. In addition, there has been less electoral pressure to adopt quotas. The Conservatives have not suffered from a consistent deficit in women's votes. Until the post-1992 campaign by Labour to revamp its image among women voters, the Conservatives had not even perceived a challenge over women's votes. In addition, the Conservative women's organization has not pressured for quotas because they do not view quotas as an appropriate mechanism to increase their numbers in the delegation to Parliament. When interviewed, a top-ranking woman within the Conservative Party organization stated she and many of her colleagues reasoned that a quota policy would diminish women's status in the party, and that Tory women prided themselves on rising through the party ranks on the basis of their qualifications alone. This party official lamented that quotas seemed to be out of reach, reasoning that she did not see any effective mechanism to increase women's representation in the near future. Rather, women would have to continue building their qualifications and wait for their opportunity in the future.

Conservative insiders point out that a rule change implemented by the central party organization may be the only way to encourage reluctant local party organizations to promote more women, but such central leadership is unlikely in the form of public rules. One former women's officer revealed that the party is between a rock and a hard place in finding formal mechanisms to increase women's participation; quotas for internal party offices are out of the question given the party's overriding laissez-faire ideology, while the party's wait-and-see approach yields few women among the leadership.

Relative to the gains made by women in the Labour Party, the underrepresentation of Conservative women in the House of Commons results from less vociferous pressure on the party leadership from both internal and external women's groups, and the Conservative ideology that precludes any intervention into the process of promoting women through the party ranks.

Conclusions

The British case illustrates the importance of electoral pressure *plus* women's strategic activism in the party leadership. Party competition from the Liberal Democrats set women's presence on the agenda. The Conservatives sense electoral pressure but have taken few direct measures to incorporate women, because Conservative women have been less vociferous on this issue and because special measures are largely antithetical to their ideology. The successes of women in the Labour Party demonstrate how women pressured the party leadership for greater representation within the party, and how women use their influence inside the party to improve the opportunities for women in the party's parliamentary delegation. Specifically, internal quotas for party offices were key to getting more women into powerful positions, and those women pitched women's parliamentary presence as essential to Labour's electoral success. The importance of women's mobilization and rule changes within Labour supports Joyce Gelb's (2002) analysis. Yet Gelb also cautions that numerical representation does not automatically translate into political power. She asserts that British women MPs need to rebel a bit more, pushing feminist claims. Presence may not equal power, but with the addition of an alignment with the dominant party faction and strategically pitched claims, British women were able to shake up the party culture and reconfigure the rules.

6

Germany: Women, Parties, and the Bundestag

Parties are especially important to women's parliamentary presence in Germany because among the German Volksparteien, the traditional route to the Bundestag leads directly through the party hierarchy. Diligent duty to the party through a succession of party offices for several years—aptly named by party activists as the *Ochsentour,* or "working like an ox"—is prerequisite to parliamentary office (Kolinsky, 1991). This process made it difficult for women, who often shouldered additional family responsibilities, to dedicate so many years of service to the party organization (Kolinsky, 1993). Further, because women often viewed the party organization as a male domain, they did not participate at the same levels as men (Kolinsky, 1993). The situation appeared dire in the late 1970s, and Hall (1981) wrote, "West German politics is populated by men; women appear as isolated individuals with little influence and lacking the presence of other women, able to affect little changes only with support of their male colleagues" (176). Yet the situation has changed dramatically in recent years, and greater numbers of women have reached the top echelons of the German parties.

Women's presence in the Bundestag underwent a sea change since the mid-1980s. Figure 6.1 displays the trends in the percentage women in the Bundestag from 1969 to 2002. German women began the 1970s with a presence

Figure 6.1 German Women in the Bundestag, 1969–2002

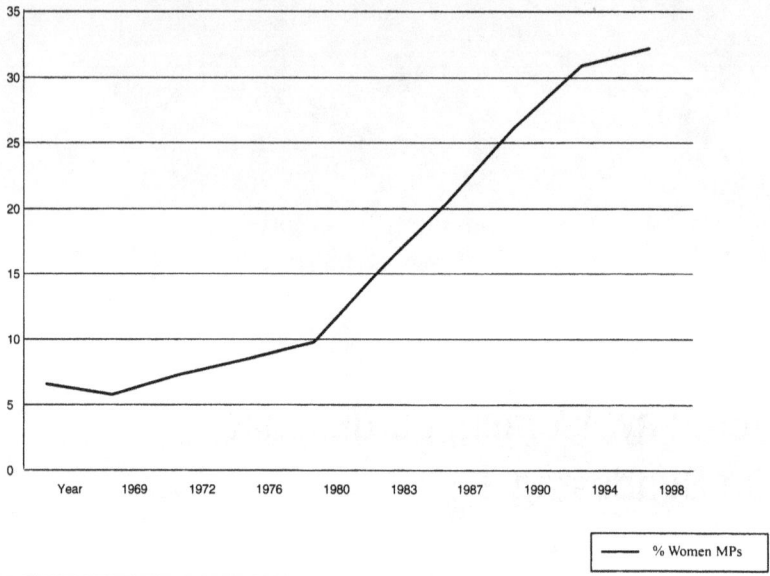

Source: Inter-Parliamentary Union (1997), updated with data from www.ipu.org.

of only 6% in parliament. Between 1983 and 1987, the proportion of women in parliament from the three major parties—SPD, FDP, and CDU/CSU—nearly doubled. Women made steady and significant gains throughout the 1990s, ending up composing nearly a third of the Bundestag by 2002.

Why did German women make such strides in the 1980s and into the 1990s? This chapter shows increases have resulted from German women's intensified efforts within political parties; the chapter also illustrates women's recognition of the strategic importance of joining forces with the powerful party leadership. Further, women heightened their efforts at an opportune point in time—with the fault lines in voting patterns shifting, party competition heating up, and parties in search of loyal bases of support.

The German case offers a unique feature, the unification of the East and West in 1990. In the East, one-third of the members of the national legislature were women, yet this high level of numerical representation did not reflect a more fundamental change in the political culture as it did in the West. Kolinsky (1993) writes that "unification revealed that the presumed advantage of women in the East was in reality a disadvantage: an agenda of hidden inequalities and state administered discrimination had short-changed East German women of their opportunities" (113). Thus, although the West and the East were shaped by very different political forces in the postwar period, women in both countries suffered barriers to full participation. In each case, fundamental change within the party channels was necessary to increase women's parliamentary presence.

The German Women's Movement

Although German women had won the right to vote and run for office under the Weimar Republic in 1918, the proportion of women in the Bundestag remained below 10% until the mid-1980s. It was not until the women's movement upped its energies in the electoral arena that women's presence in the Bundestag began to increase. The second wave of the West German women's movement was sparked by a growing concern over the issue of abortion, which eventually led to demonstrations and to the formation of several women's organizations and groups (Kaplan, 1992; Rueschemeyer, 1998). Growing out of the student movement, the German women's movement launched its first coordinated campaign in 1970 (Randall, 1982). Similar to the movement in Britain, the German women's movement is characterized by its radical nature and by a historical penchant to remain autonomous from mainstream institutions such as political parties (Katzenstein and Mueller, 1987; Kaplan, 1992; Rueschemeyer, 1998). Yet in contrast to the British movement, feminists held weaker bonds with the Socialists. In Germany, women's concerns were not as well represented among the "Old Left" (Randall, 1982; Davis, 1997).

While many women sought to keep the movement completely autonomous from conventional political channels, by the 1970s an increasing number of women had entered party politics as activists and party members (Rueschemeyer, 1998). In 1976 the German Women's Council launched a campaign called "Vote for Women" and circulated this message in a young women's magazine called *Brigitte*. In 1980 another campaign, entitled "More Women in the Parliaments," was launched (Hall, 1981). Women across the parties emphasized their numerical underrepresentation, rather than focusing on "women's issues" per se. Across the system, the number of women in the highest party echelons, including the Bundestag, became a more general symbol of the party's commitment to women's equality (Kolinsky, 1993). As a consequence, the three most electorally successful parties in the German system, including the two Volksparteien—the Social Democrats (SPD) and the more conservative Christian Democratic Union (CDU)—and the shifting coalition partner, the Liberal party (FDP), responded, to varying degrees, to women's demands for greater representation.

Political Background

The German governmental structure is parliamentarian, yet it differs from the British system in its federal structure. In addition to the national parliament, the Bundestag, the regional parliaments play a key role in policymaking. The electoral rules offer district representation and proportionality among parties. Researchers often refer to the German system as a mixed-member proportional system (MMP). There are two ballots, one in which a voter casts a ballot for an individual representative (*"erstimme"*), and one in which the voter casts a vote for the political party (*"zweitstimme"*). Seats are first awarded to those individual candidates who won their districts, and then additional seats are awarded to parties on the basis of the second ballot outcome, in order to make the party's share of seats proportional to its share of votes. Thus, the outcome is "identical to that of straight nation-wide allocation" (Taagepera and Shugart, 1989: 130). Constituency candidates are selected by the local party organizations, and the party lists are composed at the regional level. The constituency candidates tend to be more powerful within the party. Women historically gained fewer constituency nominations than positions on the party lists, where parties can balance among different interest groups. Yet women were often placed low on the party lists because constituency candidates are often placed first (Hall, 1981).

In German politics, the parties play the dominant role in the democratic process (Dalton, 1993a; Wildenmann, 1987). Relative to the British party system, the German system offers to voters a greater selection of parties. There are four major parties that span the ideological spectrum from left to right: the Alliance 90 (the Greens),[1] the Social Democrats (SPD), the Free Democrats (FDP), and the Christian Democratic/Christian Social Union (CDU/CSU).[2] Through the early 1980s, the SPD and CDU/CSU dominated, with the smaller FDP acting as a coalition partner in most governments. At that time, the established parties drew their support mainly from economic and religious interests, the SPD from the working class, and the CDU/CSU from middle-class and religious voters. Yet it is important to note that since the mid-1960s, the major parties, and especially the CDU/CSU, had been true "Volksparteien," or people's parties, which are less programmatic and more oriented toward capturing a broad spectrum of voters (Dalton, 1996; Kolinsky, 1993). The Greens' entrance in 1983 brought new issues to the German political agenda. The Greens emphasized issues such as the environment, nuclear disarmament, and women's rights—all issues with no clear fit into the existing partisan alignment (Dalton, 1996). German unification further altered the traditional party alignments. The CDU/CSU drew support from the middle class in the West, and the PDS from the working class in the East (Dalton and Cole, 1993).

German Women's Voting Patterns and Parliamentary Presence

A majority of German women consistently voted for the Christian Democrats (CDU) in the 1950s and 1960s—the "traditional" gender gap. Yet by the 1970s, many women had moved left, toward the SPD (Kolinsky, 1989; 1993). As the SPD moved toward the center of the ideological spectrum in the wake of the Godesberg program, more women came to view the SPD as a viable alternative to the CDU. The SPD's march toward the Center continued into the late 1990s with Schroeder's "Neue Mitte," or new middle approach, much like Blair's "New Labour" (Cole, 2002). Herbert Kitschelt (1999) points out that this turn away from traditional, class-based leftist politics characterizes social democratic parties in general as they search for new groups of support. By the mid-1970s, women's voting patterns became increasingly volatile, and young women increasingly joined the SPD as part of a new constituency. In the immediate aftermath of unification, the CDU enjoyed an advantage among East German women, but slowly lost this advantage to parties of the Left (Rueschemeyer, 1998).

Perhaps this shift in women's voting behavior parallels women's gains in the Bundestag. Figure 6.2 investigates this relationship by tracing the gender gap in women's votes and the percentage of Social Democratic and Green Party women in the Bundestag from 1970 to 1998. I measure the gender gap as the percentage of women who intend to vote for the Social Democrats or

Figure 6.2 German Trends in the Gender Vote Gap and Women MPs from
　　　　　　Leftist Parties, 1970–98

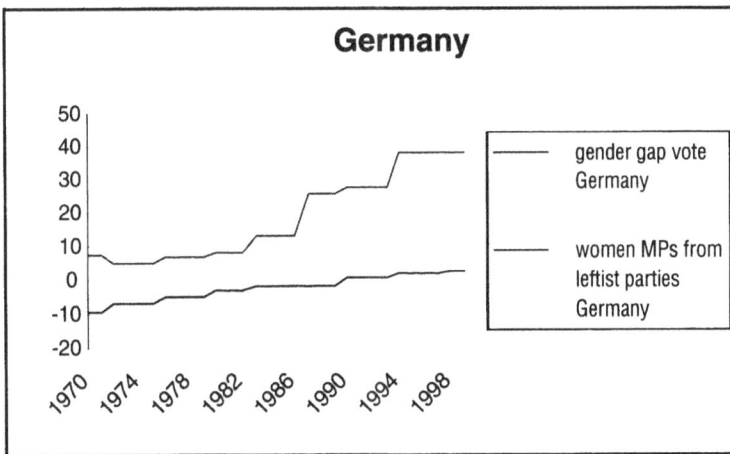

Source: Eurobarometer Studies, IPU (1997). See Appendices for details.

Figure 6.3 German Trends in Left Vote among Supporters of the Women's
Movement and Women MPs from Leftist Parties, 1970–98

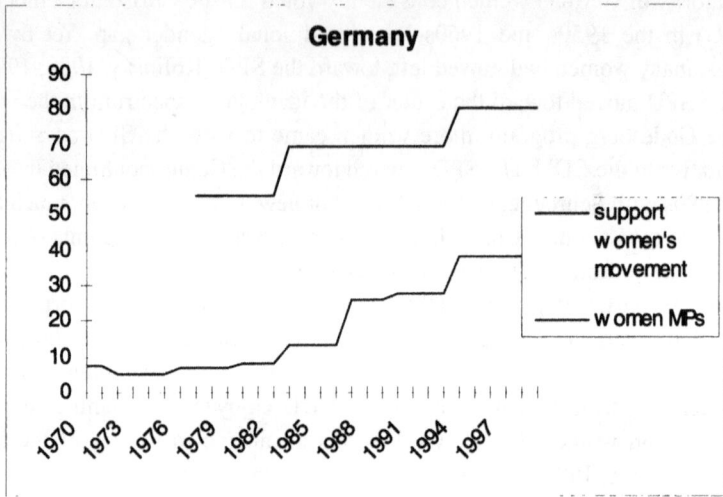

Source: German Election Studies, IPU (1997). See Appendices for details.

Greens (the Left), minus the percentage of men who intend to do the same.[3]
The higher the vote gap line reaches, the better the SPD is faring among
women voters. One can observe steady gains both in support for the Left and
in women's parliamentary presence. Since the early 1970s, the gap in favor of
the CDU has diminished, and the SPD and the Greens have enjoyed a slight
benefit since the early 1990s. The increase in support for leftist parties began
in the 1970s, and increases in women's parliamentary representation among
those leftist parties followed in the late 1980s. Although these two trends
appear related, certainly one must be careful to avoid inferring causality.

Values and Party Preferences

Rather than simply gender, it may be that those who support the women's
movement are even more likely to vote for the Social Democrats. As in the
analysis of Britain in chapter 5, I measure support for the women's movement.[4] Figure 6.3 displays the trends in the Left vote among those who support the women's movement, similar to the analysis of voter support in the
previous section. In addition, the trends in women MPs from the leftist parties
are graphed as well, for comparison. The graph shows that the percent Left
vote among those who support the women's movement grows evenly over
each time point. Mirroring this steady increase is the growth of women MPs
from leftist parties. As compared with the British trends, the earlier rise in

support for the German women's movement on the Left is paired with an earlier rise in levels of women's representation among those leftist parties. The increases in representation take off in 1987, after the largest increase in support for the movement.

Party-Level Forces for Increasing Women in the Bundestag

Certainly mass-level forces underpin women's gains in the Bundestag through shifting voting patterns and support for an increasingly mainstream women's movement. Yet just as in the British case, a closer look at the direct party-level mechanism behind women's gains gives us a more focused picture.

Party Competition

Although the CDU/CSU lost and SPD gained women's votes, neither party automatically responded to women's demands for greater representation. It was not until many young women shifted their votes to the Green Party in the early 1980s that SPD officials began to take serious notice of women as a specific constituency. Officials from the SPD cite the Green Party as playing an integral role in sparking greater competition for women's votes. As the Greens gathered strength in the early 1980s, they emphasized women's equal representation by mandating 50% women in party offices and in parliament. In the early 1980s, the Green electorate remained predominantly male. However, with the jump in the proportion of Green Party women in the Bundestag, many young women who had previously voted for the SPD shifted their loyalty to the Greens. The unprecedented number of women in the Greens' parliamentary delegation set a new benchmark for women's expectations, and their success in gaining young female voters triggered a response from rival parties (Kolinsky, 1989; 1993).

In an attempt to regain the votes they lost, the SPD sought to promote women candidates for office, though intraparty opposition held up direct action for one election cycle. By the 1994 election, the SPD featured women MPs in their media campaign to project a progressive image and to persuade female voters that the SPD placed highest priority on women's interests.

Under pressure from Green and SPD efforts, other parties across the ideological spectrum attempted to show their support for women. The FDP and the CDU both pledged to increase the number of women in office throughout the 1980s. In interviews, CDU leaders revealed that the party had dismissed the loss of young women voters to the SPD in the 1980s by predicting that these women would return to the party later in life, after their life experiences led them away from the Left. Yet after a decade, CDU leaders realized that young women were not reverting back to the party fold over the course of their lives, as the leaders had once expected. Consequently, the CDU leadership took greater initiative to cater to women voters, especially by offering conservative professional women for office.

Women in the Party Hierarchy: Strategy in Intraparty Alignments

Certainly women have not been passive recipients of party concessions by way of electoral forces. As more women have become active in German party politics since the 1970s, women have acted as agents on their own behalf, pressing for gains within the party hierarchy and in the Bundestag. The following section details women's efforts with the SPD, FDP, and CDU from the 1970s through the 1990s.

Social Democrats (SPD)

Of the German parties, the SPD gained the largest influx of women members during the 1970s and 1980s. Women's membership in the SPD rose from 17% in the early 1970s to nearly 30% in the early 1990s, where it remained through 1998 (Kolinsky, 1989, 1993; Rueschemeyer, 1998). As more women joined the SPD, they became increasingly active and wanted to hold office. While women made up about 25% of the SPD's membership in 1983, they accounted for only 15% of the party's national executive committee (NEC) over the same period (Lovenduski, 1986: 150). In 1972, the proportion of women in the SPD's delegation to the Bundestag hit rock bottom (5%), which marks a turning point for Social Democratic women. Although SPD women consistently gained nomination to the party lists, their low position on the rank order of those lists meant that few women were elected to office.

At this time, the SPD's women's organization (ASF) shifted from simply toeing the party line toward voicing greater demands for women's equality. At the 1971 party congress, ASF women won the right to vote for their own officials (Hall, 1981). Increasingly active by 1972, the ASF lobbied the NEC for a greater voice. In 1975, the women's organization got a commitment in the party program for sex equality, but it proved largely rhetorical (Lovenduski, 1986). In 1977 the ASF officially demanded quotas (Rueschemeyer, 1998). After the 1977 party congress, a working group called the "Commission for Equality" was set up to look at the problem of women's underrepresentation (Hall, 1981). Leader Willy Brandt not only offered to launch the commission, but also to co-chair it with Elfriede Hofmann, a longtime SPD activist (Kolinsky, 1989). Women from the ASF supplied half of the members to the commission. Yet to the ASF's chagrin, the commission produced a 1978 report that yielded no concrete measures, and women continued to lobby (Hall, 1981).

The ASF's strategy within the party strengthened its efforts to promote women. One key difference between the British Labour Party's women's organization and the German SPD's ASF is that the ASF had fewer links to outside women's organizations. The larger German women's movement's greater reluctance to align with a Socialist party, or with party politics in general, precluded strong ties to outside groups that could support those on the inside. Counterintuitively, the lack of strong ties to the more radical, outside-the-mainstream feminist movement may have led to the earlier advances by party women in the SPD, relative to Labour. As discussed in the previous chapter, the radical nature of Labour's women's organization through the mid-1980s precluded its alignment with the more moderate and increasingly powerful faction of the party. In contrast, the women in the SPD were free to align themselves with the dominant centrist party coalition, and this alignment, coupled with the electoral pressures, proved a powerful combination for women's advancement within the party. Important alignments with the central party leadership led the central party to encourage the regional party organizations to promote women within the party. Because the regional power holders were reluctant to give up entrenched positions, the central party leadership needed to launch a coordinated top-down effort to spark real changes for women in the SPD.

By the late 1970s and early 1980s, a new generation of young women activists joined the SPD and met great disappointment as their high aspirations and hard work failed to win them promotions within the party (Kolinsky, 1991). Unmet expectations brought renewed efforts for sweeping changes to the party organizations. Traditionally, women in the SPD followed a distinct "women's track" within the party, working within the special women's section (established in the 1890s). The women's organization effectively separated women from the party's mainstream, the center of decision making.

The new group of young women professionals disliked the isolation and protective nature of this separate track, and they insisted the party lift its policy to send four women to special women's seats on the national executive committee (Kolinsky, 1989). Interviews with former party activists revealed that these young women activists reasoned that these de facto members of the NEC had no real decision-making power, and they desired a real say in party policymaking. However, these young women were shocked when women gained only two seats in the next (1976) election for the NEC. This loss of power sparked re-energized efforts to increase women's representation, and the SPD became the first party in the German system to move women's underrepresentation to the main party agenda.

At a succession of party congresses in the mid-1980s, the SPD passed a series of resolutions designed to assist women to gain prominence in the party and seats in the Bundestag. Paralleling each decision, the proportion of women among the party's higher ranks grew. In 1984, the Social Democratic leadership pledged its support to promote women within the party and requested regular reports on the state of women's equality at all levels within the party. In a propaganda move, the SPD placed its women candidates in the front row of pictures in party election posters (Lovenduski, 1986). In 1985, the party instructed the district and regional parties to give preference to women in the nomination process. The ASF continued to pressure the party leadership through the equality commission, stating in a 1986 party document, "To grant women full equality within its ranks has now become a question of credibility for the SPD . . ." (Kolinsky, 1993: Appendix). By 1986, the party finally agreed upon the necessity of direct mechanisms to increase women's presence (Kolinsky, 1989).

As detailed in the previous section, the final straw that broke the SPD's back was the Green Party's success among young women voters (Kolinsky, 1989; 1993). Finally, after ten years of challenging the SPD, in 1987 SPD women achieved formal party rule changes that would bring even greater power to women within the party. The low proportion of women (7–14%) on the NEC through the 1970s and 1980s, as discussed at the outset of this section, increased to 30% at the beginning of the 1990s and to almost 50% by 1994. Yet McKay (2004) points out that women have had an easier time gaining accession to collective bodies, such as the NEC, than into the real top individual leadership positions.

Free Democrats (FDP)

Of the three German parties in this study, the FDP has the worst record regarding women among its highest ranks (Kolinsky, 1989). For the most part, the party is male. Officially, the FDP does not record membership by gender (Hall, 1981). Estimates reveal the number of female members has ebbed and flowed from 20% to 30% over time as a function of the FDP's coalition partners; when the FDP joined the CDU/CSU, women's membership fell, relative to when the FDP joined the Social Democrats. By 1995, Marilyn Rueschemeyer (1998) estimates 30% female members. In the early 1900s, the FDP had a rule to ensure a few women sat on the NEC, but this clause was removed in 1954 (Hall, 1981). Through the 1980s, women made up only about 10% of the party's national executive committee (Kolinsky, 1989; 1991). Interviews with party leaders revealed that the current state of affairs is no better—the party's regional and district offices are staffed overwhelmingly by men.

Despite women's lack of representation in the party ranks, FDP women currently have no separate organization within the party. The original women's organization was dissolved during the 1950s (Hall, 1981). Interviews with an FDP election coordinator revealed that the strategy of FDP women has traditionally focused on work within the mainstream organization, side-by-side with men. This strategy is consistent with the FDP's ideological distaste for preferential treatment for special groups. Yet a few Free Democratic women formed the Association of Liberal Women in the early 1990s. The association is designed to pressure for women's political equality, but it officially works outside the party hierarchy (Rueschemeyer, 1998).

Yet one segment of FDP women, disgruntled by their years of unrewarded service, organized outside the party to pressure party leaders to address the issue (Kolinsky, 1989; 1993). Under muted calls for reform, the party's 1986 conference endorsed a programmatic statement called "Putting Equal Rights into Practice." The FDP strictly rejected any formal rule changes to improve women's status, stating that "liberals consider it a mistake to believe that special rights and protective clauses can create equal participation" (quoted in the Appendix of Kolinsky, 1993).

Women in the FDP still sought more than rhetoric. In 1987, women members pressed for a Frauenforderplan (Plan for the Advancement of Women) (see Kolinsky, 1989). As part of the plan, the party established an equality office, adjusted the dates and times of party congresses to minimize the conflict with family obligations, and adopted informal procedures to increase women's representation among the party's internal hierarchy (Kolinsky, 1993).

As part of this plan, the FDP drafts an annual report on the status of women within the party. In interviews, top party officials revealed that the party currently continues to file these reports, even though the reports have had little effect. Little more than lip service, these reports keep women's representation on the party's agenda, albeit on the back burner in many instances. Following the lead of the FDP, parties across the ideological spectrum began drafting similar annual reports on the status of women. In some other parties, these reports set the stage for quotas. Many women activists remarked that the reports are an annual reminder of the problem of women's underrepresentation and a symbol of the importance of women in German party politics. In 1995, the FDP launched a new campaign called "More Opportunities for Women in the FDP" (McKay, 2004). Yet in the 1998 report, it was revealed that women's presence in the top echelons and in parliament remained stagnant.

The FDP has yet to match the substantial gains of the SPD regarding women in the party leadership or in the Bundestag. Yet in the 1990s, the proportion of women on the NEC did climb to 20% from its original 10% in the 1970s and 1980s. According to interviews with a party election strategist, the

FDP has few future plans to increase women's representation within the party. The party argues that because there are so few women members, there are few women in higher party posts.

Christian Democrats (CDU)

Through the 1960s, as part of the conservative ideology, the dominant attitude among CDU members and officials was that women's proper place was in the family, taking care of children, or at church, participating in community service activities. At this time, women made up a large share of the CDU's loyal and active membership. Increasingly in the 1970s, pressures from secularization and from the women's movement into paid employment challenged these traditional attitudes (Wiliarty, 2001). As a result of changing attitudes, many women members left the CDU, weakening its loyal base of women's support. The proportion of women members grew from 13% in 1969 to 20% in 1976. Yet since the late 1970s, women's membership has largely stagnated. By comparison, women's membership figures are lower in the more conservative CSU—reaching only 16% by 1995 (Rueschemeyer, 1998).

Relative to women in the SPD, women in the CDU have fewer representatives in the party hierarchy. Throughout the 1970s, up to only 10% of the NEC members were women. Although the CDU's party program contained a provision early on that women should be "adequately" represented on party bodies, this clause was removed at the 1967 party conference (Hall, 1981).

The CDU's women's organization, the Frauenunion, has played a strong role within the party, but it has not demanded increases in women's representation as strongly as the ASF. Established in 1947, the Frauenunion was successful in recruiting women members, so that the proportion of women members in the CDU grew through the 1970s. All CDU women are automatically members of the Frauenunion, which publishes a monthly magazine called *Frau und Politik* and has served as a training ground for some women who have risen to positions of leadership (McKay, 2004). Since 1972, the Frauenunion recommends women as potential parliamentary candidates, but the central party organization is not required to accept these recommendations (Hall, 1981).

For women in the CDU, the traditional track to gaining posts within the party led through the Frauenunion, to an even greater extent than in the other German parties. The party traditionally elected a representative of the Frauenunion as a deputy member of the party's executive committee, giving women a voice among the top leadership, but not the power to execute decisions. While an honorary position on the NEC appears at first glance to be conducive to forwarding women's issues, Kolinsky (1989) suggests that this outlet, in some respects, kept women from making stronger claims within the party, almost co-opting their support on party policies.

The tradition of giving women an honorary seat on the party's NEC may stem from the CDU's established norm of representation and control. Desiring to unite Catholics and Protestants under one umbrella for maximum electoral support, in the 1950s the CDU formed a system of proportional representation ("proporz") by ensuring adequate Protestant influence on the party's highest decision-making bodies (Wiliarty, 2001). The CDU continued as a "loose alliance of regional and interest organizations" until Helmut Kohl intensified the process of centralization under his leadership in the 1970s (Clemens, 2000: 68). The CDU's historically segmented organization has shaped its response to new contenders today, and has laid the foundation for the separate track for women within the party.

Although the SPD began debating women's representation in the early 1970s, the CDU did not take up this issue until the 1980s. Simply put, women inside the CDU had made less-direct claims for parity. Yet in the late 1980s, CDU women, increasingly professional, and increasingly frustrated by the CDU's glass ceiling, made stronger arguments for representation. The influx of working women transformed the Frauenunion from an organization that had served primarily as a forum for socializing and campaigning to a more politicized organization with an admittedly weak feminist agenda. The more political and strategic the Frauenunion became, the more power it gained among the party structure (Wiliarty, 2001). Although the Frauenunion pressured the CDU leadership for a role in the decision-making process, party leaders offered few concessions through the late 1970s and early 1980s. Yet by the mid-1980s, when the Frauenunion forged an alliance with the controlling factions, party leaders took notice. Rather than aligning with the internal opposition, the Frauenunion connected itself with those who had the power to change party policies. Thus, the CDU's position on women's participation was shaped by internal interest group bargaining (Wiliarty, 2001).

Together, increased demands, the Greens' success, and the Frauenunion's new position in the dominant party coalition sparked a series of increasingly effective concessions from party leaders. In the first concession in 1985, the CDU forwarded a new plan called the "New Partnership" and placed the minister of youth, family, and health in charge of the operation. The "New Partnership" document states that the "political equality of women, however, must not remain a matter for women alone, but it has to become an issue for the party" (Kolinsky, 1993: Appendix). The new initiative catapulted more women to higher party positions, and at the 1986 party congress, the CDU committed to some target percentages for women's representation. The targets stopped short of quotas, which were viewed as too stringent, even by the majority of women within the party (Kolinsky, 1989).

Women within the party certainly have grounds upon which to base their claims for a more feminine face in parliament. Punctuating a steady decline, the 1998 election marked a sharp drop in women's support for the CDU/CSU. Their support dropped in both the East and the West. Research has pointed out the value of women's votes to the Right. In an analysis of the 1998 voting data, Mary N. Hampton (2000) states, "It is clear that eroding support among women for the CDU/CSU made a real difference in the election's outcome. With a loss in support of approximately 10% among women in less than 10 years, the outcome is dramatic and in need of further explanation" (159). If key women within the party can tie these electoral losses among target groups to a lack of women in the parliamentary party, they may gain greater concessions from the party leadership. Rita Sussmuth publicly argued for this connection, stating "those who do not move will be moved aside" (quoted in Hampton, 2000: 170).

Although Helmut Kohl had gone back and forth with a leading female figure in the party and former parliamentary president, Rita Sussmuth, party insiders revealed that Kohl emerged as a surprising force for attention to women's underrepresentation in the CDU. Rita Sussmuth's efforts to convince Kohl of women's electoral importance eventually paid off. In the next set of party concessions, in the mid-1990s Helmut Kohl opened the "Frauendebatte," stating that women's support was integral to the party's future (Hampton, 1994). He led the party to adopt more direct measures to promote women in the party hierarchy.

Because CDU women's claims came later and more moderately than those in the SPD, CDU women's gains in the party and in the Bundestag have come later as well. Yet relative to its sister British Conservative Party, women in the CDU have fared well. As a result of the CDU's women's inclusion as part of the dominant party faction, women's share of the seats on the CDU's NEC reached almost 35% by the mid-1990s. The importance of women's organized alignment within the party illustrates the strategic necessity of gaining voice within the party leadership, denoting a process led from the top, rather than the party's grass roots.

Alliance 90/The Greens

The West German Green Party was founded on the principles of equality, including parity for women within the party and in office. Within the Greens, the Federal Women's Council oversees women's equality in politics and organizes a conference each year (McKay, 2004). Women make up 50% of the Green Party at all levels—as federal chairs, delegates, conference speakers, party employees, and candidates. The Greens win nearly all of their seats from their lists, and they ensure women's representation by zipping, or alternating male and female candidates within the list. However, if there are insufficient candidates of either sex, the zipping procedure can be abandoned (McKay, 2004). In fact, at the time the West and East German Green parties merged in 1993, Alliance 90 claimed quotas were too stringent at that time, and they won an exemption for two years (McKay, 2004).

Party Rule Changes: A Diffusion of Gender Quotas

Candidate gender quotas characterize the German party system's response to women's claims for greater representation. And, as the following sections illustrate, the adoption of gender quotas was not limited to the more egalitarian Left. Instead, rule changes have diffused across the German party system. Certainly a climate of competition for women's votes provided the backdrop for the adoption of quotas.

Alliance 90/The Greens

Quotas were first introduced into the German system by the Green Party, which entered the Bundestag in 1983 with a firm commitment to women's equal representation. From the start, women gained prominent positions in the party organization, such as the joint leader of the parliamentary party and chair of the parliamentary committee, and women always held half of the positions at the executive level (Kolinsky, 1989). Yet at the parliamentary level, the Greens' commitment to equality at first fell short. As a consequence, at their federal party congress in 1986, the Greens introduced a formal candidate gender quota of 50% for candidates. At each election, the party list was to alternate the names of men and women. As a result, in 1987 the Greens attracted voters' attention by entering the election with an unprecedented number of female candidates. Women in rival parties, who for years had been pressing their parties to increase women's representation, envied the Greens' quota policies, which allowed women to achieve parity in a very short time.

Social Democrats (SPD)

The SDP most acutely felt pressure to adopt quotas because of their attempts to compete for young women voters. Young women in the SPD prized equal participation in the party, especially at the top ranks. Women rose to the higher ranks of the SPD organization in greater numbers under Willy Brandt's leadership beginning in 1969, yet these increases were not matched at the parliamentary level (Kolinsky, 1989). After the SPD's 1972 election success, the ASF focused on rule changes to mandate more women candidates. Interviews with party activists revealed that the quota debate originated within the ASF as female members became disillusioned with their lack of representation in positions of power. Women who had been elected to party positions such as deputies and party managers climbed to the top of the party ranks. By 1987, women on the party's NEC directly lobbied for quotas. One of those women who rose to power, Anke Martiny, issued a report that cited the structural barriers to increasing women's representation, which she called "Comrade Obstruction"; she called for structural measures to rectify the situation, yet little action came from these recommendations (Kolinsky, 1989; Hoeker, 1998).

After the Greens introduced quotas, the SPD leadership began to follow suit. Yet rule changes came in increasingly stringent steps. The first response to the Greens came during the SPD federal party congress in Nuremburg in 1986, when the SPD accepted the principle of quotas, but did not yet adopt the logistical plans for a real policy (Kolinsky, 1993). Finally, in 1988 the party congress voted to implement a 40% quota for both internal and parliamentary offices. The quotas were to be achieved in two stages, 33% women in the Bundestag by 1994, and 40% by 1998. Although the ASF oversees the quota policy, the party has no sanctions if it is not enforced (McKay, 2004).

These changes in party rules altered party practices and norms of operation. Kolinsky (1993) notes that, in the case of the SPD, efforts to promote women quickly through the party ranks necessitated changes in the party's recruitment patterns. Quotas cleared out the long-standing backlog of women potential candidates for upper and midlevel elite positions among the party's local ranks. Therefore, in subsequent years it became necessary to promote women who had not served the traditional "Ochsentour" through the party ranks, thus creating a new route to the top, cleverly titled "from the side" by party insiders.

Free Democrats (FDP)

The FDP was the first party to react to the Greens' quota policy, but merely at a rhetorical level. At first, the FDP leadership used the issue of women's representation to vie for women's votes. The party congress in Hanover in May 1986 endorsed a formal recommendation to advance women's opportunities. However, the FDP denounces quotas, claiming that these rules downgrade the importance of the quality of candidates (Kolinsky, 1989). Yet at the next party conference in 1987, the FDP did adopt a rule for "target" numbers of women, a policy that allowed the party to stop short of formal quotas but to demonstrate symbolic support for women candidates.

The FDP's ideological orientation toward individual rights and individual achievement means the party will continue to shun formal quotas. Instead, women are expected to make gains based upon their own merit, rather than through protective measures. Yet party leaders do express a desire to gain women members. The FDP is entangled in a catch-22—no direct measures to promote party women, few women members, and even fewer women in the Bundestag. As a result, the FDP's record on women's advancement is likely to continue to proceed at a snail's pace.

Christian Democrats (CDU)

Compared with the SPD, the CDU felt less pressure for quotas from its women's organization. Like women in the FDP, on the basis of ideological consistency, CDU women do not support quotas as a mechanism of special treatment. In a survey of women candidates, Kolinsky (1991) finds that both CDU and FDP women dislike the idea of quotas and would rather wait for selection based upon merit. While 95% of Green and 70% of SPD women candidates support quotas, only 10% of CDU and FDP women express the same support.

Without women's pressure, the CDU members denounced quotas at their 1986 party congress. Yet, as detailed in the previous section, by the 1990s the CDU began to covet the votes of young professional women and perceived a need to update the party image. In 1994, when Chancellor Helmut Kohl opened up the "Frauendebatte," he threw his support behind direct mechanisms to promote more women. At a party conference, Kohl reasoned, "If we want to get a start into the future we have to do it now . . . The image of the CDU is colored by how it deals with change in society" (as quoted in Davis, 1997). And with that, the Conservatives had moved to promote women. At first, the party rank and file rejected a loose quota rule at the 1995 party conference (Hampton, 2000). Under Kohl's leadership, in 1996 the CDU finally agreed to adopt a lighter form of quotas. Stopping short of actual quotas, the CDU called their new affirmative action policy a "quorum" in order to bypass the leftist term they had eschewed for years (Davis, 1997; Hoeker, 1998). The new selection rules called for 30% women at all levels of the party and among the party's parliamentary candidates (Hampton, 1995).

Conclusions

Battling for women's votes, and challenged by women within the party, the German Greens, the SPD, and eventually the CDU changed their selection rules to bolster women's parliamentary presence. Similar to the story of British Labour, to ignite the process of quota diffusion, electoral pressure was complemented by party leaders' realization that women's votes are essential to building a winning coalition, and that running more women candidates would be an effective method of attracting those women's votes.

In this way, electoral pressure and women's activism worked in a dynamic process in Germany. Importantly, the German case is an exemplar for the importance of strategy by the party women's organization. Selecting the right intraparty coalition partners proved key to getting women's parliamentary presence on the political agenda, and to gaining enough organizational power to change the party selection rules.

7

Finland: Women, Parties, and the Eduskunta

Finland provides an intriguing contrast to the British and German cases. Although the push for women's parliamentary presence did not make much progress in Germany until the late 1980s, and in Britain until the late 1990s, women saw great gains in the 1960s in Finland—an early leader in Western Europe. Figure 7.1 details the proportion of women in the Finnish Eduskunta from 1966 to 2003. Already in 1966, Finnish women made up nearly 17% of the Eduskunta. By the end of the 1970s, women's presence had grown to 26%. By 1991, that percentage leaped to an all-time high of 39%. Yet the figure dropped a bit in 1995, and it has largely stagnated since then. In 1996, all three speakers of the Finnish Eduskunta were women, and in 1999 Finland elected its first woman president.

This chapter will demonstrate the efficacy of a concentration of women's efforts on party politics to women's substantial gains in parliamentary office. Rather than focusing on protest politics, Finnish women concentrated on electoral politics and on parties in particular. Finnish women gradually changed the party culture as they entered party politics full force in the 1960s (Sundberg, 1995b). Finnish women's preference for electoral politics is part of a larger Finnish state-centered tradition. Together, women's party activism and the establishment state-level equality bodies have raised women's status in Finland.

Figure 7.1 Finish Women in the Eduskunta, 1966–2003

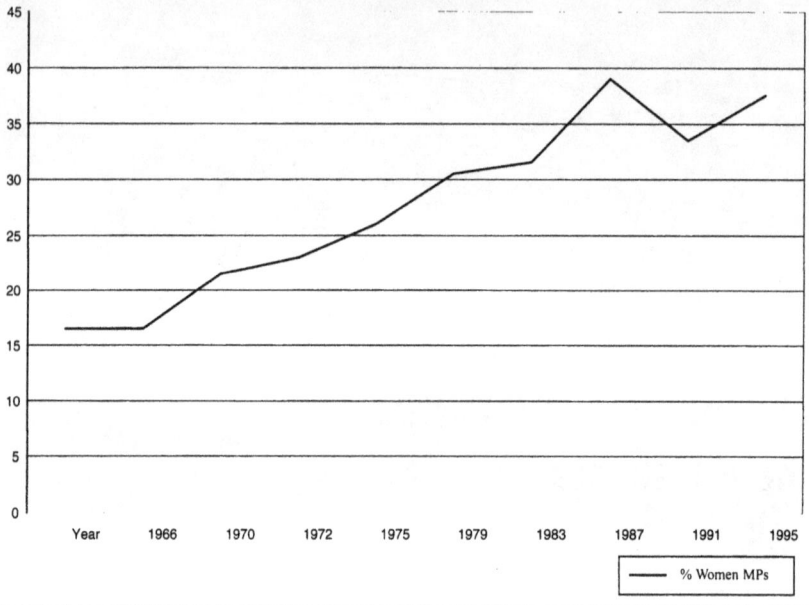

Source: IPU (1997), updated with data from www.ipu.org.

Certainly Finnish women have encountered barriers in party politics. Yet their earlier entry into the public arena, relative to women in other Western European nations, encouraged higher numbers of women in politics. By giving women the right to vote and to run for office in 1906, Finland was the second nation to enfranchise women and the first to allow women's candidacies (Kuusela, 1995). Women's enfranchisement coincided with that of most men, and as a result, women encountered fewer entrenched interests in their initial elections than women in other Western European nations (Haavio-Mannila, 1981).

As part of an effort to pay off Finland's debts after World War II, the Finnish government strongly encouraged women to enter the paid workforce. Likewise, Finnish women entered higher education in record numbers a decade earlier than their counterparts in other Western European nations. In addition, spending on healthcare, family allowances, national childcare, and other social transfer payments decreased women's dependence on the traditional family structure. These strong national policies are a unique feature of Finnish society and set women's situation in Finland apart from their situation in other Western European nations.

Many casual observers chalk up Finnish women's high levels of representation to an egalitarian culture in Scandinavian nations. Yet if a general ethos of gender equality alone accounts for the high percentage of women in parliament, then one might logically expect to observe a high level of equality in other public spheres as well. However, women have not achieved record levels of power in every arena. Women's gains in elected office have not been mirrored by gains among the business, media, academic, or scientific elite (Karvonen, 1995). A 1998 report found a statistically significant deficit for women in almost all of its measures of social status, including family responsibilities (Meklas, 1999). In addition, akin to its European neighbors, gender inequality in Finland continues to manifest itself through income disparity (Haavio-Mannila, 1981). In 1997, although women accounted for 48% of the members of the Central Organization of Finnish Trade Unions, they only made up 20% of the union's executive committee, and that underrepresentation stands in other unions as well (Nordic Council of Ministers, 1999). In a 1998 survey, 83% of women and 65% of men felt that Finnish women did not enjoy the same status as men (Meklas, 1999). Women's achievements in positions of power in the Finnish Eduskunta appear unique, and it is important to examine the mechanisms behind women's early rise to political power.

It is also important to note that although Finland has historically been tightly linked with Sweden, Finland is not uniformly regarded as Scandinavian. Finland also shares a common history with its eastern neighbor, Russia, which occupied Finland intermittently over the eighteenth and nineteenth centuries. However, for all intents and purposes, Finland was granted autonomous status in the nineteenth century (Pesonen, 2000). In 1917, Finland declared itself independent. The confluence of Western (Swedish) and Eastern (Russian) traditions in Finnish society contributes distinct conceptions of gender roles; women's position in Scandinavian society has historically been more powerful than in Russian society.

Political Background

The Finnish governmental structure is both parliamentary and allows for the direct election of a president. In some respects, the president depends upon the prime minister and executive cabinet, yet policymaking is segmented, so that the president leads in foreign policy, and the parliament largely controls domestic policies (Pesonen, 2000). Finland's proportional representation (PR) electoral system uses "open lists." Rather than voting for a predetermined slate of candidates, Finnish voters may cast their votes for an individual candidate on the party's list. Parties receive seats in proportion to their share of the vote, and the first candidates to receive seats are those on the party's list who received the most votes (Pesonen, 1995). Since 1978, Finnish law has required parties to hold primary elections among their members to select candidates.

With a largely homogenous ethnic population and common Protestant heritage, the Socialist/non-Socialist division, often referred to as the "Red-White cleavage," grounds Finnish voting behavior. This division differs from the traditional Left/Right cleavage dominant in other Western European nations, because there is a strong political center which belongs to the non-Socialist side. Finland is a multiparty system, and no single party has dominated. Coalition governments are common (Pesonen, 1995). There are six major parties in the national parliament, and they can be categorized as follows: the Social Democrats (SDP) and the Left Alliance (VAS), which follows from the Finnish People's Democratic League (SKDL), fall into the Socialist category; the Center (KESK) and the Conservatives (KOK) fall into the non-Socialist category; and the Green Party (VIHR) falls into its own, independent third group. The Green Party's popularity coincides with the rise in new issues that are not part of the traditional social class framework. The "Red-White" cleavage has further attenuated in the past two decades with a decline in the number of working-class voters (Pesonen, 2000). Together, the rise of new issues and the deterioration of the class cleavage encouraged a visible process of partisan convergence toward the center of the ideological spectrum by the major Finnish parties over the last fifteen years (Pesonen, 2000). This convergence is best illustrated by the 1987 and 1995 coalition governments made up of the SDP and the Conservatives, without the mediating Center Party.

Finnish Electoral Rules and Women's Presence in the Eduskunta

Certainly Finland's unique electoral rules aided women's early achievements. In PR systems, parties have a distinct incentive to include women on the party list to appeal to a broad stratum of voters. Yet while women in other party-list, proportional representation systems were bound to "closed lists" and ranked toward the bottom by party officials, Finland's "open" list meant women could receive individual preference votes. Thus, Finnish women avoided the trap of being ranked so low on the list that they could not be elected. Instead, women candidates proved highly popular among women voters and were often elected by a distinct women's constituency (Haavio-Mannila, 1981). By the 1972 election, there was no difference in the candidate success rates among male and female candidates (Haavio-Mannila, 1981). In a 1970 poll, 40% of women and 7% of men said they would vote for a female candidate (Haavio-Mannila, 1981). By 1991, those percentages had risen to 57% of women and 25% of men ("Women Members of the Finnish Parliament"). Finnish parties responded to women candidates' popularity by running even more women in subsequent elections. In essence, electoral rules in Finland did not present the same barriers for women that they did in other Western European nations.

Finnish Women's Voting Patterns and Parliamentary Presence

Women's political activity has been high since the 1970s, and women's voting rates caught up with those of men in the 1950s (Haavio-Mannila, 1981). Relative to voting patterns in Germany and Britain, the gender gap has played such a small role that the major studies of voting behavior do not emphasize gender differences (Pesonen, 1995; for reviews, see Borg and Sankiaho, 1995; Pesonen, 1999). Past research on the gender gap in Finland shows women are only gradually moving toward the leftist parties, yet these differences are not large enough to be called a "gap" (Oskarson, 1995).

Figure 7.2 displays the trends both in the Finnish gender gap in voting and in the proportion of women MPs from leftist parties. I measure the gender gap as the percentage of women who intend to vote for leftist parties (the Social Democrats, the Greens, and the Left Alliance) minus the percentage of men who intend to do the same.[1] The higher the vote gap line reaches, the more support the Left enjoys among women voters. Indeed, the graph supports previous research. There is virtually no difference in support for the Left between men and women. And still the proportion of women in leftist parties' delegations to parliament grows considerably over this period—jumping in 1980 and the early 1990s. Electoral forces do not appear to underlie women's rise to political leadership in Finland.

Figure 7.2 Finnish Trends in the Gender Vote Gap and Women in the Eduskunta, 1970–95

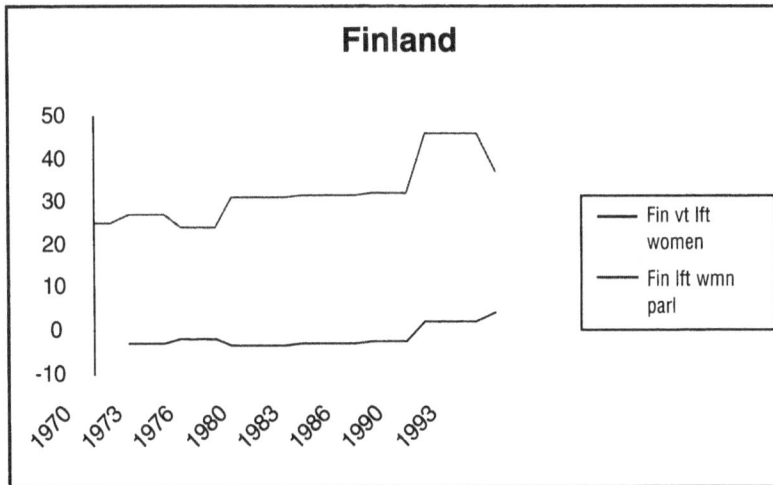

Source: Finnish Election Studies and IPU (1997). See Appendix B for details.

107

CHAPTER 7

Party-Level Forces for Increasing Women in the Eduskunta

In contrast to Britain and Germany, Finnish parties made fewer visible efforts to promote women candidates. In several interviews with party officials and MPs from each of the major Finnish parties, there was little indication that the party directly acted to promote women candidates in the 1980s and 1990s. Finnish party leaders and women activists did not perceive women as a special constituency, nor as a key to electoral success. As such, no media campaigns (such as Labour's "Winning Words") specifically targeted women voters as a collective. Further, women's representation in parliament never became a highly salient issue in party politics. In part, there was less need for efforts to boost women's presence—by the 1960s Finland was already a world leader. Finnish women's head start by way of an integrationist strategy in party politics earned them great strides early on.

Party Competition

Like the German Greens, the Finnish Green Party began by running a nearly equal proportion of women and men for election to parliament. Yet the Finnish Greens did not ignite competition for women's votes through political presence. The distinction is that in Finland, running a high proportion of women candidates was not unprecedented. By the time the Greens entered politics, Finland was already a world leader in women's numerical representation.

Women's Strategies in Party Politics

In contrast to the women's movement in most Western European nations, the Finnish movement emerged later and was quite small, even proportionate to the population. Importantly, the Finnish women's movement pursued a strategy unique to Western Europe. In the early days of the movement, while the German and British movements overwhelmingly remained autonomous, Finnish women advocated integration into the existing party structure. As a consequence, Finnish women's ties to political parties have long been stronger than in other Western countries (Jallinoja, 1986; Holli, 1992; Weldon, 2002). Drude Dahlerup (1985) notes that feminism in Finland has been even more closely integrated in the traditional political institutions than it has been in its Nordic neighbors. An interview with a former director of the Council for Equality revealed that this strategy was often referred to by activists as "gaining influence from within."

Rather than dividing efforts outside and inside institutionalized channels, women's movement activists focused attention on women's organizations within the parties and used the political parties to press for women's equality. Many women in the movement believed that women's oppression was best addressed in a larger package of social and political reforms (Parvikko, 1991). Because parties are issue-aggregating institutions by their nature, they offered the most natural site for women's claims.

Following the Western European pattern, the Finnish women's movement's renewal is rooted in the New Left movement of the 1960s, which was grounded in the universities and attracted a great number of young people (Jallinoja, 1986; Siisiainen, 1992). It is important to note that the integrationist strategy is not limited to the women's movement—it characterizes the entire Finnish New Left more broadly—including the ecological, peace, and antinuclear movements. Further, even students interested in addressing social problems were routed through their school councils into party politics, rather than more fluid protest movements. In short, the New Left in Finland was "not a movement outside the established parties" (Paastela, 1987: 6). This integrationist strategy is rooted in the broad Finnish tendency to look to the state as the ultimate provider of the collective good and social justice (Holli, 1992).

The first main organization of the women's movement, called the "Association 9," was founded in 1966. Its membership peaked in the late 1960s with 800 members (Holli, 1992). Association 9 was characteristic of the Finnish movement in its strategies and demands. They advocated the adoption of equality between men and women, rather than difference. To back up their equality claims, the Association allowed men to join, and ended up with 28% male membership (Paastela, 1987). Association 9 looked to the state to bring equality to women and therefore oriented itself toward changes in public policy (Holli, 1992).

The Association collapsed in 1970 when its activists opted to move solely into party politics. Women activists saw parties as the true site for decision-making power, and thus party politics provided the best opportunity for the movement's goals to be translated into reality. The presence of women in the Eduskunta became key to "real" equality (Holli, 1996). Most of the members of the Association 9 joined the political parties, and my interviews uncovered that many of these former members went on to elected office. Most women politicians and party officials revealed in their interviews that their political careers began in the university movements and shifted soon after to the party organizations, where they worked their way to the top, often eventually running for office. Bergman (1991) refers to this process in the Finnish system as the "party politicization of protest." Subsequent outside women's organizations were founded, but none ever achieved more than a few hundred members (Jallinoja, 1986). Laurel Weldon (2002) notes that it is "difficult for women to simultaneously maintain strong intraparty organizations and autonomous organizations" (79). With few outside women's organizations, women activists in later years had little choice but to take their demands to the political parties (Sundberg, 1995).

Each of the Finnish parties has a women's organization. And these organizations have been well funded. In 1975, the government mandated that one-ninth of all state support for political parties be given to the party women's organization. This policy did not prove especially popular among men and women alike, but it was adopted, nonetheless (Holli, 1996).

Certain factions of Finnish women in party politics shunned intraparty women's organizations altogether. Some women felt that women's organizations, by their nature, inhibit women's progress. This belief is rooted in the dominant ideology of the Finnish women's movement that equal status is achieved through equal treatment (Haavio-Mannila, 1981). Among Finnish women there has been a long-standing preference for men and women to work together to further party goals (Dahlerup, 1985). The main principle of the Finnish sex role debate has been to de-emphasize gender difference in favor of equality and sameness (Eduards, 1985; Holli, 1997).

Many activists in the 1970s subscribed to this attitude and regarded the women's organizations as separatist, and thus contradictory to their goals of equality (Parvikko, 1991). Dahlerup (1985) points out that official party histories make scant mention of the women's organizations. In my interviews, few party officials, regardless of party, offered details on the women's organization within the party, and they had to be prompted to mention these organizations at all. In short, even with subsidies, there appears to be less focus on separate women's organizations than in other Western European nations.

Yet many women have joined forces to keep women's equality on the current political agenda. In 1988, women across the political parties came together to form the Network of Women in Finland's Parliament (NYTKIS). Several women MPs from each political party were interviewed, and they mentioned the role of NYTKIS in getting women parliamentarians together to discuss women's issues and equality. Yet surprisingly, no interviewee could remember when they last met, nor who the current leader was, suggesting a diminishing role for NYTKIS in the late 1990s. NYTKIS works with the Council for Equality to bring attention to women's voice in politics. During the 1991 elections, women MPs described a NYTKIS-sponsored campaign called "Elect 101 Women to the Eduskunta." With 200 members total, winning 101 seats would mean the number of women representatives would exceed 50%. The campaign built quiet support, but it certainly did not achieve its ambitious goal.

While women's early and massive entrance into party politics underscores the history of women and parties in Finland, there are differences in women's roles in the three major parties of the Finnish system—the Social Democrats (SDP), the Center Party (KESK), and the Conservatives (KOK), and the following sections will briefly lay those out. The focus of this section is to understand how women gained power within the Finnish parties. Women's presence on the NECs of the Finnish parties is especially important for women's parliamentary representation, because the NEC has the power to demand that regional party lists contain more women (Sundberg, 1995). By 1975, women already averaged 10–15% across the Finnish parties' NECs.

The Social Democrats

Women's membership in the SDP has increased considerably—from 34% in 1977 to almost 40% in the 1990s (Sundberg, 1995). Yet women's representation in the party's leadership has not always matched their participation at the local level. In the 1970s, women made up less than 10% of the party's NEC. Through mobilization within the party, SDP women achieved powerful positions.

The SDP was the first party to establish a women's organization at the turn of the century. In 1891, the SDP was also the first to call for women's right to vote and stand for election in their party program. The SDP women's section traditionally recruited new women members and campaigned for the party, and since the 1970s, the women's organization has acted as an interest group by pushing for greater influence within the party (Haavio-Mannila, 1981b). In addition, the women's organization has backed women candidates for office, and several SDP female parliamentarians have benefited from this support.

The SDP's women's organization was quite influential in the 1970s, especially at the district level, where many women worked in student and city politics. For their support, the women's organization made demands on the party leadership since the 1970s. The number of "women's issues" discussed at party conferences, such as abortion rights and childcare, jumped noticeably since the women's organization pressed its claims (see Ramstedt-Silen, 1990, as quoted in Sundberg, 1995).

Although the SDP women's organization is stronger than in rival Finnish parties, it has wielded less influence than its sister organizations in Britain and Germany. While the women's section exerted some power in the 1970s, even in the leftist SDP some women were reluctant to participate in a separate women's track, preferring to work within the mainstream party organization. According to at least four different Social Democratic MPs interviewed, the women's organization has lost some power and size over time as it became more popular to work only within the mainstream party organization. SDP women increasingly came to believe that real change would only come through cooperation between women and men.

The SDP has close ties with Finnish trade unions, and unions have not been terribly supportive of women. The opening of this chapter described the underrepresentation of women in union decision-making bodies. In interviews, SDP members of parliament revealed that their female presidential candidate (and eventual victor in the February 2000 election) did not gain the full union support that was automatically granted to the party's presidential candidates in the past. These women MPs suspected that the tempered support of unions was caused by the fact that the presidential nominee was a woman.

SDP women's strategies to channel the bulk of their energies and resources within the regular party organizations earned women significant and early progress within the party hierarchy, culminating in women making up 33% of the NEC by the early 1990s. The lack of ties to outside women's groups allowed women to concentrate their full effort on climbing in the party ranks. However, by 1995 women's representation on the NEC dropped to less than 13%. Without strong and sustained claims from women, the party has allowed women's representation to ebb and flow, rather than maintaining women's gains.

The Agrarian/Center Party

The KESK does not officially record membership by gender, and thus it is difficult to assess women's presence at the party's grass roots (Sundberg 1995). Elina Haavio-Mannila (1981b) estimates women's membership at 46% in 1980. While the SDP experienced the largest increase in women members, the KESK began with a high number of women members even in the early 1980s. Yet, according to women in the party, the proportion of women activists in the KESK appears a bit lower than in the rival parties. Women activists from these rival parties revealed that the KESK's low number of women stems from its base of support in the rural areas of Finland, where historically fewer women were active in politics altogether. The influx of women into politics came primarily from the urban areas, especially Helsinki, where the university students joined parties in record numbers. Low levels of women's activism were matched by low levels of women's representation on the party's NEC in the 1970s and 1980s—under 15%.

While women members may not be the most visible political activists in the party, the KESK houses the largest women's organization of all Finnish parties. A grassroots organization, centered in the rural localities, the women's section earns its title as a "federation." The KESK Women's Federation had 70,000 members spread among 860 local branches in 1980 (Dahlerup, 1985). Although the KESK women's federation is large, its size is not indicative of its power. The KESK women's section differs from its leftist counterparts in its very limited demands for greater representation.

Similar to women in the SDP, the majority of women achieving higher posts in the KESK followed the central party track to higher party posts.

Those KESK party officials interviewed rose to higher party posts through years of work, and did not make use of the women's organization. Rather, these women considered the mainstream party channels as far more conducive to a party career. In an interview, a KESK party official scoffed at an old initiative to increase women's participation in the party. Branded "one woman politics," the policy sought to get each committee and electoral list to contain one woman. Yet women in the party soon realized that one woman on a party body was simply token representation, and thus they urged the party to abandon this practice in favor of encouraging women more generally. KESK women desired equality—equal access for men and women alike, rather than special, token gestures.

Although they made few claims, the quiet and weakly organized strategy of women in the KESK led to some progress through the party hierarchy. By 1995, women made up 23% of the NEC. The limited progress is not only a function of the weak women's federation, but also to the dominant party ideology that stresses the importance of promotion through the ranks based solely on an activist's "merit" and a reluctance to intervene to promote women to higher positions within the party.

The Conservatives (KOK)

In the late 1970s, women's membership in the KOK was estimated to be the highest of all Finnish parties (Dahlerup, 1985). Yet the KOK has not realized the same increases in women members as the SDP. Further, women's membership figures were not matched by presence among the party decision makers. While women made up about 50% of the membership, the KOK had 18% women on its NEC in 1975.

The Finnish Conservative women's organization was established after its counterpart in the SDP, yet it grew larger by the late 1970s (Dahlerup, 1985). The Conservative women's organization is independent and enrolls its own members. While women have had a strong presence at the party's grassroots, the women's organization applies weaker pressure on the party leadership than does its SDP counterpart.

In interviews, party officials and MPs made it clear that, like the KESK, the KOK's conservative ideology shapes women's views on their role within the party. Most contend that they do not desire any special treatment, nor do they strongly mobilize around women's issues. To an even larger extent than other Finnish parties, Conservative women eschew the separatist route, in favor of mainstream institutions.

Although the Conservatives began the 1970s with almost 20% women on the party NEC, without further pressure from women within the party, women's share of the NEC stagnated and never approached the 50% goal that was supposed to evolve naturally over time, based upon women's talents and hard work. Instead, the proportion of women bounced between 20% and 10% throughout the 1980s, and it culminated in the 1990s with the same 20% they began with in the early 1970s. In an interview, a leader in the KOK, and speaker of the Eduskunta, Riita Uosukainen, stressed that there were no future plans to promote women within the party hierarchy, as those who were motivated to attain higher office would find no significant barriers.

Party Rule Changes

While Germany was experiencing a contagion of quotas across the party system, and the British Labour Party was tinkering with its short lists, Finnish parties avoided quotas altogether. In interviews, party officials and women MPs from each of the parties insisted that there had been little discussion of such a policy within their party. Because there were no formal party rule changes in Finland, one might be tempted to gloss over this aspect of the Finnish case. Yet the case in which an event did not occur—Sherlock Holmes's "dog that didn't bark"—may shed considerable light on the absence of key conditions identified in the previous narratives. It is important to examine why the Finnish parties appear to have avoided the quota debate altogether.

Chapter 6 revealed that the German Green party was important in setting a precedent for quotas. However, the Finnish Greens did not follow the same path: they have not adopted formal quotas for candidates for parliament. Sundberg (1999) reports that the Finnish Greens adopted quotas for internal party positions. Yet in interviews, several high-ranking Green Party officials indicated that the policy was less a formal quota, and more an informal, agreed upon norm for achieving gender balance within the party—part of the party ethos in equality for all. So in short, the Finnish Greens have not served as an impetus for formal rule changes.

Another important influence on the adoption of quotas in Britain and Germany was growing volatility among female voters. Finnish parties felt little electoral pressure based on a constituency of women voters. Relative to Britain and Germany, women's votes have been consistently spread more evenly across the party system. Thus, electoral competition has not played the same role in encouraging quotas as in the other two cases.

Further, among the Finnish parties, the women's organizations made fewer publicized claims for representation and never mounted a campaign within the party. Interviews with party officials revealed that the Finnish parties lacked the high-profile party women advocating quotas that we found in Labour and the SPD. Yet one still might ask why the women on the National Executive Committees of the Finnish parties did not press for quotas. This question is especially intriguing for the Finnish SDP, whose leftist ideology suggests that quotas would be an acceptable practice to increase women's representation.

The same reason behind the reluctance to form strong women's organizations in Finland may partly explain the lack of a debate over quotas: Finnish women's strategy has been to integrate into the mainstream institutions of the party, and to downplay any form of women's separatism. The predominant ideology surrounding any Finnish discussion of gender relations is that equality is preferable to special treatment for women (Parvikko, 1991). Hence quotas, which offer women special protection, are considered an anathema to equality.

Even more important than being incongruent with ideology, quotas in Finland may not have been deemed necessary, given Finnish women's high levels of representation in parliament by the 1970s, relative to other Western European countries. The great strides by Finnish women early on relieved much of the pressure for candidate quotas. Further, parties often resort to stringent (and thus more controversial) quotas when women are continually ranked low on the party list. With Finland's open list, party gatekeepers could not keep women in unelectable positions on the list.

State-Level Forces for Women's Equality

A discussion of women's role in the Finnish political arena would be incomplete without some attention to the state's engagement in promoting equality. This book focuses on the party level, but it is essential to examine state-sponsored bodies, because they have often been sites where party women have struggled to make their claims.

Although the Finnish state has been quite active in devising policies to promote gender equality, women have still had to push for increasingly more effective policies over time. In 1962, the principle of equal pay for equal work was introduced through the Equality Act. Yet even with such a policy early on, in the 1990s, the difference between male and female full-time wage earner's salaries averaged 19% (Office of the Ombudsman for Equality, 1999). In 1966 the Council of State commissioned a study of the state of women (Ministry of Social Affairs and Health, 1999). The study amounted to little more than lip service, and a state body was deemed necessary. In 1972, the Finnish government established the Council for Equality. Under the direction of the prime minister's office, the 13 member council is made up of representatives from all of the major political parties. It is charged with promoting equality between men and women, and it makes regular reports to the Eduskunta (Council for Equality, 1999; Raevaara and Taskinen, 2004). However, the council had little power to enforce policies, and such power was clearly necessary to achieve real gains.

In 1987, the Act of Equality Between Men and Women set up a monitoring mechanism to track women's progress and eliminate discrimination (Ministry of Social Affairs and Health, 1999). To ensure the act was carried out, the office of Ombudsman for Equality was established. The idea for an Ombudsman's office originated in the equality movement of the late 1960s (Raevaara and Taskinen, 2004). With the ombudsman now reporting directly to the prime minister, the council took a backseat on gender equality policy (Holli, 1996).

While Finnish parties have not adopted candidate gender quotas, in 1995 a national law to promote equality was adopted. The constitution was altered to allow for positive actions to achieve gender equality in social activities and decision-making bodies. However, the amendment does not apply to elected bodies. The law requires at least 40% of each sex in government committees, advisory boards, and "corresponding bodies," and within the boards of state majority companies (Raevaara and Taskinen, 2004). As a result, the internal bodies of all Finnish parties rose to 40% women.

The stronger role of the state in Finland, relative to other Western European nations, is largely caused by two factors. First, the common first response to social problems among most Finns is to look toward the state. In other words, there is a state-centered tradition within Finnish culture. Second, in the case of women's equality, the state took a more active role because women had already established a foothold in state institutions early on, especially in the parliament. By the time the 1995 gender equality law was adopted, women had already made inroads at the highest echelons of parliamentary politics. In a circular fashion, women's political gains have reinforced themselves through a reconfiguration of state policies.

Conclusions

Taken together, women's strategy and favorable electoral rules contributed to strong gains for Finnish women in the Eduskunta. The Finnish women's movement illustrates how national contexts exert strong influence over movements, which in turn shape efforts within parties. Specifically, the larger movement's full-force focus on party politics heightened women's presence in all parties from the 1970s. This early strategy is unique to the Finnish parties. What is striking about the Finnish parties' women's organizations is that while they are fairly large and well financed, their role appears weaker than in other countries where women have made successful claims. A common theme in all of the party narrative is that many party women avoided the women's organizations, for fear of being labeled isolationists.

Importantly, the rules of the game favored women in Finland. Women have less need to pressure parties for parliamentary presence. Instead, women can lobby female voters. In Finland, parties have less control over nomination than in the rest of Western Europe, because of party primaries among party members. Further, Finnish parties have no control over the ranking of candidate lists. So the rules give parties incentive to offer women on candidate lists, through the logic of balancing lists to appeal to voters. And the rules allow voters to specifically select women candidates, no matter where they appear on the party list.

Women achieved substantial representation through Finnish parties early on, yet women still have a way to go in Finnish politics. Over the last three decades, women in the British Labour and German SPD and CDU have come close to achieving 50% women among the top party leadership. Similarly, since the 1970s, women's parliamentary presence has been nearly stagnant, and Finland has been surpassed as the world leader. In some respects, the Finnish case may represent the "tortoise and the hare" fable. As chapter 1 illustrated, women's representation in the Eduskunta leaped ahead of other Western European countries in the 1970s. While women in other countries were galvanizing and organizing against their underrepresentation, Finnish women had already made gains. The absence of a strong women's movement outside partisan channels precluded the reinvigoration of party women's organizations. In short, the reluctance of women in the Finnish party system to make strong claims for representation based on their identity as women, and their reluctance to call for new party rules, has made it difficult for women to gain truly "equal" representation.

8

Increasing Access to Parliaments: A Model for Change

After examining women's activism within the party ranks, and formal rule changes in party policies to select candidates, this chapter moves on to examine the end result—women's parliamentary presence. Systematic comparison across parties and over time illuminates some common characteristics of parties that lead to increases in women's representation. By using the party as the unit of analysis, one can examine those influences at two levels, the party system and individual party behavior and characteristics. Importantly, many previous cross-national statistical analyses of women's parliamentary presence are essentially static. Yet chapter 1 made clear that women have made great strides in recent years. This chapter takes a dynamic perspective, analyzing both levels of women's parliamentary presence and changes over time.

Explanations for the Increase in Women's Representation

This chapter provides a multifaceted explanation of change in women's representation within the parties of advanced industrial nations. Explanations for the increase in women MPs may be categorized within both the political and institutional opportunity structures, as laid out in chapter 2.

Political Opportunity Structure Explanations

Theoretically, the set of political opportunity explanations represents a shift in the power balance, which may open up windows of opportunity for women to gain seats in parliament. These forces may operate outside or inside the party itself.

Political, Exogenous to Party

Shifts in women's voting patterns may open up opportunities for women's parliamentary gains by highlighting the potential or realized benefits of obtaining a bloc of women's votes. Time-line analysis of patterns in women's voting behavior in the case study chapters suggested that women's shift to the Left in Britain and Germany might be related to their parliamentary gains. It may be that, controlling for other factors, the gender gap in the vote is a strong influence.[1] I test the hypothesis that a party's accumulation of women's votes (a women's electoral "bonus") heightens women's parliamentary representation.

The British and German case studies also reveal that established parties sometimes respond to new issues after there is pressure from a new rival party. Past cross-national research on other issues suggests that new rival parties play a role in spurring change among the established parties. Thus, I expect that the entrance of a New Left party into the party system will spur parties within the party system to highlight issues of gender equality by running more women for office.

Political, Endogenous to Party

Case studies revealed that women's mobilization at the party's grass roots is important to women's ascendance through the party structure. The women's organizations of the German Social Democrats and Christian Democrats, British Labour, and the Finnish Social Democrats were instrumental in putting forward women's demands for greater representation. The women's organization channels women's demands and presents them to the party leadership. Thus, one might expect that pressure generated by women's organizations may prove important when examined systematically across parties, especially when controlling for other factors such as the party's ideology.

In addition, changes in the number of women among the top party ranks may prove important. Women's entrance represents a change of the guard among the party leadership, opening up new opportunities for parties to change the status quo. Chapter 3 illustrates how women's participation in the decision-making bodies within political parties has increased over time. Caul (1999) finds that across twelve advanced industrial democracies, the proportion of women among party leaders strongly influences the proportion elected to parliament. By gaining power within the party, the opportunities and resources increase substantially for women to lobby for increased representation at the parliamentary level. Further, women's activity within the party creates a larger pool of politically experienced women from which the party can draw for candidate lists. Women's activity at the elite level may act as a mechanism of change. As the number of women among the party's leadership increases, I expect the number of women among the delegation to parliament will increase, as well.

Institutional Opportunity Structure Explanations

Structural characteristics of parties provide the context for women's parliamentary gains. The rules within some parties are more conducive than in others. Although structural characteristics may not directly lead to change, they can be conceptualized as intervening variables that make it more likely for a party to take a strategic action.

Institutional, Endogenous to Party

Parties can take direct action to ensure a greater proportion of women candidates by creating formal rules, such as candidate gender quotas. Chapter 4 suggests that candidate quotas bring substantial increases in women's parliamentary presence. For example, the strong and rapid effect of quotas is illustrated by the British Labour Party's adoption of its "all-women shortlists."

In addition, the organizational characteristics of the intraparty opportunity structure—the degree of centralization, fractionalization, programmatic orientation, and New and Old Left ideology—are drawn out in chapter 2 and tested in chapter 3 regarding women's representation among the party's national executive committee. These structures, in addition to a few factors that are unique to women's parliamentary representation, will be examined in this chapter.

First, a party's degree of centralization may impact women's access to parliament. Centralization describes the distribution of control over the decision making among levels of the party hierarchy. Chapter 2 suggested that a centralized party might allow party leaders the leeway to promote women candidates—when they perceive the need to do so. Without a centralized and coordinated effort, the Labour Party would have failed to coerce local constituencies into nominating female candidates. Further, chapter 3 revealed that centralized parties are more conducive to women's representation on the party's NEC.

In addition, because fractionalized parties have more links to outside groups, they might provide more points of access to new groups who wish to enter their ranks. Chapter 4 revealed that fractionalized parties are indeed more conducive to women's ascendance to the party's NEC, and by extension, this feature may also be conducive to women's ascendance to parliamentary office.

Similarly, a more pragmatic, as opposed to more rule-bound, party is more likely to support women. Although the pragmatic nature of a party was not found to be instrumental to women's gains inside the party, it may still be important to their gains in parliamentary office.

One conditional factor unique to women's parliamentary representation is the level of candidate nomination. Candidate nomination can be controlled mainly by the local party organization, as illustrated in the British Labour Party, or at some other level. For example, in the German Social Democratic Party, the regional party organization has a great degree of control over nomination to the party lists. Further, the central party leadership may have more control over the process, as illustrated in the Dutch Labour Party (PvdA). The level of candidate nomination may intervene to influence party behavior. A more localized level of nomination makes it more difficult for party leadership to implement a new rule, such as candidate gender quotas. For example, when the British Labour Party adopted all-women short lists, party officials from headquarters in London had trouble persuading local constituencies to follow the policy. Without direct control over nomination, this policy was difficult to enforce.

Another contextual variable is the party's ideological framework. Chapters 3 and 4 revealed that leftist parties are more likely to have women among the party's leadership and to adopt quota policies. By extension, one can expect leftist parties to have higher rates of increase in women's parliamentary representation than rightist parties. In previous research (Caul, 1999), I find that across twelve advanced industrial democracies, leftist parties, and especially those with New Left values, had higher proportions of women in parliament from 1975 to 1992. Likewise, Darcy and Beckwith (cited in Darcy, Welch, and Clark, 1994) find that even when controlling for a party's electoral gains and losses, Socialist, Communist, and Green parties elect one or two additional women per election, compared with parties in the Center and to the Right. Although the leftist orientation of a party is a fairly stable influence and may not be directly related to change, it is likely that the mechanisms that do lead to change are adopted by leftist parties. As such, party ideology is an intervening variable through which other influences are filtered.

Institutional, Exogenous to Party Itself

Research on the representation of women often emphasizes the effects of the electoral system. Several studies have established that party-list, proportional representation systems (PR) with large district magnitudes lead to more women in parliament than plurality systems (Lakeman, 1994; Duverger, 1955; Rule and Zimmerman, 1994; Beckwith, 1994; Matland, 1993; Matland and Studlar, 1996). Rule (1987) concludes that the method of election, when compared with socioeconomic indicators, is the strongest influence on women's parliamentary representation. The standard explanation is that parties are less likely to run a woman in a single-member district because parties worry that they will lose the seat to a male competitor. In contrast, in party-list, PR systems, parties are more likely to add women to the list of candidates in an effort to broaden the party's appeal and to balance the ticket. Women candidates are often viewed as benefits to the party by attracting votes, without forcing established politicians to step down.

For example, in the Finnish party-list, PR system, party officials revealed in interviews that it is the accepted practice to balance their lists—not only balanced in terms of gender, but also age, occupation, and factions of the party—to broaden the party's appeal among all types of voters. This penchant to balance the list, by way of what we might call a "logic of proportionality," has become the established norm, and the Finnish parties are unlikely to conceive of composing a ticket that was not balanced in such a way.

Although the electoral system does not appear to be the direct mechanism of change because of its largely static nature over time, party-list systems may be the most fertile soil in which the proportion of women can grow. Darcy, Welch, and Clark (1994) contend that party-list, PR systems are more conducive to women's representation because legislative turnover is higher than in single-member district plurality systems. The authors reason that for women to win a seat, established male politicians must lose a seat. In single-member districts, there is more emphasis on the personal appeal and constituency work of the incumbent, and thus the party has less power to select or deselect officeholders. In contrast, in those systems where candidates are slated on a list, rather than representing a constituency, there is less emphasis on the candidate. Therefore, it is easier for a party to replace past MPs on a list. For example, the low proportion of women in the U.S. House can be explained, in part, by the drag of incumbency. In the United States, where incumbents are overwhelmingly reelected and are slow to retire, the opportunities for women to run for open seats are few. So, one expects that party-list, PR systems will be associated with larger increases of women MPs owing to greater electoral turnover. Among the set of countries analyzed here, all but one uses a form of PR (the exception is, of course, Britain). Thus, the impact of degree of proportionality will be tested here. This impact is measured using district magnitude, which ranges from 1 to 75 across this set of countries.

In a related manner, where there are swings in the distribution of seats among candidates, independent of electoral system, there is an opportunity for newcomers such as women to be elected to parliament. Conversely, when members are reelected, there should be little change in the gender composition of the party's delegation to parliament. At the level of the nation, Darcy and Beckwith (cited in Darcy, Welch, and Clark, 1994) establish that electoral turnover is indeed a powerful explanation for increases in women's representation over time. In a study of eleven nations from 1970 to 1984 and in an in-depth study of seven Danish elections, the authors find a clear pattern between party gains at elections and increasing numbers of women in parliament. Therefore, I expect that when a party gains seats, there will also be an increase in the number of women that party sends to parliament. This process is best exemplified by the British Labour Party, which swept the 1997 elections, winning an unprecedented number of seats. Candidates in marginal, and even not-so-marginal, seats were elected. As a result, the Labour Party went from 37 women in their 1992 delegation to parliament, to 101 in 1997. However, the expectations for future women's gains are dismal, because Labour is not likely to win many new seats, and thus there are fewer opportunities for more women to be elected.

It is important to note that parties with open nomination slots will not automatically nominate more women—other factors must be present to encourage them to do so. Thus, as discussed in chapter 2, the electoral rules and seat turnover only create the context in which party-level forces operate.

Data Analysis

Setting up the "puzzle of women's representation," as described in chapter 1, I argue that past cross-national research missed important clues in explaining the increase in women's representation by focusing only on static, national-level percentages between nations. Taken together, this research established that party-list, proportional representation systems are the most conducive to the election of women. Indeed, the method of election does matter for comparative levels of women's representation. Yet problematically, while women's representation has systematically increased since the mid-1970s across advanced industrial nations, the electoral systems have remained fairly stable. Therefore, in addition to examining the actual levels of women's representation by party, in this section I examine change in the proportion of women from one election to the next.

In this section, I systematically analyze the mechanisms that influence the proportion of women among a party's MPs. A pooled cross-section of data that includes observations for all national elections between 1975 and 1997 in the ten Western European nations in our study is analyzed.[2] This pooled

Table 8.1 Multivariate Model Explaining Women's Representation as Party MPs

Explanatory Variable	Levels		Change	
	Model 1a	Model 1b	Model 2a	Model 2b
Political Opportunity Structure				
Gender and Vote (Women's Bonus)	.15**	.14**	.10*	.10*
New Left Party	.06		.11*	.09*
Presence of Party Women's Organization	.01		.00	
Women in Party Leadership	.49**	.47**	.16**	.12**
Institutional Opportunity Structure				
Gender Quotas	.07		.09*	.08*
Candidate Nomination Level	-.14**	-.14*	-.09*	-.04
Party Centralization Index	.23**	.61**	.08*	.10**
Party Fractionalization Index	.01		.00	
Party Programmatic Index	.02		.01	
Old Left Ideology	.03		.01	
New Left Ideology	.01		.01	
Electoral System (District Magnitude)	-.12		.01	
Seat Turnover (Change)	.06		.05	
Lagged Percentage of Women by Party			.61**	
Adjusted R-Squared	.37	.57	.74	.75

Note: Table entries are standardized regression coefficients. Dichotomous country variables are also included in Models 1b and 2b but are not shown. Denmark and Finland are significant in each. Dichotomous country variables are not included in Models 1a and 2a because the presence of country-specific variables such as electoral system serves as a proxy-country dummy variable. See chapter notes for full explanation. Significance Levels: ** = $p < .05$, * = $p < .10$

cross-section of 547 cases provides enough observations to control for several factors. Measures were collected from published national statistics and other data sources for each of the independent and dependent variables. A full explanation of the variables and data sources of the data can be found in Appendix A.

Multivariate Analyses

The goal is to determine which influences affect both levels of women in a party's parliamentary delegation and change in the proportion of women, and how these influences work together. Using the hypotheses outlined in the previous section, I create multivariate models to test the combined influence of these explanatory factors. The dependent variable in the first set of models (Models 1a and 1b) is the percentage of women in parliament by party—the actual numbers. In the second set of models (Models 2a and 2b), the dependent variable is also used as a lagged variable in the equation—to explain change in the levels.

The multivariate analyses are presented in table 8.1.[3] Model 1a contains all of the hypothesized influences on the level of female party MPs.[4] Among the political opportunity structure explanations, there are two statistically significant predictors, a party's share of women's votes, and the proportion of women among the party's leadership (NEC). Neither the presence of a New Left Party nor a women's organization within the party is a significant predictor of levels of women's representation. Further, among the institutional opportunity structure variables, both a decentralized level of candidate nomination and a centralized party structure emerge as statistically significant influences on the number of women in a party's delegation to parliament.

The strongest and most significant explanatory variables from this original "full" model are entered by themselves in a separate equation to assess their importance without the interference of the weaker variables. Model 1b presents the results of the scaled-down model. The same explanatory variables remain significant in this model, the predictive power of a centralized party organization skyrockets, and the explained adjusted variance climbs to nearly 60%.

In search of mechanisms to increase women's representation, the second set of equations examines *change* in the proportion of women. As expected, in the "change" models, the lagged percentage of women by party is the strongest variable, and it explains the cross-sectional variance.[5]

First, the results of the "full" model predicting change (Model 2a) reveal that a women's bonus in party's votes (or a deficit in men's votes) is a significant predictor of increases in women's representation. Further, increasing numbers of women in party leadership positions is a strong and significant predictor of increases in parliament. Importantly, although not significant when explaining static levels of representation, when it comes to explaining change, the presence of a New Left party in the system and the use of gender quotas are statistically significant and therefore appear to be mechanisms of change. As observed when examining static levels of women's representation, a decentralized level of candidate nomination and a centralized party structure are the most conducive for women. Surprisingly, neither a party's ideology nor the electoral system's district magnitude proves statistically significant in explaining change.

As with the first set of models, the strongest explanations from the full model are entered separately in a scaled-down model (Model 2b). The results reveal that the explanatory variables that were significant in the full model remain so in the scaled-down model, except the level of candidate nomination.

It appears that a decentralized level of nomination is not a consistent or robust indicator of change in women's representation. The model's explanatory power holds constant, and together these influences explain 75% of the adjusted variance in party-level change in women's parliamentary representation.

Discussion

The multivariate models reveal that both political and institutional opportunity structure influences are important influences on change in the gender composition of a party's delegation to parliament. Further, forces both in the party system and within the party itself heighten women's opportunities for office. Select explanatory variables from each category are found to be statistically significant across the different models constructed in the data analysis. From the political side, parties that garner more women's votes, relative to men's, have higher numbers of women MPs and have experienced greater increases in women MPs over time. Clearly electoral forces are at work here. Because the difference (or "gap") in women's and men's votes is a lagged indicator, meaning it is taken from the previous election, this sequence suggests that having more women among a party's supporters leads to more women in office, rather than the other way around.

Overall, one of the strongest and most consistent indicators of both "levels" and "change" is the increase from the previous election in the percentage of women on the party's national executive committee.[6] Having more women in the party's leadership before the elections appears to be key to getting more women elected. After women become more entrenched in the higher ranks of the party hierarchy, women then also gain entrance into the parliament in higher numbers. The results of this model indicate that women's presence is key at the top of the party hierarchy, but the mere presence of a women's organization is not as important. This finding lends support not only to the importance of political factors within the party, but also to the elite-led, top-down theory of party change. It appears that women among the party decision makers can lead the way toward women's gains in parliament.

Further bolstering the important role of party leadership is the finding that centralized parties have higher numbers of women in office and experience greater increases in women's representation. This finding suggests that where party leaders have the power, they can support women candidates for office and can compel the local and regional party organizations to follow their lead. As part of the institutional opportunity structure, a centralized organization creates a context conducive to women's efforts from above to pressure and gain results in parliament.

An important difference follows from separately examining the levels and change. The impact of New Left parties and quotas is limited to the statistical model that measures change in women's parliamentary presence from one election to the next. New Left parties and quotas are mechanisms for women's gains. As the New Left party brings gender equality to the top of the agenda and runs a high number of women for office, other parties appear to follow their lead and run more women. In addition, parties that adopt candidate gender quotas register larger increases in women's progress.

Because decentralized candidate nomination loses its significance in one model, it is one of the weaker indicators. Yet it may loosely shape women's parliamentary representation. How can one square this finding with the finding that a more highly centralized party leadership is conducive to women's representation? The central party leadership can take an active role in responding to women's demands for more equitable representation, even when nomination is largely conducted at the local levels. In a centralized party, national authorities have the power to persuade local constituencies to implement standard policies to promote women.

Although I predicted that ideology would strongly condition women's opportunities within the party, measures of both New and Old Left values in the party were weak and insignificant in each instance. While chapters 3 and 4 find ideology impacts women's opportunities for ascendance through the party ranks to the national executive committee and impacts the likelihood that a party will adopt quotas, ideology does not emerge as an important factor in predicting women's parliamentary presence, *ceteris paribus.* Parties further to the left on the ideological scale do *not* appear to be registering higher levels of women in parliament than other parties across the ideological scale. Perhaps the center and rightist parties had more ground to make up—overall, rightist parties started out at lower levels in the 1970s, and there was much more room for progress. Some leftist parties, especially those in Scandinavia, began in the 1970s with levels that left them with less area to cover in their progression toward 50% women in parliament.

It is also surprising that many of the other institutional opportunity structure explanations prove weak and insignificant in the quantitative analysis. Specifically, past research emphasized the importance of electoral rules and seat change for creating the space for women to make gains. In this analysis, a party's overall gain of seats in the legislature relate weakly to women's gains. In a similar fashion, proportionality in the electoral system (as measured by district magnitude) exerts little influence. Although past research establishes that party-list, PR systems with high district magnitudes are strong indicators of *levels* of women's parliamentary representation, this does not appear to be the most direct mechanism of *increases* in the proportion of women in parliament. Despite the fact that the proportionality of the electoral rules is a fairly stationary variable, it was included in the model to predict change, not only because it is an important control variable, but also because theoretically a PR system should provide the opportunity for other mechanisms of change, such as quotas, to work.

All in all, the results of the multivariate model point toward simultaneous bottom-up pressures and top-down strategies behind efforts to promote women for office within a changing political opportunity structure. Women's role in this process proves vital—women are important to increasing their representation in parliament, both as a voting bloc and as leaders within the party hierarchy.

9

Conclusions: Implications for Party Theory and Underrepresented Groups

At its core, this book concerns challenges from new contenders for voice within the party and in parliament by focusing on one group—women. Changes in women's roles have been one of the fundamental social transformations across postindustrial democracies. The surge in women's participation within parties called attention to women's political voice and placed this issue squarely on the mainstream political agenda. Demands to alter the status quo threaten powerful interests within the party organization, and parties have been reluctant to meaningfully address this issue. Yet at various points over the past three decades, certain parties across Western Europe have focused attention on raising the number of women candidates. To be sure, it has been a contested process, full of debate and rancor. Women have not only challenged party organizations for greater voice in party politics, but also, in some cases, ultimately changed the party rules and transformed the face of parliament.

Chapter 1 began by arguing that parties have been given short shrift in many previous systematic, cross-national studies of women in parliament. As gatekeepers to parliamentary office in Western Europe, parties can promote or hinder women's efforts. From the perspective of how new challengers find access in democratic party systems, I asked how the political and institutional structures within parties facilitate women's access. From the perspective of party change, I asked why some political parties took steps to promote women candidates while others did not, and why they did so at the time they did. These questions were considered by assembling an extensive body of evidence from published statistics, opinion surveys, and interviews with party officials and politicians. Drawing together the findings from the systematic multivariate analysis and the in-depth case studies, this chapter connects those findings to the larger theoretical implications. This chapter begins with the three case study nations, identifying the key forces behind the motivations of party elites to initiate party-led campaigns to promote women candidates for office. In the final section, these forces are tied to the strongest explanations found in the statistical analyses.

Party Change in Britain, Germany, and Finland

The case studies generate important insights into women in party politics. Some of these insights reinforce the relationships yielded by the statistical analyses, and others are valuable because they tap forces that are not easily measured with quantitative data. In all three party systems, women's mobilization was key to gaining party efforts to promote women within the party, and to support them for elected office. Women's renewed claims on the party systems of these three countries brought the issue of women's parliamentary presence onto the mainstream agenda and kept it there. Shifts in attitudes, women's voting patterns, and women's grassroots party activism explain *why* parties might have incentive to promote women candidates, but to a large extent, the varying strategies of women within parties explain why women made gains *when* they did.

First, the British and German case studies highlight the importance of changing party leaders' perceptions. Electoral pressures generated by women's shifting voting patterns alone are not sufficient to ignite change. Years of gaining more women's votes brought little response from the British Labour and the German Social Democratic parties. The key to translating electoral shifts into women's parliamentary gains was highlighting the value of women's votes. In the German Social Democratic Party in the late 1980s, the British Labour Party in the early 1990s, and, to a lesser extent, the German CDU in the late 1990s, key women within the party appealed to the party leadership by framing women's votes as part of a winning electoral strategy. Further, these women convinced party leaders to expect that more women's votes might be gained if the party had more women MPs. British Labour's quintessential "Winning Words" campaign was an unabashed strategic maneuver to win women's votes by running women for office.

While extrapartisan activities are not the focus of this project, the renewal of the women's movement serves as the backdrop for women's participation in party politics in all three cases. The case studies recount how the women's movement infused parties with a new generation of women in party politics—a group with a common identity as women, and a concern for representation among the party ranks. Importantly, the timing of this shift toward party politics differs across the three cases. Finnish women entered parties full force in the 1960s, while German and British women's movements focused more on protest activities until the late 1970s. As a result, Finnish women made inroads within parties much earlier, and this progress was reflected in the country's position as a world leader in women in parliament in the 1960s.

The infusion of feminist women into the party women's organizations of the British Labour Party and German Social Democratic Party in the 1970s injected the traditional party women's organizations with a renewed politicism. Yet selecting the right allies within the party is essential to making parliamentary gains. When the women's organizations aligned with the more radical factions within the party, their success was limited. When the women's organizations aligned with the up-and-coming faction of party "modernizers," they made greater inroads. Party modernizers prized winning control of government, even if this goal meant more centrist policies. In other words, by framing women's demands for office as part of the party's plan for electoral success, women were often able to achieve their goals. A similar case was illustrated on the Right by the German Christian Democrats, where a group of young professional women led the traditional women's organization to engage in power politics by aligning with the dominant party coalition for a short time.

As women gained positions of power within the party, they gained greater ability to transform party rules. In the British Labour Party, women made great strides on the national executive committee, and their lobbying efforts resulted in a quota-type policy for candidates. As a result of the new candidate selection rules, women's presence in the party's delegation to Parliament jumped from 14% in 1992 to 24% in 1997. The German SPD also adopted a series of quota policies in the late 1980s, culminating in the 1987 candidate gender quota that boosted women's representation from 18% in the 1987 election to 27% in the 1990 election. Women in the highest echelons of the CDU lobbied Chancellor Helmut Kohl and won a quota-esque policy for women's candidacies.

The Finnish case proved to be a bit of a contrast to the British and German cases and deserves some special consideration. Despite the absence of overt party efforts to promote women candidates, Finnish women made great gains in party politics and parliament in the 1960s. First and foremost, as in Britain and Germany, women's activism in party politics was key to gaining access to the parliament. In addition, a predominant national ideology oriented toward women's "equality," rather than women's difference, played an integral role in this process. The penchant for women across the ideological spectrum to favor mainstream party channels reduced the role of the women's organizations within Finnish parties and reduced the need for special measures to support women. The early and full-force integration of the women's movement into partisan channels precluded the aggressive challenges generated within the leftist parties of Britain and Germany. This process is supported by evidence from previous research on the opportunity structure for new social movements (NSMs) in Western Europe. Kriesi et al. (1992) conclude that states that use an inclusive strategy, or accommodate some NSM demands, tend to preempt protest activity. Here, the more inclusive Finnish parties preempted the more vociferous and organized claims for gender parity that emerged in other Western European parties.

Importantly, Finland's unique electoral rules also clearly enhanced women's progress. First, parties have a distinct incentive to include women on the list—to broaden the party's appeal among women voters. Finnish women have turned out to vote at higher rates than their male counterparts since the 1970s (Sundberg, 1995a). And through the Finnish "logic of inclusion," parties developed an early and enduring norm to balance the party list by including women. While women in other party-list, proportional representation systems were bound to "closed lists" and ranked toward the bottom by party officials, Finnish candidates receive individual preference votes. Finnish women avoided the trap of being ranked so low on the list that they could not be elected. And women voters were able to support women candidates. In essence, electoral rules in Finland did not present the same barriers that they did in other Western European nations. Because the barriers were lower, women in Finland made great strides early on and did not press for candidate quotas.

Challenging Parties and Recognizing Opportunity

Taken together, the statistical and case study findings show that women's efforts interact with parties' opportunity structures to shape the effectiveness of women's demands for increased representation. The broader implications shed some light on how new contenders can best lobby party channels to gain access to parliament.

The case study evidence pointed toward the importance of the party women's organizations in channeling and articulating women's demands for greater representation. In addition, the multivariate models in chapter 8 showed that growing numbers of women among a party's voters are linked to increases in their representation among a party's delegation to parliament. Both influences depict a bottom-up flow of party change as they represent citizen-initiated pressures on the party.

Party institutions condition the effectiveness of these bottom-up forces. Cross-national statistical analysis in chapter 3 shows that parties with New Left ideological values are more hospitable to women within the internal party ranks. Thus, women rise to top positions more quickly in parties with a standing commitment to new, noneconomic issues. Further, the case study evidence suggests that the leftist parties such as Labour, the Socialists, and the Greens have paid most attention to women's demands for equality. In addition, women make greater gains in the hierarchy of permeable party structures. The statistical evidence in chapter 4 shows that more factionalized parties have more women on the top decision-making committees. Long-standing ties to outside groups may provide women more points of access and may establish a norm for incorporating new groups.

Women's presence among the top party leadership strongly influences the statistical likelihood a party will adopt candidate gender quotas and will send more women to parliament. The case studies demonstrate that women in top party positions can highlight the problem of women's underrepresentation and keep this issue on the party's agenda. Specifically, as best illustrated by the British Labour Party, a few well-placed women who are interested in "letting the ladder down" to other women can be a catalyst for change. What is more, strategy in the form of timing and framing proved essential to making substantial gains. Women in powerful positions gain the ear of their counterparts, and they can convince the party leadership to listen to women's claims for parity in parliament. These women may point out that rival parties are running more women, or that a deficit in women's votes can be attributed to the party's male-dominated image. Women in the party leadership shape party leaders' perceptions, and they can "sell" improving women's representation as a part of a package to enhance the party's image among female voters. Thus, women's parliamentary presence is framed as part of a larger, modern transformation to benefit the party at the ballot box.

Given the importance of women among the party leadership as a direct mechanism of change, and given the time series evidence in chapter 4 demonstrating that internal quotas lead to more women on the NEC, these internal quotas may be more effective in the chain of influences than previously thought. Plus, internal party quotas tend to be far less controversial than the highly visible candidate quotas. In short, the more contentious candidate quotas may be less imperative where there are internal quotas.

This process is most effective in a centralized party structure. Chapter 3 shows women climb the party ladder more easily in a centralized party. Chapter 4 shows quotas are more likely to be adopted in a centralized party. Finally, chapter 8 shows that women's parliamentary presence is higher among centralized parties, all other things being equal. Linking these findings together suggests that parties that are centralized can effectively implement measures to ensure that women are nominated for office—when they are willing to do so. Yet chapter 4 also shows women within the party hierarchy make greater gains if the party organization is permeable to new interests, more "factionalized." Factionalization and centralization seem to work at cross-purposes. It is important to note that although a permeable structure allows for more points of access for new contenders, a closed and centralized structure allows a party to act decisively in promoting women to parliament. So, a permeable (but not centralized) structure may allow women to make gains at the party's grass roots, but it may not yield top-down campaigns to promote women candidates.

Furthermore, the final institutional opportunity structure factor is a party's ideology. Parties with "New Left" value orientations are more likely to adopt quotas and prove to be more conducive to women's promotion to the party national executive committee. Although chapter 8 shows that a leftist ideology is not directly related to women's parliamentary presence, the *mechanisms* that lead to increases in women's representation are more likely to be found in leftist parties. As such, a leftist orientation appears to be more fertile ground for women's efforts to attain parliamentary office.

Social change forces appear to be a necessary, but not always sufficient, condition for party change. Pressures from voters and women's organizations proved important. In the Finnish case, they proved sufficient. Thus, mass-level forces may suffice where the new contenders focus all of their energy and resources on partisan channels, and where the electoral rules provide just the right mix to facilitate women's election. Yet in other cases, the demand for greater presence explains why parties moved to promote women, but not why they moved when they did. These pressures mounted, yet year after year party women realized few gains. Many of the early barriers to women's advancement in party politics remained in place. Thus, the thrust of this book was to search for agents of change.

Where women didn't make gains early on, electoral forces proved important so far as they motivated top-down efforts. Specifically, electoral instability and new party competition open up new opportunities for new contenders. Chapter 2 detailed some possible pressures generated by internal party dynamics. Party elites are concerned with the party's electoral fortunes. A change in that membership, or reorganization of power, introduces new perceptions that responding to new issues will benefit the party. Specifically, more women among the party's decision makers proved the vital ingredient in producing change. Women leaders can use their power to implement changes in a top-down process. In some cases, new policies such as quotas were adopted and implemented by mandating that the local party organizations follow the central party leadership's lead.

The fact that having women in positions of power within the party is so integral to each step in the process of promoting women for office suggests that women's gains are long-term. If policies designed to promote women candidates stemmed only from the party's desire to change its image among women voters, then efforts to increase women in parliament would appear to be short-term, symbolic strategies designed by party leaders to gain women's votes. Yet because these new party policies are directly related to increases in women who are firmly established in powerful positions within the party, the growth reflects a more fundamental shift in the party culture. As women have become more entrenched in higher positions, it has become more difficult to erase women's representation from the agenda.

Where women have focused their attention on parties, rather than on the outside movement, and where the party women's organizations have strategically framed the issue of women's political equality, women have made the greatest strides in achieving representation in parliament. This idea suggests a tradeoff long debated by social movements. As women work within the mainstream, male-dominated party institutions, they may conform to the existing standards of practice and make greater gains. In some cases where women have eschewed the mainstream party channels, their demands may remain more stringent, yet their party gains may be circumscribed.

Women have certainly made gains in parties and parliaments across Western Europe. The intent of this book has been to assess their gains in achieving presence and a voice in politics. The degree to which women have transformed party and national policy is left to future research. Yet one way in which women have changed party organization is by reconfiguring the institutions. As women challenged for equal voice in parliament, their demands were often heard, and where direct action was taken, the party recruitment policies were changed to mandate a certain proportion of women candidates. Not only does this type of policy change signal a commitment to women, but also to fair and equal representation of underrepresented groups in general.

In conclusion, movement groups *can* effectively take their demands to political parties. Women's successes demonstrate that parties are permeable structures, and not necessarily the stalwart, patriarchal bastion of entrenched interests as often characterized by the feminist movement and theories of institutionalization. Parties do respond, given the right conditions. The finding that women's efforts were matched by party responses speaks volumes for the health and vibrancy of our contemporary party organizations. Scholars of Western European parties note that parties appear to be losing the historical, encapsulated social cleavages upon which they traditionally relied for votes (Dalton et al., 1985; Crewe and Denver, 1985; Franklin et al., 1992). The erosion of groupings based upon class and religion that used to provide the stable partisan loyalties appear to be giving way to shifting coalitions of disparate interests. The "unanchoring" of women's votes without a clear gender realignment reflects this trend toward more ephemeral bases of electoral support that parties face in a new era. Salient new issues such as women's parliamentary presence can clearly be used by parties on an election-by-election basis, informed by public opinion polls and focus group research. In short, political parties need women. In turn, women need political parties if they are to change the face of parliaments. Rather than using citizen interest groups as an alternative to party politics, the findings of this book suggest that new contenders can take their demands to the parties, and that parties have the capability to respond—when they perceive the need to do so.

Theories that contend that parties are indeed thriving as their social bases shift often speak of party "adaptation." However, the evidence from this case does not support the idea of an evolutionary adaptation. Instead, in most cases, real gains for women largely follow a "change from above" pattern, in which the party itself is a deliberate actor that shapes its own environment. In short, political parties in Western Europe will remain important actors in the democratic process, and new challengers demanding a political voice should design strategies to promote their interests within parties, bearing in mind that parties are complex sets of institutions, embedded within an ever-changing political context. In turn, with an increasingly shifting social base, the future electoral successes of established parties depend upon their ability and willingness to incorporate new issues and new groups.

10

Afterword: Women and Parties Navigate in a New Era, 1998–2004

In Western Europe, the period from the 1970s to the 1990s represents a unique era of unprecedented growth in women's parliamentary presence and in political parties' adoption of new policies to promote women candidates. Since this wave, characterized by party-centered change, there have been some noteworthy developments. First, many nations have witnessed a stubborn plateau in levels of women's representation. For example, in the 2002 British general elections, women lost ground in parliament for the first time in twenty years, slipping from 120 women in 1997 to 118 (Childs, 2003). In the 2002 German elections, women won 32% of the seats, a number virtually unchanged from the 1998 elections. This stagnation stands in contrast to women's steady gains in the Bundestag in the 1980s and 1990s—particularly, a sixteen percentage point gain over the decade leading up to the 1998 election.

In a broader shift, women have increasingly focused their claims for greater presence in parliament toward the institutions of the state and have won constitutional changes (Beckwith, 2003; Klausen and Maier, 2001). For example, following women's losses in the 2002 election, Britain passed the Sex Discrimination (Election Candidates) Act in 2002, which allows political parties to adopt a form of gender quotas for candidates, if they so choose. In France, a new constitutional amendment requires parties to offer an equal number of women candidates.

Have constitutional changes and state institutions replaced party-level mechanisms to improve women's parliamentary presence? In a word, no. The evidence in this chapter suggests that where claims on institutions of the state are coupled with continued efforts within political parties, they are most likely to be effective. When it comes to women's entrance into parliaments, parties are still the "gatekeepers" to elected office and still the most effective target for women's efforts (Lovenduski and Norris, 1993). Nevertheless, whether at the party or state level, a strategic recognition of the opportunity structure makes or breaks women's efforts to gain ground. In fact, it is such a recognition of the opportunities that has prompted women to double their efforts by targeting new points of access as power shifts up to supranational institutions, and down, through devolution (Beckwith, 2003).

In this chapter, I examine select developments in women's efforts to gain political equality since 1998. The organization of the chapter is as follows: the first section returns to our starting point—cross-national trends in women's parliamentary presence as of 2004; the second section focuses on post-1998 strategies in Britain, Germany, and Finland; and the fourth situates the unprecedented reforms in the case of France within the theory of party opportunity structures developed in this book.

Women's Parliamentary Presence, 2004

The "rising tide" in women's socioeconomic achievements and in citizens' support for women's role in politics (see Inglehart and Norris, 2003) suggests that women will continue making gains in the parliaments of established democracies. Table 10.1 displays trends in women's parliamentary presence up to 2005 in twenty-four postindustrial democracies. The first column displays the percentage of female MPs in the lower chamber of the national legislature in the general election most proximate to 2005. The second column gives the percentage point difference between the elections closest to 1975 and 2005. Each nation has witnessed gains—most in the double digits. Some of the greatest strides were made by Belgium and Spain, both nearly thirty percentage point jumps. The United States posted only moderate gains, climbing from not quite 4% women in the House in the election closest to 1975 to 15% by 2005.

In a comprehensive long-term study, Ian McAllister and Donley T. Studlar (2002) examine women's parliamentary presence across twenty established democracies from 1950 to 2000, and they point out that the same nations that led in the 1950s remained leaders in 2000. While the proportional electoral formula and parties' candidate gender quotas exert influence over the number of women in office, McAllister and Studlar argue that an egalitarian political

Table 10.1 Percentage of Women in Parliament, 2005

Nation	% Women MPs, 2005	% Point Increase since 1975	1975 Ranking	2005 Ranking
Australia	24.7	+24.7	24	13
Austria	33.9	+26.2	7	8
Belgium	34.7	+28.1	10	7
Canada	21.1	+17.7	19	15
Denmark	36.9	+21.3	3	3
Finland	37.5	+14.5	1	2
France	12.2	+ 9.5	20	21
Germany	32.2	+26.4	12	9
Greece	14.0	+12.0	22	19
Iceland	30.2	+25.2	14	10
Ireland	13.3	+10.5	21	20
Israel	15.0	+ 8.3	9	18
Italy	11.5	+ 7.7	17	22
Japan	7.1	+ 5.7	23	23
Luxembourg	23.3	+16.2	13	14
Netherlands	36.7	+27.4	5	4
New Zealand	28.3	+23.7	15	11
Norway	35.8	+20.3	4	6
Portugal	19.1	+11.1	6	16
Spain	36.0	+30.0	11	5
Sweden	45.3	+23.9	2	1
Switzerland	25.0	+18.0	8	12
United Kingdom	17.9	+13.6	16	17
United States	15.0	+11.3	18	18

Source: International Parliamentary Union, 3/1/2005

culture, measured by a nation's early propensity to enfranchise women, can explain why the leaders retain high proportions of women over time. The data presented here in table 10.1 support McAllister and Studlar's contention that among established industrial democracies over this period, the "rich get richer," and those with low numbers of women in parliament in 1975 tend to remain toward the back of the pack by 2005. Certainly egalitarian values exert some influence.

Yet comparison of the rankings of countries in 1975 and 2005 (displayed in the final two columns in table 10.1) reveals that several countries have made great leaps. Australia bounced up from last place in 1975 to thirteenth place by 2005, for a gain of twenty-five percentage points. Canada rose from nearly last to fifteenth place, gaining nearly eighteen percentage points. A few "middle-class" nations rose to leadership positions. For example, Spain rose from eleventh to fifth. Still, countries such as Finland, Denmark, Sweden, Norway, and the Netherlands remain the leaders, and Japan, France, and Greece remain the laggards. Despite the great gains in the 1997 election by Labourites, Britain remained in the middle of the pack. Germany moved up a few notches from twelfth to ninth place, gaining over twenty-six percentage points. The United States and Israel share the same rank at eighteenth, each with 15% women in parliament.

This book asked why some countries have made gains, while others lost ground, with an eye toward identifying some mechanisms for change. I have argued that political parties are key to the gains observed at the national level. Citizens' attitudes towards women's political roles certainly change over time, albeit slowly (see Inglehart and Norris, 2003). However, gains in women's representation are often the result of direct actions. This book has shown that by recognizing favorable party institutions and climate, women's organizations and women in top-level party positions can prompt political parties to adopt mechanisms and rules to increase the proportion of women in their delegations to parliament.

Political Party Efforts and National-Level Institutional Change

Broad trends across nations are quite instructive, yet it is also important to look underneath, to the progress of individual parties. To assess some of these changes since 1998, we briefly return to the three countries that were examined in-depth in chapters 5 through 7: Britain, Germany, and Finland.

British Women in Party Politics, 1998–2005

Britain has witnessed changes in its constitution regarding women's representation; also, British women have had remarkable success in two devolved assemblies. Both changes create a new context for women in party politics and have far-reaching implications for women in Westminster in the twenty-first century.

Great Gains in the Devolved Assemblies of Wales and Scotland

Although national elections have been the focus of this book, in order to fully understand post-1998 efforts to promote women in the House of Commons, we must first consider the remarkable achievements and favorable electoral rules in the newly devolved Scottish Parliament and the National Assembly for Wales. Scottish and Welsh women's success in getting the topic of women's representation on the political agenda highlights the importance of strategy in a changing opportunity structure. Under a completely new set of electoral rules,[1] all parties began competing under electoral uncertainty. Further, in each new assembly, women encountered a clean slate—few entrenched male power holders. Taken together, women faced a window of opportunity to make gains, and organized women's groups recognized this critical juncture.

Women and the Scottish Parliament

Scottish women recognized the importance of gaining positions in parliament from the start, while the resources of incumbency were still up for grabs. Women with diverse backgrounds and interests found common ground in the goal to gain presence (Brown et al., 2002; Beckwith, 2003). At the 1989 Scottish Convention, a coalition of women from parties, trade unions, churches, business, and movements joined forces under the label of the "Scottish Women's Co-ordination Group" to lobby for women's political equality in parties and the new parliament (MacKay et al., 2003). Over a ten-year period, they carefully framed the claims in their "50:50" campaign within the broader Scottish campaign for voice in the democratic process. These women claimed a "double democratic deficit": they were excluded from power both as Scots and as women (Brown et al., 2002; MacKay et al., 2003).

Importantly, women in the Scottish campaign concentrated their efforts on political parties. Brown et al. (2002) point out that this focus stands in stark contrast to the context of the devolved assembly elections of Northern Ireland, where women focused their efforts outside of the electoral arena and made fewer gains.

Scots' criticisms of Westminster centered on its lack of inclusiveness. The rallying cry for a "new politics" of power sharing, access, and equal opportunities characterized the movement for devolution (MacKay et al., 2003). If parties competing in this "new politics" arena were to exclude women in the new Scottish Parliament, they would appear hypocritical (MacKay et al., 2003). By situating women's representation within the justifications for the broader campaign for devolution and by taking parties to task on their inclusiveness, women made their parliamentary presence a highly salient electoral issue.

Alice Brown (1999) describes a competition among Scottish parties for women's votes based on rhetoric concerning women's parliamentary presence. Pressured by women's organizations and competing for women's votes, Scottish Labour and the Scottish Liberal Democrats gained media attention by signing an electoral agreement to balance their candidates in terms of gender. The Scottish Liberal Democrats proposed that for every two men who stood, two women would be nominated to match. However, the party did not end up implementing this policy. Formally, the Liberal Democrats said they could not muster enough women candidates. Brown (1999) contends that in reality, the party was afraid they might be subject to the same legal appeal under the Sex Discrimination Act as experienced by the British Labour Party, with its all-women short lists.

Scottish Labour faced the same legal uncertainties, but the party went beyond rhetoric to forge ahead with positive action measures for women. Meg Russell (2003) suggests several reasons. First, women MPs were a symbolic part of "New Labour's" more modern face. Conservatives had argued that the entrenched interests of Scotland and Wales would prevail in a devolved system, and Labour was not about to let this prediction come true. Second, Labour visibly committed itself to equality with the electoral agreement and did not want to renege on its promises. Finally, Labour women activists, many now in high-level positions (as detailed in chapter 3), kept the pressure on the party leadership.

To get around the possible legal challenges, Labour devised a process called "twinning." First, Labour matched up twin constituencies based upon geography and their chances for a Labour seat. Then, in the selection process, nominees from the twin constituencies were pooled; the woman applicant with the greatest proportion of the votes gained one candidacy, and the male applicant with the greatest proportion of votes gained the other candidacy.[2] The Scottish National Party stopped short of a formal quota rule, but because of the strong lobbying efforts of women within the party hierarchy, women's representation remained a priority on the party's agenda, and informal targets were largely adhered to in the party's nomination process (Russell, 2003).

In the first election to the Scottish Parliament in 1999, women won a strong presence with 37% of the seats. The Scottish Liberal Democrats, who relied on rhetoric only, ended up with 12% women MPs. In contrast, the Scottish Labour Party, with its direct rules, sent 50% women among its delegation (Brown et al., 2002). Despite a lack of quotas, women in the Scottish National Party fared well, gaining 43% of their party's seats. The Scottish Conservative Party ended up with only 17% women in its delegation (Russell, 2003; MacKay et al., 2003).

With a solid presence in the parliament, women organized a cross-party group of women to discuss relevant issues, which contributed toward planning "women-friendly" legislation and institutionalizing women's gains in the next election. In the second election, in May 2003, women inched up to claim nearly 40% of the seats.

Women and the National Assembly for Wales

Although women played a slightly less visible role in the process of establishing the National Assembly for Wales, they still played a central role, calling for presence in the newly elected body (Russell, 2003). In contrast to the Scottish case, women's networks were not as well established in Wales, and the established politicians made little public commitment to equality early on (Russell, 2003). While few in numbers, key members of the Welsh women's movement and women active inside the political parties strategized to push parties to take positive action to promote women's political equality (Chaney, 2003).

Women began their push early in the process of constitutional reform. In 1994, at the Parliament for Wales Campaign's Democracy Conference, women placed the equality issue on the agenda. Despite a lack of resources and organization, in the 1997 cross-party "Yes for Wales" prodevolution movement, women launched a complementary "Women Say Yes" campaign, pressing for party and electoral rules favorable to women's election (Chaney, 2003).

The "Women Say Yes" campaign persuaded the Welsh Labour Party to formally commit to promoting women's representation. After considerable debate and the threat of legal action from within, the Welsh Labour Party agreed to use twinning. In contrast, the Welsh Liberal Democrats only required gender-balanced short lists and offered women special training programs. Not only did the Welsh Conservative Party stay away from any form of quotas, they also avoided any debate over it altogether. The Plaid Cymru agreed on a measure called "zipping" to promote women on its regional lists. On each list, a woman occupied the number one and three positions. Yet importantly, the Plaid Cymru had no gender rules for constituency seats (Russell, 2003; Chaney, 2003).

The first election to the National Assembly for Wales proved a solid success for Welsh women—they won 40% of the seats. With "twinning," women from Welsh Labour won 50% of their party's seats. The Welsh Liberal Democrats sent 50% as well (three of their six seats). The Plaid Cymru had 35% women in their delegation, though few women won constituency seats. Finally, with little attention paid to gender balancing, the Welsh Conservatives had no women in their eight-person delegation (Russell, 2003). Like the Scottish case, women in the Welsh Assembly were able to consolidate their gains over time. The subsequent 2003 election marked a new high—women won 50% of the seats. As a result, the Welsh Assembly is a world leader in women's representation.

In sum, in the first elections to both the Scottish Parliament and the Welsh Assembly, women achieved strong parliamentary presence through party channels. Key groups of women found success within parties because they made their claims for presence resonate within a broader process of democratization. As a result, the inclusion of women became an integral part of parties' attempts to achieve a more modern face and an electorally salient issue. And women in some parties were quite adept at gaining formal party rules to ensure women's presence. Certainly the lack of incumbents in the fresh assemblies provided the ideal conditions for these forces to work within.

The House of Commons

The devolved assembly elections primed the agenda for the British general elections. Meg Russell (2003) notes that the lively debate over women's presence in the new assemblies kept the issue of women's political equality on the parties' radar screen. Without this debate, she argues that women's representation would not have been mentioned after the 1997 general elections until 2001.

After its landslide victory in 1997, the British Labour Party entered government with a broad agenda to democratize British politics, from reforming the House of Lords to devolution, and sending more women to the House of Commons fit well within this package (Russell, 2003). In the 2001 general election, Labour was the only party to employ formal measures to promote women. Although they did not go back to the all-women short lists (AWS) of the 1997 election, Labour mandated gender-balanced short lists in all vacant seats. This policy was not nearly as effective as AWS, and the number of Labour women MPs dropped from the historic 101 down to 95.

Setbacks at Westminster stood in contrast to the great gains in Wales and Scotland, and it became apparent that some form of positive discrimination was necessary to break the status quo. Given the fact that an industrial tribunal found AWS to be in violation of the 1975 Sex Discrimination Act, any new party-level rule changes would require a change in national law. The drive for national-level legal change came from the Labour Party. In early 2000, Joan Ruddock (Labour's former minister for women) spearheaded an initiative for such legal reform, and she persuaded 100 MPs from all parties to sign on. Bolstering Ruddock's efforts, legal research showed that a law permitting positive discrimination would not break European Union or international human rights law (Russell, 2003). Meg Russell (2001), a former Labour Party official-turned-scholar at the Constitution Unit, argued that the European Court of Justice was not likely to take up the issue based upon the precedent established by the new French law (discussed below), which actually mandated equality for women. Further, she showed that the United Nations' Convention on Elimination of All Forms of Discrimination Against Women allows for positive action measures (Childs, 2003).

With heightened pressure from women across the spectrum and seemingly free from legal challenge, in October 2000 Labour's annual conference voted to support a new law to allow parties to implement policies to improve women's representation. By early 2001, Labour's election manifesto documented their support, and the Queen's speech publicly voiced Labour's commitment to introducing this new legislation (Russell, 2003).

In October 2001, the Sex Discrimination (Election Candidates) Bill was introduced to the House of Commons. The bill amends the original Sex Discrimination Act, clarifying that the act does not apply to measures adopted by political parties designed to reduce inequality among men and women. The new act allows parties to use positive discrimination measures—but only if they wish to do so (Women and Equality Unit, 2002). It applies to national and regional elections (except for mayor). A sunset clause ensures that the measure is temporary, and it expires in 2015.

To build greater support for the bill, several organizations disseminated research pointing toward the effectiveness of quota-type policies in facilitating women's election. The Equal Opportunities Commission published a report in 2001 that concluded the AWS policy and quotas in the EU were the "decisive factor" in increasing women's numerical representation. Similarly, the Fawcett Society distributed a report arguing that the only way to increase women's representation was through the use of some form of quotas (Women and Equality Unit, 2002).

Next the bill came up for debate in the House of Commons. Ironically, this formal proceeding is more accurately characterized by a lack of debate over party use of gender quotas. Few male MPs attended the debate, and women spoke disproportionately, most in favor (Childs, 2003). The majority of those in favor argued for positive action measures on the grounds of leveling the playing field for potential female candidates (Childs, 2002).

Passing both houses with cross-party support, the Sex Discrimination (Election Candidates) Bill became law in February 2002 (Russell, 2003; Childs, 2003). The lack of controversy over the bill stems from its voluntary nature—no party is obligated to adopt quotas. Indeed, most MPs agree that there should be more women's faces in their midst, but there is partisan disagreement over the means to achieve gender balance (Childs, 2002).

After the passage of this new bill, parties could now freely adopt positive action measures. Labour women renewed their efforts to gain formal measures to get more women elected. By relying solely on balanced short lists in 2001, Labour saw its percentage of women MPs slip for the first time in twenty years. MP Joan Ruddock voiced her rationale, stating, "I am certain that my party will have to re-adopt all-women shortlists because no other measure— we have tried the others that I know—will work for Westminster selections and elections" (quoted in Childs, 2003: 89). The Labour Party agreed to use

Table 10.2 British Women MPs, by Party, as of 2005

Party	% Women MPs	Change 1975–2005 (% Points)
Labour	23	+18
Conservative	8	+5
Liberal Democrat	10	+10

Source: Data for 2002 election from Childs (2003)

AWS in 50% of vacant seats in the next election, and if an insufficient number of constituencies volunteer, the central party leadership is committed to enforcing it (Childs, 2002).

Although Labour slipped in the percentage of women in its parliamentary delegation from 1997 to 2002, Labour still led the British parties in women's representation. Table 10.2 displays the percentages of women among each party's MPs after the 2002 election, and the final column denotes the percentage point increase in women MPs from 1975 to 2005. After the 2002 general election, Labour led with 23% women, the Liberal Democrats were a distant second with 10%, and the Conservatives were last with 8%. Certainly Labour made great strides, increasing by eighteen percentage points over the past thirty years.

The Conservative Party has largely stalled in improving women's position in parliament. In the 2002 election, 14% of Conservative candidates were women, but only 8% of their MPs ended up being women (Studlar, 2004). Unlike Labour, the Conservatives' manifesto made no mention of women's representation (Studlar, 2004). Yet it appears that there may be some intraparty debate over the importance of sending more Conservative women to Westminster. In the House of Commons debate over the Sex Discrimination (Election Candidates) Bill, Conservative MP Teresa May hinted at some potential changes (possibly even gender-balanced short lists) in her party over the issue of formal measures to improve women's presence, stating that "parties move on their attitudes" (quoted in Childs, 2003: 84).

Although Liberal Democratic women won few seats in the general election, women's political equality is a salient issue within the party. The Liberal Democrats' 2002 manifesto makes reference to "family-friendly and efficient working practices for Parliament" (as quoted in Studlar, 2004: 10). In addition, women within the party are growing impatient, and they have upped their lobbying efforts for a formal mechanism to improve their numbers in the House.

The Liberal Democrats voiced their support for the Sex Discrimination (Election Candidates) Bill. During the bill's debate in the House of Commons, Liberal Democratic MP and Spokesperson for Women Evan Harris said his party "recognized that we have a problem" regarding women's representation and called for some direct action to improve women's situation (quoted in Childs, 2003: 85). Despite support for the bill, the party's 2002 conference rejected the proposition of using all-women short lists (Childs, 2003).

More Women in Westminster—Does It Matter?

The great strides made by women in Westminster in 1997 prompted a wave of research to assess whether women's presence impacts politics as usual. Sarah Childs (2004) conducted interviews with the newly elected women MPs and found that these women do feel like they speak with a different voice—a less confrontational, more problem-solving tone. Yet these new female MPs note that their approach is not valued, but rather that it is perceived by male colleagues as an area in which they must improve if they are to become effective within Parliament. Cowley and Childs's (2003) analysis reveals that Labour's newly elected women MPs, when compared with Parliament as a whole, voted overwhelmingly with the government. Rather than a signal of some tendency for women to be compliant, these women's propensity to toe the party line may reflect the process by which Labour nominated and elected them in 1997. Many of the newly elected women gained nomination through the central party organization's AWS policy. As a result, the AWS women may have a stronger sense of loyalty toward the central party leadership. In addition, the constituencies in which these women were nominated complied with the AWS policy before other constituencies, and this compliance may signal the local party's already more favorable attitude toward the party leadership.

Women in the Bundestag, 1998–2005

Women made only slight gains in seats in the Bundestag into the 2002 election. The stagnation stems, in part, from women's inability to win more constituency seats. Overall, women continue to fare better on the party lists (through which women have won 61% of their seats) than in constituency seats (through which women have only won the remaining 39% of their seats).

Table 10.3 displays the percentage of women MPs for each party, and the final column presents the increase from the 1970s up to early 2005. The Social Democrats (SPD) had 38% women in its parliamentary party after the 2002 election (up from 35% in 1998). This jump represents an increase of thirty-three percentage points over thirty years. The Free Democrats (FDP) sent 21% women, largely unchanged from the 20% women in its 1998 delegation. Finally, Alliance 90/The Greens actually witnessed an underrepresentation of men, with 58% women in their parliamentary party.

Table 10.3 German Women MPs, by Party, as of 2005

Party	% Women MPs	Change 1975–2005 (% Points)
Social Democrat (SPD)	38	+33
Christian Democrat (CDU)	23	+16
Christian Social (CSU)	21	+19
Free Democrats (FDP)	21	+16
Alliance 90/The Greens	58	+22
Party of Democratic Socialists (PDS)	100*	N/A

Sources: Data for 2002 election from McKay (2004).
*The PDS sent two MPs to the Bundestag after the 2002 election. Both are women.

Table 10.3 also shows that the Christian Democrats (CDU) and Christian Social Union (CSU) sent 23% and 21% women to the Bundestag, respectively. The CDU's "quorum" resolution (a loose form of quotas), passed in 1996, appears to have helped CDU women gain seats. The quorum became binding in December 2001, and one would expect to observe the greatest rise in women's parliamentary presence in the subsequent election. Indeed, the 23% achievement in 2002 represents a rise of five percentage points from the 1998 election. The quorum's impact focused on the list candidates, where women gained 34% of the slots. Since the resolution is not applied to constituency seats, women only made up 10% of the constituency candidates (McKay, 2004).

While the quorum resolution has been somewhat effective, it appears to be gaining only marginal legitimacy among women in the party. McKay (2004) cites a poll at the party's 1999 federal conference in which the majority of the women polled supported the resolution as a temporary measure to even the playing field, and in a 2001 survey, about half of CDU women felt the quorum had a positive impact for women in the party. The emphasis on the rule's temporary nature and the "quorum" terminology certainly help to fit the idea of positive discrimination within the conservative ideology.

In contrast to its sister party, as of 2004 the CSU still eschewed quotas in any form. Yet in the 2002 election, the CSU elected nearly the same proportion of women to its parliamentary delegation as did its partner, the CDU. One might suspect that the debate over quotas brought women's equality onto the party agenda and pointed out women's deficit within the CDU/CSU, and its saliency has brought women modest gains in nominations. In addition, the CSU may have used informal measures in an attempt to stave off calls for controversial quotas.

Although women's progress in the German Bundestag appears minimal after the 2002 election, trends in the party system and within individual parties may offer unique openings for women to make gains in the next election. First, the broad political climate lends itself to competition for women's votes. The catchword in the 2002 election was "Wechselwähler," which means the changing voter. As the traditional group bonds based upon class and religion continue to erode and party attachments further decline, electoral choice is increasingly volatile (Dalton and Bürklin, 2003). Women's votes are still up for grabs, as they have been since the CDU lost its lock on women voters in the 1980s. Where key women in party politics can connect winning women's votes to a party's greater commitment to women's political equality, women may gain stronger party measures to ensure their election.

Within this climate of electoral volatility, the German party organizations themselves have witnessed developments that offer potential changes in the status quo. Importantly, women's advancement in CDU party politics must be set against the enormous party crisis that occurred after the 1998 election. Former Chancellor Kohl was found to have an unreported personal slush fund, and he was forced to step down from control of a party that had largely coalesced around his personal leadership (Clemens, 2000). The scandal toppled the tight party leadership circle, and the top party post was up for grabs. The party elected Angela Merkel as its leader in January 2002, the first woman to hold this post in a unified Germany. Merkel's ascendance to top leadership marks a victory for women in the CDU. In fact, the CDU's general secretary has called the party "the model for other social groups who devote themselves to the promotion of women" (as quoted in McKay, 2004: 69).

However, one cannot take Merkel's election as an about-face in the traditionally patriarchal party culture. Reports surfaced of "backroom efforts to block Merkel's elevation—a secret meeting among some top male colleagues at a 'smoke-filled Ratskeller' in Lübeck . . ." (Clemens, 2000:80). Despite her popularity among the party faithful, Merkel did not win the chancellor nomination. Some suggest party insiders knew that the odds were stacked against Merkel in seeking the chancellor-candidate position (McKay, 2004). The CSU's position vis-à-vis its partner CDU was strengthened by the scandal, and a senior CSU figure, Edmund Stoiber, claimed the nomination for chancellor. Further, McKay (2004) notes that the buzz among party officials concerning Merkel continually focused on whether or not she was "up to the job," and her leadership abilities were often questioned (70). This cloud of doubt stands in stark contrast to the confidence and allegiance inspired by Kohl. Despite difficulties, Merkel was re-elected to the chair position in 2002 and is a contender for the party's next chancellor-candidate. Despite Angela Merkel's election as the head of the CDU, as of 2003, the CDU still had fewer women in top-level positions than the SPD (Rueschemeyer, 2003).

The CDU's shake-up brings potential advantages for women in the party. The scandal brought calls from outside and within the party for a process of democratization, especially in terms of increasing transparency and widening the circle of party leadership. Clemens (2000) calls this the "healthy shock effect." Women might use this larger process of democratization to frame their claims for greater inclusion and diversity in decision-making positions. Further, the absence of Kohl's uber-centralized leadership style opened up spaces for newcomers within the party. In effect, there was turnover among the party leadership, which had long been dominated by men—namely, older men loyal to Kohl. In 2000, party delegates elected ten women (37%), out of the twenty-seven total, to the executive committee. This number is more than that required by the semiquota, and six of the top ten vote-getters were women (Clemens, 2000). With a greater presence among the highest party echelons, these key CDU women may be able to tighten up the quorum policy and to help women gain more constituency seats.

Angela Merkel's rise to CDU party chair not only impacted her party, but it also sent shock waves across the German party system. Women in the Social Democratic Party (SPD) were disappointed not to have been the first major party to reach this goal, and this failure renewed debate within the SPD over gender politics (McKay, 2004). The SPD's 40% quota has been in place for fifteen years now, and it has been an effective method in creating openings for women. In the 2002 elections, the SPD's candidates composed 40% on the lists, and nearly 40% in constituency seats, as well (McKay, 2004). Yet in no election have women been able to rise above the quota "ceiling."

ASF, the SPD's women's organization, continues to lobby to keep women's equality on the party agenda, and it aims to raise the 40% goal to 50%, calling for parity for women. In 1999, the SPD adopted the principles of gender mainstreaming, and in 2001, a party commission sought to apply this principle more rigidly to party organizational development (McKay, 2004). In addition, the SPD has initiated a mentoring program for junior women.

The proportion of women MPs from the Free Democratic Party (FDP) has remained nearly stagnant since 1990, hovering around 20%. Yet the FDP remains staunchly against any formal measures to directly increase women's presence. In 2002, the FDP's party executive committee made plans to draw in more women at the party's grass roots, with the rationale that the committee could thus solve their underrepresentation problem by increasing the pool of applicants for higher party posts and elected office. These plans resulted in the 2003 Frauenkampagn, which aimed to increase women's membership from 23% to 30%. The party's top leadership circles continue to be dominated by men: women make up only 19% of the party executive committee, and there are no women among the party's deputy chairs (McKay, 2004).

The proverbial catch-22 persists for the FDP; it is not clear whether the FDP has few women at the top because there are few to draw upon at the lower rungs, or whether the FDP fails to attract more women activists because of its patriarchal image. So far, the bottom-up approach has yielded glacial results, and the lessons from rival parties point toward the efficacy of top-down strategies to promote women for powerful positions. Women within the FDP want gender quotas, but their requests have been turned down at party conferences (Rueschemeyer, 1998). However, FDP women have not yet "sold" the party leadership on a connection between the party's patriarchal structure and its difficulty in attracting women voters and members. The ability of women to connect women's party and parliamentary presence to electoral concerns is paramount. Perhaps the party's current crisis in being out of government will create a political opportunity structure ripe for women to make claims on the party to modernize its image and attract a wider range of support.

Alliance 90/The Greens made a strong showing in the 2002 election, and the rising tide lifted women's boats as well. The party sent a delegation to the Bundestag in which men were in the minority. In 1999 the party had initiated a mentoring program in which women in top party positions mentored younger colleagues, and this mentorship program was later extended to young men, as well (McKay, 2004). Yet even within the egalitarian Green Party, quotas for women still appear necessary. Only 31.5% of their constituency candidates were women, but the party made up for this figure by allotting most of the slots on the party lists to women (McKay, 2004). Still, it is important for women to gain constituency seats, and parties must look to new mechanisms to improve women's chances.

Of special note, the Party of Democratic Socialism (PDS) sent a landmark delegation to the 2002 Bundestag. Of their two seats, both were held by women. Although the Bundestag election results were disappointing for the PDS, their image has certainly emerged as quite women-friendly. By 2002, the PDS had the largest proportion of female members of any German party, at 46% (McKay, 2004). The PDS still retains its quota, calling for at least 50% women at all levels in the party, and women gained both the number one and number two slots on the 2002 party list. In a survey of women MPs, Joanna McKay (2004) finds that women in the PDS "seem unanimous in the view that the quota is still necessary. However, many feel they have to defend the quota year in, year out, because some party members consider it to be undemocratic" (63). At the local level, and especially in the East, some party workers claim it is difficult to find women candidates, and they often ask to subvert the quota regulations. Because there are no sanctions for party branches that break the rules, women often fare worse at the local level (McKay, 2004). While women in the PDS have made terrific strides in parliamentary office and in party posts, these gains are offset by lower representation at the local level and a lack of power among the party's most powerful inner circle. For this reason, McKay (2004) argues that women in the PDS lack real power, and that party rules to promote women have yet to alter the party culture.

Women in the Finnish Eduskunta, 2005

Like Britain and Germany, major changes in the political system also characterize post-1998 Finland. Finland had gradually moved from a system of shared power between the parliament and the president since the 1950s, and this trend was reinforced in the new Finnish constitution of March 2000. Under the new constitution, the Finnish president has less power in domestic policymaking (Raunio, 2001; Paloheimo, 2003). With more parliamentary control, political parties have gained power in making policy. Popular thought has often reasoned that where office holding portends more power, women will be marginalized (i.e., women's high levels of representation in the largely rubber-stamp parliaments of the former Communist nations, yet their lack of presence among the real leadership circles). Yet even as parliamentarians gained power with the 2000 constitution, women's strong presence in the Eduskunta appears institutionalized.

In the March 2003 election, women won 38% of the seats in the Eduskunta overall. This percentage is virtually unchanged from the 1999 election (37%). Women, it seems, cannot break the 40% ceiling in the Finnish parliament. The 2003 election did bring a breakthrough in women's power holding. The Center party (KESK) won the most votes, and the Center-led coalition government is led by Anneli Jäätteenmäki, Finland's first female prime minister.

A great deal of variation exists across the Finnish parties in women's numerical representation. Table 10.4 displays the percentage of women MPs in the Finnish Eduskunta for each party as of early 2005, and the percentage point gains for each party since the mid-1970s. The Finnish Green Party sent an overwhelmingly female delegation to the Eduskunta after the 2003 elections—71% women. In contrast, the prime minister's Center Party (KESK) sent only 24% women, a number that has only increased by six percentage points over the last thirty years. The National Coalition Party (KOK), which fared poorly in the 2003 election, held 38% women in its parliamentary party. This is a high percentage, relative to its sister center-rightist parties across Western Europe. Finally, the Social Democrats (SDP) nearly achieved parity, with 45% women MPs. The SDP has made some of the greatest gains over the past three decades, rising twenty-one percentage points.

Similar to the recent processes in Britain and France, Finnish women focused their efforts on both political parties *and* state-level institutions to facilitate their political representation, and chapter 7 detailed this process. The important point that sets the Finnish case apart is that women in Finland initiated this dual strategy to press both the state and political parties much earlier than in most Western European nations. For example, in 1972 Finland

Table 10.4 Finnish Women MPs, by Party, as of 2005

Party	% Women MPs	Change 1975–2005 (% Points)
Social Democrat (SDP)	45	+21
Center (KESK)	24	+6
National Coalition (KOK)	38	+13
Green	71	N/A
Left Alliance	26	+4

Source: Data for 2003 election compiled and tallied from Eduskunta website, July 30, 2004, at www.eduskunta.fi

established the Council for Equality. In 1987, parliament passed the Act on Equality Between Men and Women. In 1995 parliament passed a national law to promote equality, amending the constitution to allow for positive discrimination measures to improve women's equality in state institutions. Although that act does not apply to parliament, it did give women in party politics one more source of leverage in pressing for equality in the party hierarchy and in elected office.

In short, women still enjoy a strong position within Finnish parties and in parliament. Although rising above 40% has proven to be an elusive goal, in each election Finnish women have been able to consolidate their presence. The party-state strategy brought Finnish women early gains in elected office and provided a solid foundation. Certainly the lack of a strong movement outside of political parties has not resulted in a backlash.

French Parity and Opportunity Structures

Although France is not included in the empirical analysis in the main text (because of its exclusion from the published party data handbooks used in this study), recent developments in France provide an extremely interesting case in women's claims for parliamentary presence. With the passage of a new law, France has "one of the most radical quota policies in Europe" (Russell and O'Cinneide, 2003: 587). One of the strongest claims of this book has been that the mechanisms to improve women's parliamentary presence are best achieved through political parties. France's national-level policy sheds some light on how women can simultaneously press for change through more than one institutional channel. Further, the French case provides new evidence for the efficacy of recognizing political and institutional opportunity structures.

The Movement for Parity

At the beginning of the 1990s, the French feminist movement appeared stagnant (Gaspard, 2001). Soon, women advanced a new set of claims, and through newly formed organizations, they called for equal representation for women in politics. These efforts culminated in unprecedented rule changes in the French constitution.

According to Dauphin and Praud (2002), the parity movement was not a large social movement; rather, it began in 1992 as a set of organizations composed of women active within political parties. The women demanded parity in elected office, to be enshrined in law. The movement's approach was innovative, both in the use of new terminology and in the call for equal numbers of women. Most women across Europe pressed for 30%, or even 40%, quotas, falling short of the 50% that reflects women's proportion of the population.

The parity movement gained momentum in 1995 after the European Commission investigated women's political power in the European Union nations. Women for parity first aimed at the European level, but they later found better reception at the level of the French state and among French political parties (Jenson and Valiente, 2003). The word "parity" finds its legitimacy in long-standing French democratic ideals of liberty and equality, and thus it fit well with French political values (Jenson and Valiente, 2003).

French Parties and Rule Changes

As shown in table 10.1, France ranks toward the bottom of established industrial nations in women's numerical representation, both in 1975 and still in 2004. Without substantial pressure from women's organizations, up to the 1990s French political parties paid little more than lip service to issues of women's parliamentary presence. In 1982, the Socialist Party pushed national legislation requiring that electoral lists be composed of no more than 75% of either men or women. Although the law passed both Houses, it was struck down by the Conseil Constitutionnel, which cited the unconstitutionality of making distinctions based on sex (Russell and O'Cinneide, 2003).

French political parties have adopted some party-level rules designed to improve women's parliamentary presence. Since 1974, the French Socialist Party (PS) has had a 10% women's quota rule in its party statutes, and the bar was gradually raised to 30% over twenty years. However, the Socialists only loosely implemented the quota rule, resulting in little progress (Gaspard, 2001). In 1988, the French Green Party included a rule in its statutes requiring equal numbers of men and women (Dauphin and Praud, 2002). However, the Greens are a small party in France, and their quota policy did not ignite a process of contagion across the party system.

Rather than a push from the Greens, it was an intraparty crisis that renewed the French Socialists' debate over women's representation. After losing handily in 1993, the Socialist Party sought ways to gain new groups of voters. In the 1995 presidential elections, Lionel Jospin, leader of the PS, specifically targeted women voters. He reasoned that by increasing women's faces among the party's delegation to parliament, the PS might gain greater electoral support among women (Gaspard, 2001; Dauphin and Praud, 2002). Jospin's public support for women's equality did create competition among the French presidential candidates to state their support for more women in French politics (with the exception of Jean-Marie Le Pen). Unfortunately for women in French parties, this competition remained largely a war of words and did not yield increases for women in subsequent elections.

The Socialists' Jospin later went beyond rhetoric, pushing for 30% women candidates in the 1997 legislative elections, convincing his party to agree on a form of Britain's all-women short lists. Some electoral districts were designated "women only." The Left did return to power, but women had been nominated in largely unwinnable seats, and as a result only 16.7% of the elected Socialist MPs were women (Russell and O'Cinneide, 2003).

After the election, Prime Minister Jospin called for a revision of the French constitution to allow for laws designed to achieve parity for women in elected office (Gaspard, 2001). In early 1999, a bill was introduced calling for regional council election lists to be composed of no more than 75% of either sex. Just as in 1982, France's Constitutional Council declared this law unconstitutional.

Faced with a setback, advocates for parity set their sights on a constitutional amendment. In 1999, the French parliament passed an amendment to allow for rules requiring a gender balance, modifying Articles 3 and 4 of the French constitution (Dauphin and Praud, 2002). The new electoral law went so far as to require political parties to nominate equal proportions of men and women candidates on their local election lists. The new law brought great gains for women in the local elections of 2001.

The bill laid out a different set of rules for national elections, which are based in single-member districts, making list balancing impossible. The law stipulates that parties that nominate fewer than 49% women candidates may lose their state funding. Yet most parties used the tried-and-true loophole; they nominated women in unwinnable seats. In the first round, 39% of the candidates were women. By the second run-off round, the percentage of women candidates dipped to 24% (Russell and O'Cinneide, 2003). Other parties chose to ignore the new law, accepting the financial penalty (Russell and O'Cinneide, 2003). As a result, the new rule changes did not bring great gains for women in the French parliament in the 2002 general election. In the end, as table 10.1 shows, the percentage of women in the National Assembly amounted to only 12.3%.

The French case yields several points that are consistent with the arguments of this book. The overriding point is that political parties are still key to increasing women's presence in parliament. It was the French Socialist Party (PS) that drove early calls for rule changes, and the parity movement coupled with the PS that lobbied for the constitutional amendment. Further, electoral concerns created the context for party efforts to support women. The Socialists' fall in the polls in the early 1990s created incentives for Jospin to target women voters by presenting more women for office.

On a separate note, it appears from the French case that national-level quota laws may not be as effective as party-level quota mechanisms. Most parties violated either the spirit or the letter of the new law in the general elections. As opposed to local elections where the quotas were more easily implemented, at the national level it was more difficult to find a formula to increase the number of women than in list-based elections. In addition, national elections are high-stakes elections, and power is not redistributed without a fight. Faced with challenges, French parties ducked the gender quotas. One might suspect that in order for the true gatekeepers—party leaders—to enforce quotas, they have to be convinced of the electoral payoff for their party. In cases such as Britain and Germany, women in top-level party positions sold party leaders on the benefits of gender quotas for gaining women's votes and modernizing the party's image in the long run. In France, with the exception of the Socialists, there is no indication that the remaining parties, who were also subject to the quota laws, perceived such advantage. In short, the evidence seems to support the idea that political parties must undergo an internal process in which the party's political opportunity structure is ripe for institutional changes. Otherwise, without the proper context and central party backing, rule changes are likely to be ignored. Further, gender quota rules are ineffective if they are not backed up with real sanctions and if they allow for wide loopholes. A more specific quota that mandates an equal proportion of women in winnable seats may bring French women greater gains.

Where Do Women and Parties Go from Here?

The twenty-first century certainly brings the possibility for women in Western Europe to achieve full equality in national legislatures. With strategic pressure on parties, and on state institutions, women can gain more than incremental increases in representation. One of the clearest trends is that parties from across the ideological spectrum are seeking new issues upon which they can show a more modern face to the electorate. Including more women among their power structures is one way in which parties can appear more inclusive and democratic. Further, pressing for national laws concerning gender quotas may bring results, even if implementing quotas is voluntary. These rule changes give women another peg upon which to hang their claims. Advocates of equality for women in parliament can insist that their parties measure up to national standards.

The next general election in Britain may bring great gains for women in the House of Commons. With a legal environment favorable to rules to directly increase women's parliamentary presence, Labour's commitment to using the all-women short lists in 50% of vacant seats, and competitive pressure on the Conservatives and Liberal Democrats (who have both hinted they may use informal measures), women will at the very least face fewer barriers to election.

In Germany, candidate gender quotas helped women make rapid gains in the Social Democratic and Green Parties. However, based on interviews with German MPs, Katharina Inhetveen (1999) found that quotas were still controversial in the late 1990s. Inhetveen theorizes that the German justification for more women in elected office—equality for all—runs at odds with the use of quotas, which reify gender differences. In other words, German culture may not be hospitable to quotas. Nevertheless, they remain in use and have been quite effective. Given that quotas remained contested, it is possible that gender balancing has not become institutionalized within parties, and women may lose ground in the future without these formal rules. Indeed, Inhetveen (1999) reports that most German politicians she interviewed believe the proportion of women in parliament would slip without formal rules to ensure their presence.

In contrast, Finnish parties never adopted formal quotas. Yet a confluence of women's pressure within parties and a specific set of favorable electoral rules led to a system in which gender-balanced lists became the norm. In other words, women's political equality has become part of the party culture. Thus, even without quotas, one does not expect to see a drop in women's representation in Finland. At the same time, Finnish women are not likely to achieve full equality in parliament in the near future. Their presence seems to have hit a point of equilibrium and there is little talk of new mechanisms to bolster women's position.

The great numerical gains made by women in Western European parliaments from the 1970s to the 1990s generated a great deal of recent research on whether women MPs are different from their male counterparts. In one of the most extensive studies, Joni Lovenduski and Pippa Norris (2003) conducted a survey of 1,000 national politicians in Britain in 2001. They found significant differences between male and female politicians over affirmative action policies such as quotas, even controlling for party, social background, and age of the MP. The positive attitudes of women political elites are especially important when coupled with one of the strongest findings of this book, that women in powerful positions in parties are essential to getting more women into powerful positions. Those groundbreaking women must be willing to "let the ladder down," and recent surveys point toward a growing recognition of the effectiveness of quota policies. New quota rules may take time to change party culture, but in the interim they continue to be an effective tool for new contenders such as women.

appendix a

List of Sources for Party Variables Used in the Study

1. **Percentage women** among the total of a party's MPs and candidates were collected from Richard Katz and Peter Mair (1992) and from the published statistics from the Inter-Parliamentary Union (1997) and *Women in Parliament 1945–1995: A World Statistical Survey.* 1995. Geneva, Inter-Parliamentary Union.

2. **Party types** are taken from Lane and Ersson (1991).

3. **Percentage of a party's votes and seats** in the election closest to but before 1975 through 1997 were collected from Richard Katz and Peter Mair (1992) and from the IPU website (www.ipu.org).

4. **Percentage of women** on the party's **national executive** is collected from Katz and Mair (1992) and updated with data from Steinenger (2000) for Austria, and Galligan (1998) for Ireland. Unpublished data was collected by party experts (Professor Paul Webb of the University of Sussex for the British Conservative Party, Karina Pedersen of the University of Copenhagen for the missing data on Danish parties), and from the parties themselves (Vera Claes from the Belgian Socialist Party, Thomas Hansen of the Norwegian Liberal Party, and Rachel McLean, National Women's Officer for the British Labour Party).

5. **Presence or absence of a party quota:** Initially collected from the Inter-Parliamentary Union (1992; 1995), Katz and Mair (1992), and then checked against the case study chapters in Lovenduski and Norris (1993), and also with data collected from country experts by Professor Richard Matland, University of Houston. Where there were any discrepancies among the data sources, I relied on the knowledge of the country experts.

6. Indices of Old and New Left politics: From Laver and Hunt (1992), I have added together both elite and voter-level scores of ideology based for each of the following issue positions. For each issue, a party could be scored from one to twenty; the lower the scores, the further left the party position on the issue. (I have recoded the variables in the opposite direction so that the sign of the relationship is clearer.) The variables break down as follows.

Old Left is based upon the addition of scores on these two issues:

(a) leader and voter adjusted mean scores on *increased services*
(b) leader and voter adjusted mean scores on *public ownership*

New Left is based upon the addition of scores on these two issues:

(a) leader and voter adjusted mean scores on *pro-permissive social policy vs. anti*
(b) leader and voter adjusted mean scores on *environment vs. growth*

7. Index of party centralization: The measure of party centralization in the data analysis is taken from Lane and Ersson (1987). They call it the "index of programmatic orientation," and it is a summary variable. Parties that require a higher degree of party integration and uniformity in adherence to the party's program score higher on this measure (Lane and Ersson, 1991: 126).

8. Level of candidate nomination: 1 = nom. at low level, 2 = other levels. I have supplemented Lane and Ersson (1987) scores for this measure by filling in data for missing parties upon the same criteria. I relied upon three sources that describe candidate selection: Gallagher (1991), Gallagher and Marsh (1988), and Norris (1996).

9. Year party founded: collected from Day (1988).

10. Effective district magnitude: collected from Taagepera and Shugart (1989).

appendix b

List of Sources for Survey Data

Cross-national data on attitudinal support for the women's movement, gender, and **vote intention** were collected from the Eurbarometer Studies. These data were acquired from the Inter-university Consortium for Political and Social Research (ICPSR) at the University of Michigan in Ann Arbor. The 1970–92 Cumulative Eurobarometer Study was supplemented with later data from the Eurobarometer 39.0 (ICPSR #6195), EB 39.4 (#6194), EB 42.0 (#2563), EB 43.1 (#6839), EB 44.1 (#6536), EB 44.3 (# 2443), EB 40.0 (#6360), EB 43.1 (#6840), EB 44.0 (#6721), and EB 46.1 (#6940).

Variables on support for the women's movement and vote intention were taken from the Eurobarometer 1975 (ICPSR# 7416), 1977 EB 8 (#7604), and 1983 EB 19 (#8152).

There are two Eurobarometer surveys in most years. Therefore, the average was taken from the two observations.

Data from Britain on gender and party vote choice were collected from the British Election Studies (BESIS). These data were acquired from the ICPSR, and were originally made available by the ESRC Archive at the University of Essex, England. The cumulative file was supplemented with the British General Election Cross Survey, 1997 (ICPSR #2615).

Data from Germany on gender and party vote choice were collected from the German Election Studies. These data were acquired from the Zentralarchiv für empirische Sozialforschung (ZA), University of Cologne, Germany.

Data from Finland on gender and party vote choice were collected from the Finnish Election Studies. These data were made available by the Finnish Social Science Data Archives at the University of Tampere.

notes

Note to Chapter 1

1. The ten nations included in this book are Austria, Belgium, Denmark, Finland, Germany, Ireland, Netherlands, Norway, Sweden and the UK. See table 1.2 for a list of parties.

Note to Chapter 2

1. Although the focus of this book is on opportunity structures within political parties, it is important to mention Karen Beckwith's (2003) application of the restructuring of opportunities at the state level to women's "parliamentary presence" (as she so aptly titles this issue) in Britain, France, and the United States. Beckwith argues that as power has shifted up to supranational bodies, and down through devolution, women have recognized and used these new points of access to press for greater representation.

Notes to Chapter 3

1. Kunovich and Paxton (2003) find that the degree of women among the party elite affects women's numerical representation in parliament only in nonproportional representation systems. Their tempered support for the importance of women among party decision makers likely results from their worldwide analysis and their focus on national-level patterns. Rather than examining women activists at the party level, the authors average the percentage of women party elites for all parties in the system.

2. The data is arranged first by nation, then by party, and then by year, providing a stacked series of observations for each party over time.

Notes to Chapter 4

1. Parties have adopted not only candidate quotas, but internal quotas, as well. Intraparty quotas aim to increase the number of women in high-level party positions. Some parties have set gender quotas for their national executives (e.g., the Irish Workers' Party), and others have set quotas for their party conventions (e.g., the U.S. Democratic and Republican Parties). The quota system has been much more commonly used within party structures than for legislative elections (IPU, 1994). However, these quotas are an indirect way to increase women's parliamentary representation. In addition, several parties with internal quotas have essentially created token positions for women within the party. Candidate quotas are more comparable because they are standard across parties. While internal party quotas are important on their own, we will concentrate on candidate quotas and targets in this research.

2. Surprisingly, these three sources differed in some cases. For example, while the IPU data indicate that the Norwegian Christian People's Party has a 50% quota on women candidates, the Katz and Mair data indicate that there is no candidate quota at all. Because of the inconsistencies among sources, my coding decision was to register a quota where one source cites a quota, even if another source mentions nothing about it.

3. The number of parties analyzed in this chapter is ten higher than the fifty parties analyzed in the rest of the book. The reason is that data on the proportion of women MPs by party is not published for all parties, limiting the scope of other chapters. However, I was able to obtain data on the adoption of candidate gender quotas for a broader spectrum of parties. In particular, this chapter adds the Austrian Socialist Party; Belgian Francophone and Flemish Socialist Parties, Christian Social, and Flemish and Francophone Ecology Parties; Irish Progressive Democrats and Greens; Dutch Radical Political and Green Left; and Swedish Environmental Party.

4. In my earlier research on gender quotas (Caul, 2001), Italy was part of my analysis, but it is not included here. The quota analysis of this book significantly updates and expands my early research. The Italian party system suffered a major shake-up in the 1990s, rendering updated, consistent analysis all but impossible.

5. For policy analysis, the standard practice is to use discrete-time models, which treat the unit at risk at predefined times (Box-Steffensmeier and Jones, 1997). These models are estimable using logit, and the interpretation of the coefficients is only slightly different.

6. The estimates are based on the following EHA model: ADOPT $i,t = \Phi$ (b_1 % Women MPs National Level 1975 $_{i,t}$ + b_2 %Women MPs 1972 Party Level + b_3 % Women Party Leadership 1975 $_{i,t}$ + b_4 Electoral System (District Magnitude) $_{i,t}$ + b_5 Year Quotas First Adopted in Party System $_{i,t}$ + b_6 Old Left Index $_{i,t}$ + b_7 New Left Index $_{i,t}$ + b_8 Level of Candidate Nomination $_{i,t}$ + b_9 Index of Institutionalization $_{i,t}$ + b_{10} Age of Party (Year Founded) $_{i,t}$). The conceptual dependent variable, ADOPT $_{i,t}$, is the probability that party i will adopt quotas in year t, given that the party has not adopted quotas prior to this point. It is measured by a series of zeros up to the year in which quotas are adopted (if at all). The symbol signifies the cumulative normal distribution of the function.

7. When the index of New Left politics is substituted for Old Politics, the overall model remains significant (log likelihood = 82.5, p = .001), and the coefficient yield-

ed by New Politics is comparable to that of Old ($B = -.45$, Exp (B) $=.64$, $p = .02$). Thus, for every point toward the left on the New Politics scale, a party is 26% more likely to adopt quotas.

8. Because they were established after 1972, the parties not included in the analysis presented on table 4.2 are the Greens in Austria, Belgium, Germany, Ireland, Italy, the Netherlands, and Sweden, and the Danish CD, the Finnish KOK, the Irish PD, the Italian DP, the Dutch CDA, and the Norwegian SV and Progress Parties.

9. The same analyses were also run for a larger set of parties by only examining the years 1982 to 1995. As such, parties established after 1972 and before 1982 are added to the dataset. The results are similar to those in the model in table 4.2. The year quotas were first adopted by a party in the party system, New Left values and electorally large parties are still found to be significant and strong indicators of the likelihood a party will adopt quotas or targets. By limiting the time frame most Green parties are included in the analysis, the number of parties increases to fifty-eight, and 57% of the cases score as adopting quotas or targets. Further, the -2 (log-likelihood ratio) is 142.35 and is significant.

10. The transformation of the logit coefficient (raising the number e to the B power), displayed under the label "Exp(B)," is the change in the hazard rate for a unit increase in the particular covariate. To find the percentage change as a function of a one-unit increase in the variable, one is subtracted from exp(B) and the difference is multiplied by 100. For dichotomous variables, this is called the "relative risk," and it is the ratio of the estimated hazard for a case with the characteristic of interest to the case without that characteristic.

11. Parties other than the Greens that score highly in terms of their concern for New Left values are the Danish Socialist People's Party and the Social Democrats; the Finnish People's Democratic Party; the Irish Labour Party; the Italian Progressive Democrats, Communists, and Radical Party; the Dutch Communists, Labour, Pacifist Socialist, Radical Political, and Democrats 66; the Swedish Communist Party; and the British Liberal Democrats.

12. Further evidence for this 20% threshold is in Thomas (1991; 1994), who finds that when women constitute 20% of the legislature in the United States, the legislature is more likely to pass bills concerning women.

Notes to Chapter 5

1. Unhappy with Labour's centrist drift, a faction of the party had broken away in 1981 and formed the Social Democratic Party (SDP). The SDP formed an electoral alliance with the Liberal Party, and those two parties finally merged to form the Liberal Democratic Party.

2. Data on gender and vote choice collected from the British Election Studies. See Appendix B for details.

3. Data on gender, support for the women's movement, and partisan preferences were collected from the most comprehensive cross-national source possible in terms of availability over time—the Eurobarometer Studies. By using these studies it is possible to track gender and attitudinal differences in the vote for the entire period of this study, 1970 to 1997. The advantage of the Eurobarometer is its longitudinal breadth

and consistency. Appendix B details the full list of the specific questions, variables, and studies that were used, and the archives from which these studies were obtained. The gender gap in partisan preference is measured using respondent vote intention.

4. Kaplan (1992) contends that "second wave" may be a misnomer in the case of the British and Scandinavian feminist movements, because women made continuous organized efforts to push for women's rights.

Notes to Chapter 6

1. Known as the Greens in their entrance into the German system in the early 1980s, the party's name changed in 1993 to Bündnis 90/Die Grünen after unification because of the merger of the West German Greens, the East German Greens, and an East German Civil Rights group called Alliance 90.

2. The Party of Democratic Socialism (PDS) entered the united German party system in 1990. For continuity's sake, the PDS is not analyzed here.

3. Data on gender and vote intention collected from German Election Studies. See Appendix B for details.

4. Data on gender, feminist values, and partisan preferences were collected from the Eurobarometer Studies. The advantage of the Eurobarometers is its longitudinal breadth and consistency. Appendix B details the full list of the specific questions, variables, and studies that were used, and the archives from which these studies were obtained. The gender gap in partisan preference is measured using respondent vote intention.

Note to Chapter 7

1. Data on gender and partisan preferences were collected from the Finnish election studies. Appendix B details the full list of the specific questions, variables, and studies that were used, and the archives from which these studies were obtained. The gender gap in partisan preference is measured using respondent vote intention.

Notes to Chapter 8

1. Feminist attitudes among a party's constituency might be a more powerful indicator of the proportion of women in their parliamentary delegation, yet this variable cannot be tested in a multivariate model because the long-term, consistent measures of feminist attitudes are not available for six of our ten countries.

2. The data is arranged first by nation, then by party, and then by year, providing a stacked series of observations for each party over time.

3. The sample size and resulting degrees of freedom allow for the legitimate use of ordinary least squares regression (OLS). I used a variety of time-series, cross-sectional methods. These same models were run with the dependent variable as the level of women MPs with a lag on the explanatory side of the equation (as presented), and with the dependent variable transformed into a first-differences measure. With the first-differences method, the dependent variable, the proportion of women MPs, was transformed into a measure of change from one election to the next. Through this process, most of the national-level variation is removed. Importantly, the results are fairly con-

sistent. In each model, women on the national executive committee, the gender gap, and a centralized party structure are the most important indicators. However, the model that transforms the dependent variable to a measure of change explains little of the adjusted variance.

4. Data is not published for some parties in certain years. Therefore, a pairwise deletion of missing cases is used, so that these cases are not dropped entirely from the analysis. Because data is missing from the gender gap variable for four countries, Models 1a and 1b were also run without the measure of the gender gap in votes. The results are similar to those in which the variable is included. Women on the national executive is the strongest predictor, followed by the measures of centralization and candidate nomination.

5. Country dummy-variables are not included in Models 1a or 2a, because the explanatory variable that describes the electoral system (district magnitude) is a national-level variable and appears to act as a dummy-variable. For the full model (1a and 2a), SPSS automatically drops the electoral system variable when the model is run with country dummies. Therefore, I present a scaled-down model without the insignificant electoral system variable. Dummy-variables for each country (minus one) can be included in Models 1b and 2b. Two of these country dummies are significant (Denmark and Finland). When the same model is run without country dummy-variables, the results are similar. The first-differences model was also run with and without country dummy-variables, and with dummy-variables for each year, as well (fixed-effects model). The results are consistent: again, the national executive, the gender gap, and centralization emerge as the most important.

6. A *lagged* increase in the proportion of women on the party's national executive is used in this model, because the theory indicates that women newly elected to top party positions pressure the party to increase women's parliamentary representation. The results of this pressure will not be observable until the next election. When a simple difference measure from one election to the next is used in the multivariate model, the indicator is insignificant.

Notes to Chapter 10

1. Under the new electoral system (additional member, AMS), Scottish voters elect a representative in their constituency, and there are additional "top-up" seats that complement this by adding a dimension of proportionality.

2. The twinning strategy certainly would not work in the House of Commons. This mechanism is most appropriate to a body with many open seats. Because of the single-member district system and the incumbency advantage, there is little turnover among MPs. Thus, vacancies are few and widely dispersed across the country. It would be nearly impossible to match up open seats.

references

Aberbach, Joel D., Robert Putnam, and Bert A. Rockman. 1981. *Bureaucrats and Politicians in Western Democracies*. Cambridge: Harvard University Press.

Aldrich, John H. 1998. *Why Parties?* Chicago: University of Chicago Press.

Appleton, Andrew and Daniel S. Ward. 1997. "Party Response to Environmental Change: A Model of Organizational Innovation." *Party Politics* 3(3): 315–40.

Atkeson, Lonna Rae. 2003. "Not All Cues Are Created Equal: The Conditional Impact of Female Candidates on Political Engagement." *Journal of Politics* 65(4):1040–61.

Baer, Denise. 1993. "Political Parties: The Missing Variable in Women and Politics Research." *Political Research Quarterly* 46(3): 547.

Baldez, Lisa. 2003. "Elected Bodies: The Gender Quota Law for Legislative Candidates in Mexico." Paper presented at the annual meetings of the American Political Science Association. Philadelphia, PA, August 28–31.

Bartolini, Stefano and Peter Mair. 1990. *Identity, Competition, and Electoral Availability*. New York: Cambridge University Press.

Baxter, Sandra and Marjorie Lansing. 1983. *Women and Politics*. Rev. Ed. Ann Arbor: University of Michigan Press.

Beck, Nathaniel and Jonathan Katz. 1995. "What to Do (And Not to Do) with Time-Series Cross-Sectional Data." *American Political Science Review* 89(3).

Beckwith, Karen. 2003. "The Gendering Ways of States: Women's Representation and State Reconfiguration in France, Great Britain, and the United States." In *Women's Movements Facing the Reconfigured State*, Lee Ann Banaszak, Karen Beckwith, and Dieter Rucht, eds. Cambridge: Cambridge University Press.

———. 1992. "Comparative Research and Electoral Systems: Lessons from France and Italy." *Women and Politics* 12(3): 1–33.

———. 1986. *American Women and Political Participation*. New York: McGraw Hill.

Bergman, Solveig. 1991. "Researching the Women's Movement: Considerations Arising Out of a Comparative Study." In *Moving On: New Perspectives on the Women's Movement*, Tayo Andreason et al., eds. Denmark: Aarhus University Press.

Berman, Sheri. 1997. "The Life of the Party." *Comparative Politics*. October: 101.

Berry, Frances Stokes. 1994. "Sizing Up the State of Policy Innovation Research." *Policy Studies Journal* 22(3): 442.

Berry, Frances Stokes and William D. Berry. 1990."State Lottery Adoptions as Policy Innovations: An Event History Analysis." *American Political Science Review* 84(2): 395.

———. 1992. "Tax Innovation in the States: Capitalizing on Political Opportunity." *American Journal of Political Science* 36(3): 715.

Bobo, Lawrence and Franklin D. Gilliam, Jr. 1990. "Race, Sociopolitical Participation and Black Empowerment" *American Political Science Review* 84: 377–93.

Borg, Sami and Risto Sankiaho. 1995. *The Finnish Voter.* Tampere: The Finnish Political Science Association.

Box-Steffensmeier, Janet M. and Bradford S. Jones. 1997."Time Is of the Essence: Event History Models in Political Science." *American Journal of Political Science* 41(4): 1414.

Bratton, Kathleen A. and Leonard P. Ray. 2002. "Descriptive Representation, Policy Outcomes and Municipal Day-Care Coverage in Norway." *American Journal of Political Science* 46(2): 428–37.

Brooks, Rachel, Angela Eagle, and Clare Short. 1990. *Quotas Now: Women in the Labour Party.* London: Fabian Society.

Brown, Alice. 1999. "The First Elections to the Scottish Parliament." *Representation* 36(3): 2012–36.

Brown, Alice et al. 2002. "Women and Constitutional Change in Scotland and N. Ireland." *Parliamentary Affairs* 55: 71–84.

Burrell, Barbara. 1994. *A Woman's Place is in the House: Campaigning for Congress in the Feminist Era.* Ann Arbor: The University of Michigan Press.

Butler, David and Donald E. Stokes. 1974. *Political Change in Britain: The Evolution of Electoral Choice.* 2nd Ed. London: Macmillan.

Campbell, Rosie. 2004. "Gender, Ideology and Issue Preference: Is There Such a Thing as a Political Women's Interest in Britain?" *British Journal of Politics and International Relations* 6:20–44.

Carmines, Edward G. and James A. Stimson. 1989. *Issue Evolution: Race and the Transformation of American Politics.* Princeton: Princeton University Press.

Carroll, Susan J. 2002. "Representing Women: Congresswomen's Perceptions of Their Representational Roles." In *Women Transforming Congress,* Cindy Simon Rosenthal, ed. Norman: University of Oklahoma Press.

———. 2000. *Representing Women: Congresswomen's Perceptions of Their Representational Roles.* Center for American Women and Politics. Online Posting. Retrieved 27 January 2001.

Caul, Miki. 2001. "Political Parties and the Adoption of Candidate Gender Quotas: A Cross-National Analysis." *Journal of Politics* 63(4): 1214–29.

Caul, Miki L. 1999. "Women's Representation in Parliament: The Role of Political Parties." *Party Politics* 5(1): 79–98.

Caul, Miki. 1997. "Women's Representation in National Legislatures: Explaining Differences across Advanced Industrial Democracies." Paper presented at the Western Political Science Association Meeting, March 13–15, Tucson, AZ.

Chaney, Paul. 2003. "Increased Rights and Representation: Women and the Post-Devolution Equality Agenda in Wales." In *Women Making Constitutions: New Pol-*

itics and Comparative Perspectives, Alexandra Dobrowolsky and Viven Hart, eds. New York: Palgrave Macmillan.

Charlot, M. "Women and Elections in Britain." In *Britain at the Polls, 1979,* Howard Penniman, ed. Washington, DC: American Enterprise Institute.

Childs, Sarah. 2004. "A Feminized Style of Politics? Women MPs in the House of Commons." *British Journal of Politics and International Relations* 6: 3–19.

———. 2003. "The Sex Discrimination (Election Candidates) Act 2002 and Its Implications." *Representation* 39(2): 83–93.

———. 2002. "Concepts of Representation and the Passage of the Sex Discrimination (Election Candidates) Bill" *Journal of Legislative Studies* 8(3): 90–108.

Clemens, Clay. 2000. "Crisis or Catharsis? Germany's CDU after the Party Finance Affair." *German Politics and Society* 18(2): 66–74.

Cole, Alexandra. 2002. "The German Election of 1998 and the Transformation of the German Left." *German Politics and Society* 20(1): 131–40.

Conover, Pamela Johnston. 1988. "Feminists and the Gender Gap." *Journal of Politics* 50(4): 985–1009.

Council for Equality, Finland. 1999. "Gender Equality in Work and Everyday Life." Pamphlet published by Council for Equality and Ministry for Social Affairs and Health.

Council of the European Union. 1999. "Women in the Decision-Making Process." Presidency Report. No. 11271/99 SOC 317.

Cowley, Phillip and Sarah Childs. 2003. "Too Spineless to Rebel? New Labour's Women MPs." *British Journal of Political Science* 33(3): 345–65.

Crewe, Ivor and D. T. Denver, eds. 1985. *Electoral Change in Western Democracies.* New York: St. Martin's Press.

Czudnowski, Moshe M. 1975. "Political Recruitment." In *Handbook of Political Science: Micropolitical Theory,* Vol. 2, Fred Greenstein and Nelson W. Polsby, eds. Reading, MA: Addison Wesley.

Dahlerup, Drude. 1988. "From a Small to a Large Minority: Women in Scandinavian Politics," *Scandinavian Political Studies* 11(4): 275.

———. 1986. *The New Women's Movement.* London: Sage.

———. 1985. "Women's Organizations in the Nordic Countries: Lack of Force or Counterforce?" In *Unfinished Democracy: Women in Nordic Politics,* Elina Haavio Mannila et al., eds. Oxford: Pergamon Press.

Dalton, Russell J. 1996. *Citizen Politics.* 2nd Ed. Chatham, NJ: Chatham House Publishers.

———. 1993. *Politics in Germany.* New York: Harper Collins Publishers.

———. 1991. "The Dynamics of Party System Change." In *Eurobarometer: The Dynamics of Public Opinion: Essays in Honor of Jacques-Rene Rabier,* Karlheinz Reif and Ronald Inglehart, eds. London: Macmillan.

Dalton, Russell and Wilhelm Burklin. 2003. "Wähler als Wandervögel: Dealignment and the German Voter." *German Politics and Society* 21(1): 57–74.

Dalton, Russell J., Scott C. Flanagan, and Paul Allen Beck, eds. 1985. *Electoral Change in Advanced Industrial Democracies.* Princeton: Princeton University Press.

Dalton, Russell J. and Alexandra Cole. 1993. "The Peaceful Revolution and German Electoral Politics." In *The New Germany Votes,* Russell J. Dalton, ed. Oxford: Berg.

Dalton, Russell J. and Martin Wattenberg. 2000. *Parties without Partisans: Political*

Change in Advanced Industrial Democracies. Oxford: Oxford University Press.

Darcy, R., Susan Welch, and Janet Clark. 1994. *Women, Elections, and Representation.* Lincoln: University of Nebraska Press.

Dauphin, Sandrine and Jocelyne Praud. 2002. "Debating and Implementing Gender Parity in France." *Modern and Contemporary France* 10(1): 5–11.

Davis, Rebecca Howard. 1997. *Women and Power in Parliamentary Democracies.* Lincoln: University of Nebraska Press.

Day, Alan J. 1988. *Political Parties of the World.* UK: Longman.

DeVaus, David and Ian McAllister. 1989. "The Changing Politics of Women: Gender and Political Alignment in 11 Nations." *European Journal of Political Research* 17: 241–62.

Dodson, Debra et al., eds.1995. *Voices, Views, and Votes: The Impact of Women in the 103rd Congress.* New Brunswick: Eagleton Institute of Politics, Rutgers, State University of New Jersey.

Downs, Anthony. 1957. *An Economic Theory of Democracy,* New York: Harper and Row.

Duverger, Maurice. 1955. *The Political Role of Women.* Paris: The United Nations Economic and Social Council.

Eduards, Maud. 1985. "Equality: How Equal." In *Unfinished Democracy: Women in Nordic Politics,* Elina Haavio-Mannila et al., eds. Oxford: Pergamon Press.

Epstein, Leon. 1980. *Political Parties in Western Democracies.* New Brunswick, NJ: Transaction Books.

"Explanatory Notes to Sex Discrimination (Election Candidates) Act 2002" Online Posting, British Government pages. http://www.legislation.hmso.gov.uk/acts/en2002/2002en02.htm (4/8/2004).

Franklin, Mark et al. 1991. *Electoral Change: Response to Evolving Social and Attitudinal Structures.* New York: Cambridge University Press.

Gallagher, Michael and Michael Marsh. 1988. *Candidate Selection in Comparative Perspective.* London: Sage Publications.

Galligan, Yvonne. 1998. *Women and Politics in Contemporary Ireland.* London: Pinfer.

———. 1996. "Women in Irish Politics." In *Politics in the Republic of Ireland,* John Coakley and Michael Gallagher, eds. Limerick: PSAI Press.

Gaspard, Francoise. 2001. "The French Parity Movement." In *Has Liberalism Failed Women? Assuring Equal Representation in Europe and the United States,* Jytte Klausen and Charles S. Maier, eds. New York: Palgrave.

Gay, Claudine. 1997. "Taking Charge: Black Electoral Success and the Redefinition of American Politics." Unpublished Ph.D. thesis, Harvard University, Cambridge, MA.

Gelb, Joyce. 2002. "Representing Women in Britain and the U.S.: The Quest for Numbers and Power." In *Women Transforming Congress,* Cindy Simon Rosenthal, ed. Norman: University of Oklahoma Press.

———. 1989. *Feminism and Politics.* Berkeley: University of California Press.

Githens, Marianne, Joni Lovenduski, and Pippa Norris. 1994. *Different Voices, Different Roles: Women and Politics in the US and Europe.* New York: Harper Collins.

Gray, Mark and Miki Caul. 2000. "Declining Voter Turnout in Advanced Industrial Democracies, 1950–1997: The Effects of Declining Group Mobilization." *Comparative Political Studies* 33(9): 1091–1122.

Griffin, L., H. McCammon, and C. Botsko. 1990. "The Unmaking of a Movement? The Crisis of U.S. Trade Unions in Comparative Perspective." In *Changes in Societal Institutions,* M. Hallinan et al., eds. New York: Plenum: 164–94.

Grofman, Bernard. (forthcoming). "SNTV, STV, and Single-Member District Systems: Theoretical Comparisons and Contrasts." In *Elections in Japan, Korea, and Taiwan under The Single Non-Transferable Vote: The Comparative Study of an Embedded Institution,* Bernard Grofman et al., eds. Ann Arbor, University of Michigan Press.

Guadagnini, Marila. 1993. "A 'Partiocrazia' without Women: The Case of the Italian Party System." In *Gender and Party Politics,* Joni Lovenduski and Pippa Norris, eds. London: Sage.

Haavio-Mannila, Elina. 1981a. "Finland." In *The Politics of the Second Electorate,* Joni Lovenduski and Jill Hills, eds. London: Routledge and Kegan Paul.

———. 1981b. "Women in the Economic, Political, and Cultural Elites in Finland." In *Access to Power: Cross-National Studies of Women and Elites,* Cynthia Fuchs Epstein and Rose Laub Coser, eds. London: George Allen and Unwin.

Haavio-Mannila, Elina and Torild Skard. 1985. "The Arena for Political Activity: The Position of Women in the Nordic Societies Today." In *Unfinished Democracy: Women in Nordic Politics,* Elina Haavio-Mannila et al., eds. Oxford: Pergamon Press.

Hall, Jane. 1981. "West Germany." In *The Politics of the Second Electorate,* Joni Lovenduski and Jill Hills, eds. London: Routledge.

Hampton, Mary N. 2000. "Reaching a Critical Mass? German Women and the 1998 Election." In *Power Shift in Germany,* David P. Conradt et al., eds. New York: Berghan Books.

———. 1995. "Women and the 1994 German Elections: Dissatisfaction and Accommodation." In *Germany's New Politics,* David P. Conradt et al., eds. Providence, RI: Berghahn Books.

Harmel, Robert and Kenneth Janda. 1982. *Parties and Their Environments.* New York: Longman.

Harmel, Robert et al. 1995. "Performance, Leadership, Factions and Party Change: An Empirical Analysis." *Western European Politics* 18(1): 1–33.

Harmel, Robert and Kenneth Janda. 1994. "An Integrated Theory of Party Goals and Party Change." *Journal of Theoretical Politics* 6(3): 259–87.

———. 1982. *Parties and Their Environments.* New York: Longman.

Harmel, Robert and Lars Svansand. 1997. "The Influence of New Parties on Old Parties' Platforms: The Case of the Progress and Conservative Parties of Denmark and Norway." *Party Politics* 3(3): 315–40.

Harvey, Anna L. 1998. *Votes without Leverage: Women in American Electoral Politics, 1920–1970.* New York: Cambridge University Press.

Hayes, Bernadette C. 1997. "Gender, Feminism, and Electoral Behavior in Britain." *Electoral Studies* 16(2): 203–16.

Hayes, Bernadette C., Ian McAllister, and Donley T. Studlar. 2000. "Gender, Postmaterialism, and Feminism in Comparative Perspective." *International Political Science Review* 21(4): 425–39.

Hayes, Bernadette and Ian McAllister. 1997. "Gender, Party Leaders, and Election Outcomes in Australia, Britain, and the United States." *Comparative Political Studies* 4: 299–326.

REFERENCES

Heath, Anthony , Roger Jowell, and John Curtice. 1985. *How Britain Votes.* Oxford: Pergamon Press.

High-Pippert, Angela and John Comer. 1998. "Female Empowerment: The Influence of Women Representing Women." *Women & Politics* 19(4): 51–66.

Hills, Jill. 1981. "Britain." In *The Politics of the Second Electorate,* Joni Lovenduski and Jill Hills, eds. London: Routledge.

Hoge, Warren. May 23, 2000. "Quality Time (and Diapers) at 10 Downing." *New York Times.*

Holli, Anne Maria. 1997. "On Equality and Trojan Horses: The Challenge of the Finnish Experience to Feminist Theory." *The European Journal of Women's Studies* 4: 133–64.

———. 1996. "Check-mating the State? Argumentation Strategies in Finnish Equality Policies." *NORA: Nordic Journal of Women's Studies* 4(2): 83–96.

———. 1992. "Why the State? Reflections on the Politics of the Finnish Equality Movement Association 9." In *Gender and Politics in Finland,* Marja Keranen, ed. Aldershot, England: Avebury.

Inglehart, Margaret. 1981. "Political Interest in Western European Women." *Comparative Political Studies* 4: 299–326.

Inglehart, Ronald. 1997. *Modernization and Postmodernization* Princeton: Princeton University Press.

———. 1977. *The Silent Revolution.* Princeton: Princeton University Press.

Inglehart, Ronald and Pippa Norris. 2003. *Rising Tide: Gender Equality and Cultural Change around the World.* New York: Cambridge University Press.

———. 1998. "Gender Gap in Voting Behavior in Global Perspective." Paper presented at the annual meetings of the American Political Science Association, Boston, MA.

Inhetveen, Katharina. 1999. "Can Gender Equality Be Institutionalized?" *International Sociology* 14(4): 403–22.

Inter-Parliamentary Union. 1997a. *Men and Women in Politics: Democracy in the Making.* Series 'Reports and Documents' No. 28. Geneva: IPU.

Inter-Parliamentary Union. 1997b. *Democracy Still in the Making: A World Comparative Study.* Geneva: Inter-Parliamentary Union.

Jallinoja, Riitta. 1986. "Independence or Integration: The Women's Movement and Political Parties in Finland." In *The New Women's Movement: Feminism and Political Power in Europe and the USA,* Drude Dahlerup, ed. London: Sage Publications.

Jelen, Ted, Sue Thomas, and Clyde Wilcox. 1994. "The Gender Gap in Comparative Perspective." *European Journal of Political Research* 25: 171–86.

Jenson, Jane. 1995. "Extending the Boundaries of Citizenship: Women's Movements of Western Europe." In *The Challenge of Local Feminisms: Women's Movements in a Global Perspective,* Amrita Basu, ed. Boulder, Co.: Westview Press.

———. 1982. "The Modern Women's Movement in Italy, France and Great Britain: Differences in Life Cycles." *Comparative Social Research* 5: 341.

Jenson, Jane and Celia Valiente. 2003. "Comparing Two Movements for Gender Parity: France and Spain." In *Women's Movements Facing the Reconfigured State,* Lee Ann Banaszak, Karen Beckwith, and Dieter Rucht, eds. Cambridge: Cambridge University Press.

Jones, Mark P. 1998. "Gender Quotas, Electoral Laws and the Election of Women: Lessons from the Argentine Provinces." *Comparative Political Studies* 31(1): 3.

Kaplan, Gisela. 1992. *Contemporary Western European Feminism.* New York: New York University Press.

Karvonen, Lauri and Per Selle. 1995. "Introduction: Scandinavia: A Case Apart." In *Women in Nordic Politics,* Lauri Karvonen and Per Selle, eds. Aldershot: Dartmouth.

Katz, Richard and Peter Mair, eds. 1992. *Party Organizations: A Data Handbook.* London: Sage Publications.

Katzenstein, Mary and Carol McClurg Mueller. 1987. *The Women's Movements of the US and Western Europe.* Philadelphia: Temple University Press.

Keck, Margaret E. and Kathryn Sikkink. 1998. *Activists beyond Borders: Advocacy Networks in International Politics.* Ithaca: Cornell University Press.

King, Gary, Robert Keohane, and Sidney Verba. 1994. *Designing Social Inquiry: Scientific Inference in Qualitative Research.* Princeton: Princeton University Press.

Kirchheimer, Otto. 1966. "The Transformation of Western European Party Systems." In *Political Parties and Political Development,* Joseph LaPalmobara and Myron Weiner, eds. Princeton: Princeton University Press.

Kitschelt, Herbert P. 1986. "Left-Libertarian Parties: Explaining Innovation in Competitive Party Systems." *World Politics* 40(2): 194–234.

Kitschelt, Herbert P. 1994. *The Transformation of European Social Democracy.* New York: Cambridge University Press.

———. 1989. *The Logics of Party Formation.* Ithaca: Cornell University Press.

Klein, Ethel. 1985. "The Gender Gap: Different Issues, Different Answers." *Brookings Review* 3: 33–37.

Klingemann, Hans-Dieter, Richard Hofferbert, and Ian Budge. 1994. *Parties, Policies, and Democracy.* Boulder: Westview Press.

Kolinsky, Eva. 1993a. "Party Change and Women's Representation in Unified Germany." In *Gender and Party Politics,* Joni Lovenduki and Pippa Norris, eds. London: Sage.

———. 1993b. *Women in Contemporary Germany.* Oxford: Berg.

———. 1992. "Women in the New Germany: The East-West Divide." In *Developments in German Politics,* Gordon Smith et al., eds. London: Macmillan.

———. 1991. "Political Participation and Parliamentary Careers: Women's Quotas in West Germany." *Western European Politics* 14(1): 56.

———. 1989. *Women in West Germany.* Oxford: Berg.

Kriesi, Hanspeter et al. 1992. "New Social Movements and Political Opportunities in Western Europe." *European Journal of Political Research* 22: 219–44.

Krook, Mona Lena. 2004. "Reforming Representation: The Diffusion of Candidate Gender Quotas Worldwide." Paper presented at the International Studies Association Annual International Convention, Montreal, Canada, March 17–20, 2004.

———. 2002. "Increasing Women's Political Representation: Party Competition as a Mechanism of Change." Paper presented at the 11th Annual Ph.D. Summer School on European Parties and Party Systems, ECPR Standing Group on Political Parties, Dept. Politics, Keele University, Stoke-on-Trent, UK, Sept. 9–20, 2002.

Kunovich, Sheri and Pamela Paxton. 2004. "Pathways to Power: The Role of Political Parties in Women's National Political Representation." Working Paper.

Kuusela, Kimmo. 1995. "The Finnish Electoral System: Basic Features and Developmental Tendencies." In *The Finnish Voter,* Sami Borg and Risto Sankiaho, eds. Tampere, Finland: The Finnish Political Science Association

Lakeman, Enid. 1994. "Comparing Political Opportunities in Great Britain and Ireland." In *Electoral Systems in Comparative Perspective,* Wilma Rule and Joseph Zimmerman, eds. Westport, CT: Greenwood Press.

Lane, Jan-Erik and Svante Ersson 1991. *Politics in Society in Western Europe.* 2nd Ed. Newbury Park, CA: Sage.

Laver, Michael and W. Ben Hunt. 1992. *Policy and Party Competition.* New York: Routledge.

Lawless, Jennifer. 2004. "Politics of Presence? Congresswomen and Symbolic Representation." *Political Research Quarterly* 57(1): 81–99.

Lawson, Kay and Peter Merkl. 1988. *When Parties Fail: Emerging Alternative Organizations.* Princeton: Princeton University Press.

Leijenaar, Monique. 1993. "A Battle for Power: Selecting Candidates in the Netherlands." In *Gender and Party Politics,* Joni Lovenduski and Pippa Norris, eds. London: Sage.

Lemke, Christiane. 2001. "Changing the Rules of the Game: The Role of Law and the Effects of Party Reforms on Gender Parity in Germany." In *Has Liberalism Failed Women? Assuring Equal Representation in Europe and the United States,* Jytte Klausen and Charles S. Maier, eds. New York: Palgrave.

Lijphart, Arend. 1999. *Patterns of Democracy: Government Forms and Performance in 36 Countries.* New Haven: Yale University Press.

———. 1984. *Democracies.* New Haven: Yale University Press.

———. 1977. *Democracy in Plural Societies.* New Haven: Yale University Press.

Lipset, Seymour Martin. 1962. *Political Man.* Garden City, NY: Doubleday Anchor Books.

Lipset, Seymour Martin and Stein Rokkan. 1967. "Cleavage Structures, Party Systems, and Voter Alignments." In *Party Systems and Voter Alignments,* Seymour M. Lipset and Stein Rokkan, eds. New York: Free Press.

Lovenduski, Joni. 1986. *Women and European Politics.* Amherst: The University of Massachusetts Press.

Lovenduski, Joni and Maria Eagle. 1998. *High Time or High Tide for Labour Women.* London: The Fabian Society.

Lovenduski, Joni and Pippa Norris. 2003. "Westminster Women: The Politics of Presence." *Political Studies* 51: 84–102.

———. 1993. *Gender and Party Politics.* London: Sage Publications.

Lovenduski, Joni and Vicky Randall. 1993. *Contemporary Feminist Politics.* Oxford: Oxford University Press.

MacKay, Fiona, Fiona Myers, and Alice Brown. 2003. "Towards a New Politics? Women and the Constitutional Change in Scotland." In *Women Making Constitutions: New Politics and Comparative Perspectives,* Alexandra Dobrowolsky and Viven Hart, eds. New York: Palgrave Macmillan.

Maier, Charles S. and Jytte Klausen. 2001. "Introduction." In *Has Liberalism Failed Women? Assuring Equal Representation in Europe and the United States,* Jytte Klausen and Charles S. Maier, eds. New York: Palgrave.

Mair, Peter and Gordon Smith. 1990. *Understanding Party System Change in Western*

Europe. London: Frank Cass.

Mansbridge, Jane. 1999. "Should Blacks Represent Blacks and Women Represent Women? A Contingent 'Yes.'" *Journal of Politics* 61(3): 628–57.

March, James G. and Johan P. Olson. 1989. *Rediscovering Institutions.* New York: Macmillan.

Markovits, Andrei and Philip Gorski. 1993. *The German Left.* New York: Oxford University Press.

Matland, Richard E. 1994. "Putting Scandinavian Equality to the Test: An Experimental Evaluation of Gender Stereotyping of Political Candidates in a Sample of Norwegian Voters." *British Journal of Political Science* 24(2): 273–92.

———. 1993. "Institutional Variables Affecting Female Representation in National Legislatures: The Case of Norway." *Journal of Politics* 55(3): 737–55.

Matland, Richard E. and Deborah Dwight Brown. 1992. "District Magnitude's Effect on Female Representation in the U.S. State Legislatures. *Legislative Studies Quarterly* 17(4): 469–92.

Matland, Richard E. and Donley T. Studlar. 1996. "The Contagion of Women Candidates in Single-Member District and Proportional Representation Systems: Canada and Norway." *Journal of Politics* 58(3): 707–33.

McAdam, Doug. 1982. *Political Process and the Development of Insurgency.* Chicago: University of Chicago Press.

McAllister, Ian and Donley T. Studlar. 2002. "Electoral Systems and Women's Representation: A Long-Term Perspective." *Representation* 39(1): 3–14.

McKay, Joanna. 2004. "Women in German Politics: Still a Job for the Boys?" *German Politics* 13(1): 56–80.

Meklas, Tuula. 1999. *The Gender Barometer 1998: Equality between Men and Women in Finland.* Helsinki: Statistics Finland and the Council for Equality between Men and Women.

Ministry of Health and Social Affairs, Finland. 1999. "Gender Equality in Finland." Pamphlet.

Mintrom, Michael. 1997. "Policy Entrepreneurs and the Diffusion of Innovation." *American Journal of Political Science* 41(3): 738.

Mooney, Christopher Z. and Mei-Hsien Lee. 1995. "Legislating Morality in the American States: The Case of Pre-Roe Abortion Regulation Reform." *American Journal of Political Science* 39(3): 599.

Mueller, Carol. 1988. *The Politics of the Gender Gap.* Beverly Hills: Sage.

Mueller, Wolfgang C. 1997. "Inside the Black Box: A Confrontation of Party Executive Behavior and Theories of Party Organizational Change." *Party Politics* 3(3): 315–40.

Mueller-Rommel, Ferdinand. 1989. *New Politics in Western Europe.* Boulder, Westview Press.

National Democratic Institute. (NDI) 2004. *Global Action Plan.*Q www.winwith women.ndi.org

Norderval, Ingunn. 1985. "Party and Legislative Participation among Scandinavian Women." In *Women and Politics in Western Europe,* Sylvia Bashevkin, ed. London: Frank Cass.

Nordic Council of Ministers. 1999. "Women and Men in Nordic Countries." Pamphlet prepared by TemaNord.

Norris, Phillip. 1994. *The British Polity.* 3rd Ed. New York: Longman.

Norris, Pippa. 2001. "Breaking the Barriers: Positive Discrimination Policies for Women." In *Has Liberalism Failed Women? Assuring Equal Representation in Europe and the United States,* Jytte Klausen and Charles S. Maier, eds. New York: Palgrave.

———. 1999. "A Gender-Generation Gap?" In *Critical Elections: British Parties and Voters in Long-Term Perspective,* Geoffrey Evans and Pippa Norris, eds. London: Sage.

———. 1996. "Legislative Recruitment." In *Comparative Democratic Elections,* Lawrence LeDuc, Richard Neimi, and Pippa Norris, eds. London: Sage.

Norris, Pippa and Mark Franklin. 1997. "Social Representation." *European Journal of Political Research* 32: 185.

Norris, Pippa and Joni Lovenduski. 2001. "Blair's Babes: Critical Mass Theory, Gender and Legislative Life." Working Paper for the JFK School of Government, Harvard University.

———. 1995. *Political Recruitment: Gender, Race and Class in the British Parliament.* Cambridge: Cambridge University Press.

———. 1989. "Women Candidates for Parliament: Transforming the Agenda?" *British Journal of Political Science* 19: 106–15.

North, Douglass. 1990. *Institutions, Institutional Change, and Economic Performance.* New York: Cambridge University Press.

Norton, Philip. 1994. *The British Polity.* 3rd Ed. New York: Longman.

Office of the Ombudsman for Equality and Ministry of Health and Social Affairs, Finland. 1999. "A Millennium of Gender Equality." Pamphlet.

O'Regan, Valerie. 2000. *Gender Matters: Female Policymakers' Influence in Industrialized Nations.* Westport, CT: Praeger.

Oskarson, Maria. 1995. "Gender Gaps in Nordic Voting Behavior." In *Closing the Gap: Women in Nordic Politics,* Lauri Karvonen and Per Selle, eds. Aldershot: Dartmouth.

Paastela, Jukka. 1987. *Finland's New Social Movements.* Tampere, Finland: University Press.

Paloheimo, Heikki. 2003. "The Rising Power of the Prime Minister in Finland." *Scandinavian Political Studies* 26(3): 219–43.

Panebianco, Angelo. 1988. *Political Parties: Organization and Power.* Cambridge: Cambridge University Press.

Parvikko, Tuija. 1991. "Conceptions of Gender Equality: Similarity and Difference." In *Equality Politics and Gender,* Elizabeth Meehan and Selma Sevenhuijsen, eds. London: Sage.

Paxton, Pamela. 1997. "Women in National Legislatures: A Cross-National Analysis." *Social ScienceResearch* 26: 442–64.

Paxton, Pamela and Sheri Kunovich. 2003. "Women's Political Representation: The Importance of Ideology." *Social Forces* 82(1): 87–114.

Perrigo, Sarah. 1995. "Gender Struggles in the British Labour Party from 1979 to 1995." *Party Politics* 1(3): 407–17.

Pesonen, Pertti. 2000. "Politics in Finland." In *Comparative Governance,* W. Phillips Shively, ed. New York: McGraw Hill.

———. 1995. "The Evolution of Finland's Party Divisions and Social Structure." In

The Finnish Voter, Sami Borg and Risto Sankiaho, eds. Tampere, Finland: The Finnish Political Science Association.

Philipps, Anne. 1995. *The Politics of Presence.* New York: Oxford University Press.

Pitkin, Hanna. 1967. *The Concept of Representation.* Berkeley: University of California Press.

Piven, Frances Fox and Richard Cloward. 1977. *Poor People's Movements.* New York: Pantheon Books.

Poggione, Sarah. 2004. "Exploring Gender Differences in State Legislators' Policy Differences." *Political Research Quarterly* 57(2): 305–14.

Powell, Walter W. and Paul J. DiMaggio, eds. 1991. *The New Institutionalism in Organizational Analysis.* Chicago: The University of Chicago Press.

Raevaara, Eeva and Susanna Taskinen. 2004. "The Situation of Women in Politics." *Women, Politics and Policies of Equality in Europe.* Online Posting. http://www.helskinki.fi/science/xantippa/wee/weetext/wee252.html

Randall, Vicky. 1998. "Gender and Power: Women Engage the State." In *Gender, Politics, and the State,* Vicky Randall and Georgina Waylen, eds. London: Routledge.

———. 1987. *Women and Politics: An International Perspective.* Basingstoke: Macmillan Educational.

———. 1982. *Women and Politics.* New York: St. Martin's Press.

Ranney, Austin. 1965. *Pathways to Parliament.* Madison: University of Wisconsin Press.

Raunio, Tapio. 2001. "The Changing Finnish Democracy: Stronger Parliamentary Accountability, Coalescing Political Parties and Weaker External Constraints." *Scandinavian Political Studies* 27(2): 133–42.

Reynolds, Andrew. 1999. "Women in the Legislatures and Executives of the World: Knocking at the Highest Glass Ceiling." *World Politics* 51(4): 547–72.

Riker, William H. 1965. *Democracy in the U.S.* New York: Macmillan.

Rochon, Thomas R. 1998. *Culture Moves.* Princeton: Princeton University Press.

Rohrschneider, Robert. 1993a. "The Impact of Social Movements on European Party Systems." *Annals of American Academy of Political and Social Change* July. Vol. 528.

———. 1993b. "New Party versus Old Left Realignments: Environmental Attitudes, Party Policies, and Partisan Affiliations in Four West European Countries." *Journal of Politics* 55(3): 682–701.

Rose, Richard and Derek Urwin. 1975. *Regional Differentiation and Political Unity in Western Nations.* London: Sage.

Rueschemeyer, Dietrich, Evelyne Huber Stephens, and John D. Stephens. 1992. *Capitalist Development and Democracy.* Cambridge: Polity Press.

Rueschemeyer, Marilyn. 2003. "Women in Politics in Post-Communist East Germany." In *Reinventing Gender: Women in Eastern Germany Since Unification,* Eva Kolinsky and Hildegard Maria Nickel, eds. London: Frank Cass.

———. 1998. *Women in the Postcommunist Eastern Europe.* Armonk, NY: M.E. Sharpe, Inc.

Rule, Wilma. 1987. "Electoral Systems, Contextual Factors and Women's Opportunity for Election to Parliament in Twenty-Three Democracies." *Western Political Quarterly.* September, 477–98.

———. 1981. "Why Women Don't Run: The Critical Factors in Women's Legislative

Recruitment." *Western Political Quarterly* 34: 60–77.

Rule, Wilma and Joseph Zimmerman. 1994. *Electoral Systems in Comparative Perspective: Their Impact on Women and Minorities.* Westport, CT: Greenwood Press.

Rush, M. 1969. *The Selection of Parliamentary Candidates.* London: Nelson.

Russell, Meg. 2003. "Women in Elected Office in the UK, 1992–2002: Struggles, Achievements and Possible Sea Change." In *Women Making Constitutions: New Politics and Comparative Perspectives,* Alexandra Dobrowolsky and Viven Hart, eds. New York: Palgrave Macmillan.

Russell, Meg and Colm O'Cinneide. 2003. "Positive Action to Promote Women in Politics: Some European Comparisons." *ICLQ* 52: 587–614.

Sainsbury, Diane. 1993. "The Politics of Increased Women's Representation: The Swedish Case." In *Gender and Party Politics,* Joni Lovenduski and Pippa Norris, eds. London: Sage.

Sanbonmatsu, Kira. *Democrats, Republicans, and the Politics of Women's Place.* Ann Arbor: The University of Michigan Press.

Schwartz, Nancy L. 1988. *The Blue Guitar: Political Representation and Community.* Chicago: University of Chicago Press.

Short, Clare. 1996. "Women and the Labour Party." In *Women in Politics,* Joni Lovenduski and Pippa Norris, eds. New York: Oxford University Press.

Siisiainen, Martti. 1992. "Social Movements, Voluntary Associations, and Cycles of Protest in Finland, 1905–91." *Scandinavian Political Studies* 15(1): 21–39.

Skjeie, Hege. 1991. "The Rhetoric of Difference: On Women's Inclusion into Political Elites." *Politics and Society* 19: 233–63.

Skjeie, Hege and Birte Siim. 2000. "Scandinavian Feminist Debates on Citizenship." *International Political Science Review* 21(4): 345–60.

Squires, Judith. 1996. "Quotas for Women: Fair Representation?" *Parliamentary Affairs* 49(1): 71–88.

Steininger, Barbara. 2000. "Representation of Women in the Austrian Political System, 1945–1998: From a Token Female Politician Towards an Equal Ratio?" *Women and Politics* 21(2): 81–106.

Steinmo, Sven, Kathleen Thelen, and Frank Longstreth, eds. 1992. *Structuring Politics: Historical Institutionalism in Comparative Analysis.* Cambridge: Cambridge University Press.

Strom, Kaare. 1990. "A Behavioral Theory of Competitive Political Parties." *American Journal of Political Science* 34(2): 565–98.

Studlar, Donley T. 2004. "Women and Westminster: Descriptive Representation in Great Britain." Paper presented at conference, "Women and Westminster Compared." University of Ottawa, Ottawa, Canada, June 10–12, 2004.

Studlar, Donley T. and Ian McAllister. 2002. "Does a Critical Mass Exist? A Comparative Analysis of Women's Legislative Representation since 1950." *European Journal of Political Research* 41: 233–53.

———. 1998. "Candidate Gender and Voting in the 1997 British General Election: Did Labour Quotas Matter?" *Journal of Legislative Studies* 4(3): 72–91.

Studlar, Donley T., Ian McAllister, and Alvaro Ascui. 1988. "Electing Women to the British Commons: Breakout from Beleaguered Beachhead?" *Legislative Studies Quarterly* 13(4): 515–28.

Studlar, Donley T., Ian McAllister, and Bernadette C. Hayes. 1998. "Explaining the

Gender Gap in Voting: A Cross-National Analysis." *Social Science Quarterly* 79 (December): 779–98.

Studlar, Donley T. and Susan Welch. 1992. "The Party System and the Representation of Women in English Metropolitan Boroughs." *Electoral Studies* 11(1): 63–69.

Sundberg, Jan. 1995a. "Organizational Structure of Parties, Candidate Selection and Campaigning." In *The Finnish Voter,* Sami Borg and Risto Sankiaho, eds. Tampere, Finland: The Finnish Political Science Association.

———. 1995b. "Women in Scandinavian Party Organizations." In *Women in Nordic Politics: Closing the Gap,* Lauri Karvonen and Per Selle, eds. Aldersot, England: Dartmouth.

Swers, Michele. 2002. *The Difference Women Make: The Policy Impact of Women in Congress.* Chicago: University of Chicago Press.

Taagepera, Rein. 1994. "Beating the Law of Minority Attrition." In *Electoral Systems in Comparative Perspective: Their Impact on Women and Minorities,* Wilma and Joseph Zimmerman, eds. Westport, CT: Greenwood Press.

Taagepera, Rein and Matthew Soberg Shugart. 1989. *Seats and Votes.* New Haven: Yale University Press.

Tarrow, Sidney. 1994. *Power in Movement: Social Movements and Contentious Politics.* New York: Cambridge University Press.

———. 1989. *Struggle, Politics, and Reform.* Ithaca: Center for International Studies, Cornell University.

Tate, Katherine. 2001. *Black Faces in the Mirror: African Americans and Their Representatives in the US Congress.* Princeton: Princeton University Press.

———. 1994. *From Protest to Politics: The New Black Voters in American Elections.* Cambridge: Harvard University Press and the Russell Sage Foundation.

———. 1991. "Black Political Participation in the 1984 and 1988 Presidential Elections." *American Political Science Review* 85: 1159–76.

Thomas, Sue. 1994. *How Women Legislate.* Oxford: Oxford University Press.

True, Jacqui and Michael Mintrom. 2001. "Transnational Networks and Policy Diffusion: The Case of Gender Mainstreaming." *International Studies Quarterly* 45: 27–57.

Walker, Jack L. 1991. *Mobilizing Interest Groups in America.* Ann Arbor: University of Michigan Press.

Wangnerud, Lena. 2000a. "Representing Women." In *Beyond Westminster and Congress: The Nordic Experience*, Peter Essaiasson and Knut Heidar, eds. Columbus: The Ohio State University Press.

———. 2000b. "Testing the Politics of Presence: Women's Representation in the Swedish Riksdag." *Scandinavian Political Studies* 23(1): 67–91.

Weaver, R. Kent and Bert A. Rockman, eds. *Do Institutions Matter?* Washington, DC: The Brookings Institution.

Welch, Susan and Donley T. Studlar. 1996. "The Opportunity Structure for Women's Candidacies and Electability in Britain and the U.S." *Political Research Quarterly* 49(4): 861–74.

———. 1986. "British Public Opinion toward Women in Politics: A Comparative Perspective." *Western Political Quarterly* 39(1): 138–54.

Weldon, S. Laurel. 2002. *Protest, Policy, and the Problem of Violence against Women: A Cross-National Comparison.* Pittsburgh: University of Pittsburgh Press.

Wildenmann, Rudolf. 1987. "Germany" in Richard Katz, ed. *The Future of Party Government.* Berlin: de Gruyter.

Wiliarty, Sarah Elise. 2001. "The CDU: A Corporatist Catch-All Party." Unpublished dissertation thesis. University of California, Berkeley, CA.

Wilson, Frank L. 1994. "The Sources of Party Change: The Social Democratic Parties of Britain, France, Germany and Spain." In *How Political Parties Work,* Kay Lawson, ed. Westport, CT: Praeger.

Wolbrecht, Christina. 2000. *The Politics of Women's Rights: Parties, Positions, and Change* Princeton: Princeton University Press.

Women and Equality Unit, Britain. 2002. "Sex Discrimination Act." Online Posting. http://www.womenandequalityunit.gov.uk/legislation/discrimination_act.htm (4/8/2004).

"Women Members of Finland's Parliament." Online posting. Finnish Parliament. http:www.eduskunta.fi/efakta/opas/tiedotus/naisede.htm(4/8/2004).

Yamaguchi, Kazuo. 1991. *Event History Analysis.* Newbury Park: Sage Publications.

index

Page numbers in italics refer to tables or figures in the text.

Act of Equality Between Men and Women (Finland), 116
African-Americans, 15–16
Agrarian Party. *See* Center Party (Finland, KESK)
Albright, Madeline K., 1, 3
Alliance 90. *See* Greens (Germany, G)
"all-women shortlist" policy (UK, AWS), 81–83, 120–21, 144–47, 157
ASF (German SPD women's organization), 92–94, 99–100, 150
Association of Liberal Women (Germany), 95
Association 9 (Finland), 109
Australia, *3, 139*
Austria, 3–4, 139. *See also individual political parties*

Baldez, Lisa, 25
Beckwith, Karen, 121, 123, 163n1 (ch. 2)
Belgium, *3–4, 138–39. See also individual political parties*
Bergman, Solveig, 109
Berman, Sheri, 31–32
Blair, Cherie, 1
Blair, Tony, 1–2, 76, 82, 89
Bobo, Lawrence, 15
Brandt, Willy, 92, 99
Bratton, Kathleen A., 14

Britain. *See* United Kingdom (UK)
Brooks, Rachel, 80–81
Brown, Alice, 141–42

Canada, *3,* 24, *139*–40
candidate development, 9–10, 29, 77–79, 83, 151
candidate gender quotas. *See* gender quotas
Carmines, Edward, 32
Caul, Miki, 119–20
Center Democrats (Denmark, CD), *6, 43, 51*
Center Party (Finland, KESK), *6,* 13, *43, 51,* 106, 112–13, 152–*53*
Center Party (Norway, SP), *7, 44, 52*
Center Party (Sweden, C), *7, 52*
centralized party structures, 28, 34, 38; gender quotas and, 35, 56, 133; NEC composition and, 46–47, 49, 120; parliamentary presence and, 125–27, 133–34
Charlot, M., 72
Childs, Sarah, 147
Christian Democratic Union (Germany, CDU), 88; gender quotas and, 13, *51,* 53, 101, 131, 148; NEC composition of, *43,* 96–98, 149–50; party competition and, 91–92; voting patterns and,

183

PARLIAMENTS AND LEGISLATURES

Janet M. Box-Steffensmeier and David T. Canon, Series Editors